DEATH AND THE STATESMAN

DEATH AND THE STATESMAN

THE CULTURE AND PSYCHOLOGY OF U.S. LEADERS DURING WAR

JOSEPH B. UNDERHILL-CADY

palgrave

First published 2001 by PALGRAVE™
175 Fifth Avenue, New York, N.Y. 10010 and
Houndmills, Basingstoke, Hampshire, England RG21 6XS.
Companies and representatives throughout the world.

PALGRAVE is the new global publishing imprint of St. Martin's Press LLC Scholarly and Reference Division and Palgrave Publishers Ltd. (formerly Macmillan Press Ltd.).

ISBN 0-312-23928-9

Library of Congress Cataloging-in-Publication Data
Underhill-Cady, Joseph B., 1962–
Death and the statesman : the culture and psychology of U.S. leaders during war / Joseph B. Underhill-Cady
    p.   cm.
Includes bibliographical references and index.
ISBN 0-312-23928-9
    1. United States—History, Military—20th century.   2. United States—Foreign relations—20th century—Psychological aspects.
3. United States—Foreign relations—20th century—Decision making.
4. Statesmen—United States—Psychology.   5. Statesmen—United States—Biography.   6. Death—Psychological aspects.   7. War—Psychological aspects.   8. Political culture—United States—History—20th century.   I. Title.
E745.U54   2001
303.6'6'0973—dc21   2001040148

A catalogue record for this book is available from the British Library.

Design by Letra Libre, Inc.

First edition: August 2001
10 9 8 7 6 5 4 3 2 1

Printed in the United States of America.

CONTENTS

*O for a voice like thunder, and a tongue
To drown the throat of war . . .*

—William Blake

PREFACE

> ... *But there is another saying not of late understood, by which [we] might learn truly to read one another, if [we] would take the pains; and this is,* Nosce teipsum, *Read thy self ... [and] when I shall have set down my own reading ... the pains left to another, will be onely to consider, if he also find not the same in himself. For this kind of Doctrine, admitteth no other Demonstration.*
>
> —Hobbes, Leviathan, The Introduction

A s books are almost always as much about the author as they are about the subject at hand, I begin with a story I have told myself about this project's origins. The reader can judge whether what I have to say here reveals more than it obscures, and speculate about what I may have left out, for of course it is far from complete. Though this is but a small part of what has brought me to write this book and to write it from the perspective I have, it is still more than we normally get when picking up a book in political science. Autobiographical anecdote in academia is generally limited to the elder statesmen in the field who modestly assume their readers will want to know about them personally. My authorial self-reflection, in contrast, is a declaration of subjectivity, and a caveat for those readers who might be seeking here the dry bread of statistical analysis.

This is not how scholarly works are supposed to start. When poised on the ridgeline dividing the bright slope of disembodied positivism, with its claims of impersonal objectivity, from the shadowed and rock-strewn incline of human subjectivity, nearly all works in the social sciences instinctively and self-confidently stride down the former. The norm is to dive into the literature, the debate, the cutting argument, and pretend to completely separate the personal and the academic.[1] But the two cannot be separated; our lives and agendas are always there in the background, and the pursuit of understanding is not aided by denying the role of these factors. So before entering the academic battle over war, I turn, carefully, to my past. There I find something we all, in some form, share.

It is the summer of 1972, I am ten years old, and I am lying in a small bedroom in the house of my maternal grandmother, who died the previous year. The house sits up in the Berkeley, California, hills, a short walk from the rose garden and parks in which I roamed during our visits, and had imprinted in my memory the deliciously exotic smells of rose, eucalyptus, and cedar. The house feels foreign and elegant, with its view of the Golden Gate and the garden of Mediterranean plants. My family has driven across the country from New York to help settle up my grandmother's affairs, divide up her things. As a child I am kept busy with various amusements—there is an old toy train set in the basement that we get out and try to refurbish, the Olympics are on, and I am struck by the importance attached to them. But at that moment, the most striking quality to the house is a palpable absence. The person who used to live there is no longer there. There is something about the place, as a place in which a life was contained; it is a vessel now empty. This is not something we talk about as we go about the business of sorting out her belongings, but it something we sense. For the first time, I experience something of the reality of death. What death is I do not know, but what I am certain of is that the stately, warm, gray-haired woman who wore dangly earrings and brought us presents is not there, in the place where she is supposed to be. I sense my mother's grief; and my father, who lost both his parents when he was in his teens, has long kept his grief hidden. But it is no less present for its invisibility.

I cannot sleep, lying in the dark, surrounded by strange textures and smells of the house (the smell of someone's life, a human perfume of cooking, cleaning, wood, dust, dampness, the stiff linen of this guest bed), and there in the dark my thoughts drift out into the void created by my grandmother's absence. I think about how long I will be dead and realize that, as I can neither imagine an end to time nor to the universe, neither can I imagine an end to death. This dark epiphany causes my mind to seize, my back to tense. My existence, which I enjoy—my self—to which I am attached, will not last forever (and in the cosmic scheme of things will last for but the briefest of moments), and when I am gone I will never exist again. Before me and after me stretch an unending void of nothingness; an empty house.

Eventually that night I managed to fall asleep, and the next morning I rose and went about my usual business as a ten-year-old. But the thoughts remained that day and are with me still. They, in combination with other idiosyncrasies of my history, have in large part prompted the project that led to this book.

As I write about this "childhood experience," the academic voice in me winces a bit at its melodrama—these are sentiments scholars generally dismiss as clichés. Benedict Anderson, for instance, in beginning his discussion of nationalism with reference to mortality, describes these notions as "simple-minded."[2] But in academia we are perhaps a bit too quick to dismiss cliché (we must be path-breaking nonconformists, right? We revel in the abstract impersonal Idea, and the more abstract and complicated and cuttingly witty, the better.) In this case I think we dismiss these sentiments not so much because they are simple-minded, but because when faced they are really awful and painful, and the abstract and abstruse machinations of the academy are but one of the many pleasant distractions developed in modern society to divert our minds from the contemplation of the void. These are not new ideas, they have been worked and overworked in scripture, Hollywood, and the tabloids, but they are powerful nonetheless. I, at least, was chilled then by this thought of infinite nonexistence, and have never really been able to escape this realization other than through the denial and distraction at which our society is so good.

Whatever Freud may have said about the impossibility of imagining one's own death or nonexistence[3] (or was it that he just did not like that thought and repressed it himself?), I still find this thought disturbing. It is as powerful a feeling as I have had, and I gather, one not unique to myself. I would hazard that just about everyone, albeit within their own cultural context, has had some kind of similar experience. We are all mortal, and I have not seen too many people celebrating this fact, even if they have had a miserable life and an unshakable belief in heaven; and even in those cases, the possibility of infinite nonexistence remains, and troubles our dreams. From this common experience, I am hoping we may be able to extract some clues about who we are as humans and, because of the power of those experiences, perhaps better understand why we as humans do such extreme things as going to war.

For, at the same time as my grandmother's death, in the world around me other events were occurring of which I was only dimly aware, but of which I gradually became more cognizant, and that politicized my fear of death. That summer we watched the Munich Olympics, when the Israeli athletes were killed. The Vietnam War was drawing to a close, with Nixon sending the B-52s to drop 36,000 tons of bombs on Hanoi and Haiphong as part of the 1972 Christmas bombing campaign. In the Cold War crisis leading up to the Yom Kippur War, American nuclear forces were placed in a state of high alert, known as "DefCon3." And even as the SALT I Treaty had been signed, the superpowers continued to add to their arsenals of tens of thousands of nuclear weapons.

Just as these events meant little to me at the time, likewise death remained for me throughout my teenage years a distant, abstract fate. But as I entered adulthood, I apparently needed to locate and pin down this amorphous and drifting fear of death that I could not shake. Slovoj Žižek, following the linguistic psychoanalyst Jacques Lacan, refers to the reservoir of free-floating anxiety—those amorphous unsettling thoughts that lurk in the unconscious. These anxieties require some outlet, which is provided by projecting them onto some external entity.[4] The place I found to locate this fear was in the institution of war itself and in the hands of those who might send me off to battle—those making American foreign policy. This then forms the basis for part of the subjectivity I bring to this work, part of my agenda, and part of what I have had to work with as I studied these men.

The draft having ended, I was never in any direct danger of being sent off to war, although I did have to register; and my parents, especially my mother, were clearly concerned about me not going off to fight. These concerns, along with the specter of World War II and the Holocaust, of which I read and was aware, led me to fear that it was war that might kill me, rather than disease, or auto accident, or crime. Perhaps I latched onto the horrors of war because they were so remote, since war's improbability made it easier to think about. As I grew older, this fear was heightened by the prospect of nuclear war. I had nightmares about nuclear attacks, of seeing the mushroom clouds, and of trying to do something to stop the bombs from being used. I began to study war, peace, power, the arms race, and so on. I looked for ways to understand these troubling puzzles—including formal international relations theory and statistics, since they promised such certainty, and are the prevalent approaches in the field. I studied conflict resolution and war termination, and as part of that line of inquiry found that, of course, the main "cost" of war, in these expected utility theories, were casualties.[5] But the more I studied this, the less sense it made for the "body count" to be just another entry in the debit column.

I found, and continue to find, those approaches ultimately unsatisfying. They drew me away from what I understood war to be; they did not get at the meaning of war; they were a kind of abstract, disembodied set of methods, that increasingly came to seem anathema to the study of something as visceral and horrible as war. Eventually I came to see that I found them unsatisfying because they entailed a denial of the very aspect of war that had, unbeknownst to me, spurred me to take up the study in the first place—namely, death. Not death as a number, but death as an experience, a fate, a fear faced by a ten-year-old. Thus, my concerns about death brought me to study war, and my study of war has now brought me back to my thoughts on mortality.

ACKNOWLEDGMENTS

I have been blessed with a wonderful circle of family, friends, mentors, and colleagues who have been incredibly supportive of this venture—emotionally, intellectually, personally, financially, and artistically. Ken Waltz, Stan Bailis, Harold Jacobson, Martha Feldman, Ted Hopf, and David Winter all contributed to shaping to my thought. I am much the richer for the kind encouragement and good humor of colleagues such as Gary Shiffman, Jeff Spinner, Dan Lieberfeld, Ido Oren, Hayward Alker, Greg Nowell, Charles Webel, Andy Aoki, Mary Ellen Lundsten, and Norma Noonan. I am grateful for the open-minded support of institutions such as the University of Michigan, Minot State University, and Augsburg College, which make possible the pursuit of such odd and esoteric projects as this one. A special thanks to Heather Olson and Andrea Cobery at Augsburg for their able and cheerful assistance in the final stages of revising the manuscript, and to Sarah Schur and Roee Raz at Palgrave for their help throughout the process of publication. The skillful pen of Laura Lawrie has greatly improved the text. Many thanks to Toby Wahl at Palgrave for his advocacy, enthusiasm, and insightful suggestions on the manuscript. For the fact that this project has come as far as it has, I am profoundly grateful to all who have born with me along the way. That said, this remains far from perfect, but for that I have no one to thank but myself.

I have been sustained as well by an amazing family. My great-aunt Betty Shuey provided an example of selflessness and unflagging enthusiasm, even in the face of her own death, which continues to inspire. To my sisters Kate and Sarah and their families, and the whole Cady family, my thanks for their love and example. A special note of appreciation to my father for the inspiration provided by the bronze vessels he makes and to my mother for her photographs and her writing *Thirty Five Years, One Week*, about the loss of her sister Cher. Their creative efforts at coming to terms with mortality were the starting point for my own. My extended set of parents—William and Linda Underhill, Linn Underhill and Ann

Carter, Mark and Lee Cady—can all take great pride in knowing that without all of them, this book would not have happened. It has been a long time coming, and at times I did not think it ever would. My heart cannot express enough my gratitude to all of you.

Most of all, I am thankful to and dedicate this work to Palma, Meryn, and Ian, to whom it is hard to dedicate anything, for they are part of me, and I part of them, and they are here in every page.

INTRODUCTION

This is a book about war and death, fear and sorrow, and as such it has been generally a somber project. It is better not to spend too much time contemplating mortality, and most of the time we do a good job of avoiding the topic. Nonetheless, people continue to die in wars; and every day some 140,000 people die from various quotidian causes; and one day each of us will join their numbers. The pain and loss that these deaths and wars occasion seem to require some attention, even if we try diligently to avoid them in casual conversation. In fact, the apparent aversion to discussing these matters provides, for those interested in understanding painful truths, further incentive for examining them. This study of U.S. foreign policy is in part a response to the awful sorrow and loss that has at time accompanied that policy.

But this book is, in a strange way, also about a sort of laughter. As the above-mentioned aversion indicates, we are not well equipped to dwell too long on sorrow without some respite. Although it is important to examine these unpleasant thoughts, we should not be too serious about them. The humor in this investigation stems ironically from mortality itself. Reflection on the human condition, by putting human exploits and foibles into perspective, also can be liberating. In researching U.S. foreign policy, I found myself laughing about some of the material, enough so that there was a need to take account of that laughter; for it was not as though this was particularly humorous material—Teddy Roosevelt's account of crabs feeding on the corpses of men killed in Cuba, Dean Acheson's self-serving praise of Harry Truman, George Bush entertaining Arnold Schwarzenegger at Camp David prior to the Gulf War. The humor I found in these passages seemed to be a sign that they struck at something deep and powerful, and that they could therefore provide indications of what was driving me in the course of this study. I interpret these reactions, within the framework developed in this book, as related to my fears about death, my suspicion of the politicians who might be the agents of my death, the sorrow of the human condition, and my attempt to feel some kind of power in relation to these men. It is entertaining to see the powerful being as ridiculous as the rest of us. But there is an edge to this humor; this laughter elicited by the weaknesses of the powerful exists on the boundary between the sorrow of contemplating death, and the elation of having escaped it.

As the nineteenth-century poet and critic Charles Baudelaire describes it, "Laughter is satanic: it is thus profoundly human. . . . And since laughter is essentially human, it is, in fact, essentially contradictory; that is to say that it is at once a token of an infinite grandeur and an infinite misery—the latter in relation to the absolute Being of whom man has an inkling, the former in relation to the beasts. It is from the perpetual collision of these two infinites that laughter is struck. The comic and the capacity for laughter are situated in the laugher and by no means in the object of his mirth."[1] Thus it is that I take my laughter as a sign that these humorous passages relate to the human condition (infinite grandeur and infinite misery), and to a set of feelings intense enough to elicit this visceral reaction. Laughter is in this sense serious business, not just a source of relief from an otherwise dismal inquiry, but a good starting place for an investigation of something as serious as war. It is as well a way of bringing the overly serious back down to earth, again, of "humanizing" those who have managed to take themselves too seriously as a result of their success and power.

Laughter and sorrow, as Baudelaire and others have pointed out, are closely related. I have at times experienced laughter as an expression of tenuous power—power that one realizes can all too easily disappear; sorrow, following Hobbes's description (*Leviathan*, Part I, Ch. 6), generally reflects these feelings of powerlessness. We exist on the boundary between those two states of sorrow and joy, loss and triumph. To see someone else on the losing end can elicit this double reaction—a laughter to hide the same sorrow that one feels within oneself, and at the same time a visceral relief that, for the moment, the sorrow is someone else's.

In reading through the writings and biographies of these powerful men, and in writing about them, I found in certain passages a sense of power over death, and so I laughed. It was the passages that revealed these people at their most human, as mortals no different than any of us. If I was able to feel that I had understood them, uncovered their idiosyncratic motivations, then I could feel that I had in some sense mastered my fate. I have engaged in this pursuit of knowledge in order to understand human destructiveness. I have made sense of the lives of these eminent politicians in terms of their desire for power, and it is how I have made sense of my own coming to terms with war.

I know this is a potential source of bias in the work—that I would reach the conclusion that my predisposition toward disliking these individuals was supported by the historical record. Although I know sometimes I have slipped into that mode, I try as well to be as fair and balanced in my analysis as I can. I hope these prefatory remarks better prepare the reader for the evidence they are to be presented.

In a manner sacrilegious within the realm of the social sciences, and more in the fashion of feminist epistemologies suggested by Donna Haraway and Sandra Harding, the personal narrative of authors such as Susan Griffin, and the insights derived from qualitative methodology,[2] I have taken this laughter (and sorrow) as a gauge or signal for selecting material for this work. Having found controlled experiments and multiple regression, logit, and pooled time series analyses lacking in humor, sadness, and meaning, I have adopted a self-consciously subjective method—not one that tries to manipulate the data deliberately, but one that attempts to be honest both about myself and about those whom I am studying. This is not to say that I reject objectivity *qua* honesty as a goal toward which to strive but, rather, that I think a better way to try to approach objectivity is to recognize and work with the inevitable subjectivity that we all bring to our investigation—to pursue both a personal truth and a social truth at the same time, an approach indicated by George Lakoff and Mark Johnson's argument that "[t]he mind is inherently embodied. Thought is mostly unconscious. Abstract concepts are largely metaphorical."[3]

My research consisted of reading extensively about these powerful American men who made decisions about war, and finding passages or events about them that struck me as odd or interesting. This is not a replicable or rigorous method of inquiry, but it serves as a set of guidelines that allow for an imaginative reading of these foreign policy texts. I assume that these passages will offer some insights into how these people dealt with mortality, with sadness, with power, with being human. There is certainly ample colorless, dry, mundane material written and spoken by statesmen and bureaucrats, but I leave that to those with a different sense of humor. This selection criteria is not a hard and fast rule, but it was a criteria toward which I gravitated, despite (or perhaps as a reaction to) having been trained in a discipline that seems increasingly infatuated with formal models, statistics, and quantification.[4]

As I understand it, the aim of science is to work toward some conception of truth in which prior belief, superstition, dogma, and one's own personal and political agenda obscure "reality" as little as possible. While sharing the poststructuralist perspective that such a search may be overly simplistic, at times counterproductive, and occasionally used to imbue highly politicized research projects with the aura of objectivity, I certainly share this basic scientific standard of guiding my investigation by what boils down to integrity, open-mindedness, and a willingness to change my mind. Where I differ from the positivist social scientists is in how to do this, and to what degree the pursuit of pure objectivity may compromise other worthwhile goals of an investigation such as this one.

One way to minimize bias is through the use of the scientific method, to try to insulate an investigation from whatever personal, emotional, or subjective biases might be present. Social scientists urge the investigator to limit one's research to the bounds of randomization, double-blind investigation, quantification, carefully specified inferences, rigorous and formal theorization, and thorough peer review.[5] Although this approach to the study of human beings has produced all sorts of interesting insights, the trouble with it is that it does not answer my questions about life and death and meaning. To reduce the study of humans to quantified formal models almost invariably involves a certain desiccation and dehumanization. It makes it nearly impossible to analyze the emotional and ontological aspects of a phenomenon like war.

Furthermore, through its generally authoritative claims to objectivity, the scientific method elides some very important questions. The scientific method filters out some subjectivity, but it does not eliminate it; and it has the potential to obscure whatever subjectivity remains. As Thomas Kuhn, Evelyn Fox Keller, Donna Haraway, and others have pointed out, science has always involved an element of politics, and been guided often by a sense of aesthetics as much as by objective standards of truth.[6] Although the techniques of normal science clearly go a long way toward "depoliticizing" investigations, they can never completely remove one's own agenda from an investigation. There remain the inevitable elements of metamethodological choice and judgment—about what to study, how to study it, how to interpret the results, which results to report and which to ignore, how to specify models or operationalize variables. Each of these choices has political implications. The very choice to undertake a "scientific" and, therefore, ostensibly value-free investigation makes the huge choice of leaving aside (or at least claiming to leave aside) normative questions.[7]

Given the great stakes involved (from the mundane of getting tenure to apocalyptic of avoiding nuclear war), it is not surprising that we find the field is highly contested; the study of war is itself a bloodless battle between realist and liberals and social constructivists and feminists and neo-Marxists, each seeking to capture the flag of legitimacy and foundation funding. In this melee, calls for self-critical reflectiveness are welcome.[8] And although it may not win many "battles," I think it would be more constructive to simply discuss why we hold such passionate views on these issues. If we really do want to move toward understanding war or security or U.S. foreign policy, it seems we need to look at the sources of this polarization in the field.

Hence I address the issue of subjectivity by delving right into it. This involves this kind of dual agenda for any research project—investigating the subject at hand and investigating the investigator. It requires following Hobbes's dictum and, in so doing, being better able to understand how my fears, desires, and my own agenda shape my view of the world. I find this at least as honest an approach as the one that shrouds that agenda under the tapestry of sophisticated methods. This is in accord with my desire to not only understand war, but to understand myself. Hence this work is both analytic and expressive. As such, both artists and social scientists may take issue with aspects of the book, but I hope it will facilitate some conversation across the usually wide chasm that separates these fields.

SUMMARY OF THE BOOK

I have begun this process by following Hobbes's dictum and looking within. Where I proceed is to a study of the views of presidents, high-ranking State and Defense Department officials, and members of Congress toward the deaths occurring in the wars fought by Americans in Cuba, the Philippines, Korea, Vietnam, and the Persian Gulf. The aim is to facilitate a more self-conscious and thoughtful deliberation about whatever wars the United States may contemplate entering in the century we are now beginning. The particular shape those wars may take is unclear; but, despite the end of the Cold War and the transformations wrought by globalization, there are few signs that wars are disappearing completely or that the United States will somehow be able to avoid them. I hope that it is less likely that we will get involved in any unnecessary bloodshed, but, though the technology is changing, the fears and desires that drive us to war are strong and deep-rooted. The wars in which the United States may get involved may well be of a new kind—the "virtual war" of speed, media, and reconnaissance described by Michael Ignatieff, James Der Derian, and Paul Virilio—but there will still be wars.[9] As discussed in the final chapter of this book, perhaps the most significant shift is that the level of American casualties in these wars is approaching zero. Since Vietnam, and the formulation of the Weinberger doctrine that includes the minimization of American casualties, the United States has entered war only on the most favorable of terms. The invasions of Grenada and Panama involved minimal casualties; in the Gulf War, many combatants had a greater chance of dying in their home neighborhoods than they did of being shot by an Iraqi soldier; and during the NATO bombing campaign in Kosovo, there was not a single American combat fatality. Leaders and commanders were still worrying, and worrying hard, about casualties, and they took great pains to avoid them. The deaths of Iraqis or Serbs might weigh on the conscience of George Bush, Bill Clinton, William Cohen, and Madeleine Albright, but their main concern in regard to American soldiers was the risk, rather than the actuality, of casualties. This signals a new era in American foreign policy, which Edward Luttwak calls "postheroic" battle, in which the U.S. military can kill with near impunity.[10] But the potential for battle deaths remains, and the global store of destructive technologies continues to grow, spread, and become more sophisticated. As those threats and the potential for wholesale carnage and anxieties about them remain, so does the need to be aware of how fears about death may shape our thinking about foreign policy.

Ideally, to answer the question about the relationship between mortality and war, one should look at leaders from a number of countries and historical eras. Given various constraints (and the fact that I live in the United States) I focus on the United States during the twentieth century. Given that focus, I cannot generalize beyond that time and place and culture, although my sense is that the issue of mortality, given its universality, is not irrelevant to the thought of other leaders in other times and places. How a given group or culture deals with death is, of course, highly variable, but that it must come to terms with death is not. For this study, however, I limit my conclusions to a small group of people—those most centrally involved in making American foreign policy in the twentieth century.

Throughout this work, I refer to the actors I look at as the "foreign policy élite" (usually shortened to simply "the élite"), which I define as those individuals most directly involved in making U.S. foreign policy.[11] Although a diverse group in many ways, they shared the responsibility for sending soldiers off to die and, therefore, had a particular need to justify or make sense of those deaths. The group includes, first and foremost, the presidents, but also their military and foreign affairs advisors, and members of Congress actively involved in foreign policy issues. On occasion, I mention advisors—for instance, Billy Graham—not usually considered part of the foreign policy élite, but whose views still played a role in how the élite made sense of death in battle.

From the entire set of these individuals I have focused on writings during wartime, for the obvious reason that I am trying to understand how these élite made sense of the deaths of soldiers. Furthermore, I was drawn to particular individuals, either because of the availability of material by them or because they led particularly interesting lives. This is not an entirely representative sample, but lies somewhere between biographical studies, and broader survey analyses. Thus, my observations apply most directly to a few individuals—Theodore Roosevelt (1858–1919), his Secretary of State John Hay (1838–1905), Senator George Hoar (1826–1904),

Secretary of the Navy John Long (1838–1915), Secretary of State Dean Acheson (1893–1971), Secretary of Defense Robert McNamara (1916-), Lyndon Johnson (1908–1973), and George Bush (1924-). I have found enough in common among them and their colleagues to be able to describe an evolving culture among the foreign policy officials, but a more extensive survey and study of materials could change my conclusions.

Numerous works have looked at how soldiers have come to terms with death and the strains of battle, and how civilians caught up in war were affected, but virtually nothing has been written on attitudes toward death among those making decisions about war.[12] There is a widespread perception that of any group in society, the political élite of modern Western democracies should be the least susceptible to cultural or religious influences. While there are studies of the influence of culture in the decision making of the general public or of non-Western leaders, the supposedly staid and rational Anglo-Saxon leaders are generally considered above any such analysis. Various psychological studies have shown the ways that cognitive and affective dynamics, motivations, or quirks of personality can affect political decision making, but none of these works have examined how these leaders make sense of one essential element of warfare—death in battle.[13] Although those of us who now depend on the élite's sanity for the very survival of civilization have an interest in thinking of them as somehow better and different, this research works from the assumption that simply because a group is powerful, uses computers, and dresses in Western business attire does not mean that it will somehow be free from the influences of culture or the human condition. Although yet another study of the political élite may seem less useful than of some less-studied group, the élite do represent a good test case for an examination of the role of culture in politics. If we find culture playing a role even among these august "wise men" of foreign affairs, we are likely to find it elsewhere. And if this work demonstrates anything, it is that these political leaders were as much cultural creatures as anyone else.

Because I am interested in understanding U.S. military involvement abroad, I begin my investigation at the point when the United States enters the world stage as an actor capable of such actions. Although prior to the late 1800s the United States had been expanding across the continent, and had been engaged in its brutal war with the Native American tribes, it was not until the Spanish-American War that it turned its sights toward significant involvement overseas. From that time onward, the United States was an actor to be reckoned with on the world stage, and since that time has been involved in more international crises and disputes than any other country.[14] From the list of major wars that the United States fought in during this period, I focused on limited wars, as those appear to be the type of war most likely in the nuclear, post–Cold War era. We can learn more about the Gulf War, Somali intervention, and NATO bombing of Serbia by looking at the limited campaigns of the past than from the global conflagrations. I also wanted to cover enough time to explore the effects of changes in technology and the nature of warfare on the overall nature of the discourse on death and war. Furthermore, I was interested in those campaigns in which the direct threat to the United States was relatively small, and where America might actually be seen as the aggressor, for it is in those instances that justification of death in battle becomes most difficult. There are a few wars from American history in which this threat was relatively small and where the United States was sometimes on the offensive—the Spanish-American War, the Filipino-American War (1899–1902), the Korean War (especially MacArthur's push to the Yalu), the Vietnam War, and the Gulf War—and it is élite attitudes toward these conflicts on which I focus.

From this group of prominent foreign policy officials I have focused on a number of individuals who held a range of views on war, and for whom a variety of writings was available. There is more material here on those who actively supported going to war than for those opposed, and I have gathered more material on the turn-of-the-century élite than on those from Vietnam, and even less from the Korean or Gulf Wars. Because I have greater depth of material for the Spanish-American War case, I generally begin discussion of each topic with reference to four élite from that period—George Hoar, John Long, John Hay, and, most prominently, Theodore Roosevelt (TR). Roosevelt is a central figure in this study, as in his life a number of aspects of élite culture stand out in clear relief. As well, he was also a role model for the foreign policy "Establishment," which took shape in the 1920s and which has heavily influenced war and peace deliberations up to the present day. Although American culture and the values underlying the making of foreign policy have changed over the course of this century, they have changed from and in reaction to the set of traditions embodied so well by TR.

My research of the Vietnam era covered a larger number of élite, though in less depth than for the Spanish-American case. I focus on the major players in the period from early 1964 until early 1968, as this was when the most important decisions concerning American involvement and escalation were made. In addition to the president, these include Robert McNamara, Secretary of State Dean Rusk, National Security Advisors Walt Rostow and McGeorge Bundy, Undersecretary of State George Ball, Hubert Humphrey, Senator J. William Fulbright, and Senator Wayne Morse. Somewhat less material has been gathered from the Korean War era, but I include material from the writings of and on Dean

Acheson, George Kennan, Douglas MacArthur, and the first Secretary of Defense, James Forrestal. Forrestal presents a particularly interesting case, as he committed suicide in May 1949, the highest ranking U.S. official ever to do so. As such, his life provides us with a way to explore what constitutes a life worth living, by looking at a case in which one élite decided that his life was not. I include some material from the Gulf War—although in less detail—looking particularly at how George Bush dealt with his responsibilities and mortality both during and after his time in the presidency. The views and language used by these élite are supplemented by material from a range of other American leaders actively involved in twentieth-century debates over war and peace.[15]

The work draws on three kinds of sources. The bulk of the material is drawn from the writings and speeches of these foreign policy élite. In line with my attempt at reflecting on my own feelings and predispositions toward war and death, at a few points I include personal experiences and concerns as they relate to my attempt at "coming to terms with war." Finally, I include occasional reference to material drawn from American popular culture, such as John Bunyan's *Pilgrim's Progress*, James Bond, and the *Terminator* movies, as these shed light on the thinking and symbolic acts of the foreign policy élite. I do not see claim causal links between such works of popular cultural as *Kindergarten Cop* and the decision to bomb Baghdad, but find them useful (and humorous) heuristic devices.

I picked up on and occasionally refer to John Bunyan's *Pilgrim's Progress* because of the frequency of reference to that work in the writings of the élite up at least until the 1950s.[16] The central trope of Bunyan's work is that of pilgrimage as a means of transcendence and gaining immortality, and as we will see, élite at times drew on this symbolic project in structuring their own lives. All of the élite at the turn of the century had read, or at least were familiar with, Bunyan's work. The book is divided into two parts. In the first, the protagonist Christian, torn by inner struggles, leaves his family in the City of Destruction, and embarks on a journey to the Celestial City of Zion, on the way encountering a variety of obstacles and help. In the second part, his family, guided by the character Great-heart, embarks on its own journey to join Christian in heaven. Both books end with an ecstatic description of the joys of life in heaven, which stand in stark contrast to the conditions of life on earth.

The book was immensely popular throughout the eighteenth and nineteenth centuries, second only to the Bible in circulation in the United States, and it had gone through an unparalleled 1,300 English-language editions between its publication in 1678 and 1938.[17] It was common fare in educated, upper-class families and the images and characters from it run throughout their discourse. This was certainly more true at the turn of the century than in the 1960s, and more true for members of the New England Establishment than for men such as Harry Truman or Lyndon Johnson, but the sentiments and values expressed within it were surprisingly common. Bunyan's work contains numerous examples of the kind of rituals, symbolic associations, and transformative motifs common in the language of the élite. As well, the book is useful because of its explicitly geographic symbolism and what John Long would refer to as its "vivid allegory."

To account for these élite's views toward death in battle, I construct a narrative that the world views of these political élite were shaped by their attempts to construct a coherent identity that addressed concerns about their own survival and mortality. Just as it is often difficult to describe behavior as rational, our actions likewise do not always relate to concerns about death or the search for meaning in life; but we can use this conception of human behavior as another avenue for gaining greater insights into how political élite came to terms with war.

Chapter 1 offers a critique of rational choice and neorealist studies of war, and Chapter 2 develops an alternative perspective on wartime decision making, based on political culture and the ontological concerns of foreign policy decision makers. The following three chapters explore the rituals engaged in by the élite to gain some sense of immortality (what I call their "immortality projects") and further elaborates on how war itself took on ritualistic elements. The bulk of this part of the book is an attempt at reconstructing or showing the underlying logic of the mythologies used by the élite in their encounters with death and the unknown. The material is organized according to three levels at which the élite carried out their immortality projects—as private individuals, in their role as government officials, and as part of a nation at war. In Chapter 3, I examine how the élite as individuals sought to form some kind of transcendent identity as more than simply a body that would die and disappear. Part of this transcendent identity involved taking on a self-conception as an official or representative of the state and gaining a place in history, processes explored in Chapter 4. The élite's official roles in turn served as a bridge between themselves and the nation. The élite sought to protect the life and immortality of the nation, and one of the principal ways of doing so was through warfare. As the élite sought to overcome their physical limitations, they likewise attempted to ensure the nation's transcendence of its mortal bounds. Chapter 5 then examines how these concerns about mortality were evident in the élite's discourse on war and in the social construction of death in battle.

From my examination of the symbolism used and ritual engaged in by the élite, I found that war served three ritual functions—as a way of substantiating the otherwise abstract notions the nation was said to embody, as a means of rejuvenating and strengthening a nation constantly in danger of growing soft, and as a way of symbolically doing battle with death. By framing war in these ways, the deaths occurring in them could be seen as part of a larger order, which was necessary for the survival of the existing social system, and the anxieties and fears raised by those deaths could be assuaged. The three forms of the élite immortality project and these three ritual functions of war then serve to organize my reading of the foreign policy discourse. This is the sense I have made of the language I heard when listening to the discourse of war.

I conclude with a discussion of the ways in which technological and social developments are changing the way war is waged and how we think about death in battle. There is an increasing unwillingness to see Americans die overseas, and a corresponding increase in the technology to avoid those deaths; the implications of "deathless" wars, in which one side can kill with impunity, are discussed here as well. This has been accompanied by a more technologized discourse on war, which has contributed to the depoliticization of discussions of foreign policy. This depoliticization takes the form of the attempt to deny limits, isolate ourselves from others, and resist the dialogue and compromise that are central to life in the *polis*. I discuss as well how the portrayal of war as a battle against death makes it particularly difficult to oppose war at all. Likewise, I make a call for incorporating consideration of the body, mortality, and death into our analyses of international relations and foreign policy. The revision of these frameworks to include a more self-conscious consideration of mortality, leads to the reformulation of the language, ritual, and mythology surrounding the study and practice of foreign policy. As our technological and destructive abilities advance, it becomes all the more imperative that we develop our imaginative and reflective powers so that Death does not have the last laugh.

CHAPTER 1

WORDS, EQUATIONS,
BODIES, BULLETS

The particular moment in question here is that experienced when life and death hang in the balance—when the comforting illusion of life's indefinite continuity is removed. It is the moment when we face death—not the death of some distant remote other, some glamorized or sanitized death of a fictional character, but of the conscious, individual self. You are diagnosed with terminal cancer; you see a body mangled in a car accident; the soldier charges out into the open and a bullet tears through his body. Even a distant death can be unsettling, as was the case for me when walking out in a parking lot on a summer night and realizing that at that moment an execution was being carried out. I have experienced that time as qualitatively different from everyday existence—normal conventions of conversation and habitual experience break down; talk about work, or the weather, or sports becomes irrelevant. The traditional salutation, "How are you doing?" does not work with the terminally ill or the bereaved parent or spouse. It is a moment of a certain truth, and, as such, sheds some light on an element of illusion in our everyday existence—what Heidegger refers to as "fallenness," or the human tendency to be so absorbed in the quotidian business of life as to lose sight of the basic nature of our existence as finite beings.[1] The role of this illusion in our understanding of war is the focus of this work.

That we generally maintain an aversion to contemplating mortality is mirrored by the contemporary popular infatuation with illusory death. A different moment of death occurs in the numerous fictions created in popular culture. While the norm in the modern West is to assume deathlessness—to operate as if death was not a possibility—the norm in the cinema and in a good portion of fiction (such as murder mysteries and

Stephen King novels) is to experience mortality in all its many-splendored forms. The moment of death in its reassuringly fictional form (a screen event that one watches) is a mainstay of various Hollywood genres—adventures about endlessly repeated miraculous escapes from death by the hero and the rapid and systematic death of numerous Others (the more the merrier); tragedies about the death of some sympathetic or innocent character; disaster films in which lots of people die and a few deserving souls survive. The deaths we experience in the theater can be troubling on some level, in that they remind us of our own mortality, but they are much less so than death outside the theater, as we know the deaths on the screen to be filmic illusion (with documentary footage being somewhat more ambiguous), or, at a minimum, not our own.[2]

To leave the theater is to enter back into a different illusion in which as much as possible, we do not think or talk about death. As various social commentators have pointed out, this is the norm in modern Western culture.[3] It is as if we must face our own mortality, but instead of doing so consciously, choose instead to do so in our fantasy life. But that illusion of deathlessness outside the theater is of course, at times, disturbed. We are forced to face mortality in the time before the murderer or suicide pulls the trigger; when the jury hands down a death sentence; when the death row inmate is strapped to the gurney; when the hunter catches his prey in his sight; and when national leaders contemplate going to war. I look at this moment, and in particular the time before war occurs, because it is a moment of singular electricity, of horror, even some strange elation, as it involves the exercise of a profound form of power, and because it is a moment of grim, sorrowful revelation toward which we are simultaneously drawn and repulsed. It is the moment when humans either play God, by taking into their own hands the power over life and death, or feel powerless in the face of the prospect of the end of existence. The moment of our own death is not something at which most people like looking. But as one interested both in understanding why we go to war and what it means to be human, it seems as good a spot as any to start an inquiry into the meaning of war.

The eve of Operation Desert Storm, was such a time—when a group of men considered whether or not to exercise their authority to go to war, in response to a similar decision made in Iraq a few months earlier. The result of their decision would almost certainly be that many people (some young, some old, certainly some Iraqis, and probably some Americans) would die. As with any decision of this sort, it was momentous, a responsibility fraught with anxiety and tension. President George Bush, as Commander-in-Chief, the man ultimately responsible for that decision, had a lot to think about. Like William McKinley, Woodrow Wilson,

Franklin Roosevelt, Harry Truman, Lyndon Johnson (and Saddam Hussein) before him, he and his advisors would have to come to terms with war, not as an abstract concept or vague possibility or rational calculation but as an event involving deaths for which they would be at least partly held accountable. George Bush staked his claim to sole proprietorship of that grim responsibility, repeating in his journal over and over, "It is my decision. . . . It is my decision."[4]

For George Bush, despite the aggressive nature of Saddam Hussein's attack on Kuwait, it was not a simple decision. The Japanese had not just bombed Pearl Harbor; Iraqi troops were not massing on the U.S. border; Kuwait was no bastion of democracy; other countries (East Timor, Tibet, Afghanistan) had been invaded with no direct U.S. response; innocent people were dying all over the world without a kinder, gentler America coming to their aid. The Bush Administration tried a variety of justifications for going to war with Iraq—oil, jobs, rape and pillage, violation of international boundaries, the Saddam-as-Hitler analogy, and the defense of Kuwait. George Bush asserted that the war would save lives and that it was a perfectly clear case of "good" versus "evil." However questionable that Manichean characterization might have been, what *was* clear was that in this case the requisite set of conditions for U.S. intervention had been met: there was an act of aggression across an internationally recognized boundary; there was oil, and therefore a strategic interest; Hussein was a cruel man whose power was based on the use of violence; Kuwait was militarily weak sovereign nation; and Iraq was a Moslem nation located in the desert, and vastly outgunned by the United States. These reasons made intervention both strategically advantageous and politically acceptable; but still the morality of killing for these reasons remained complex.[5] It was hard to shake the "no blood for oil" slogans and the drumming of the protesters that continued outside the White House. Bush had trouble sleeping, and wrote that had to take Mylanta to calm his stomach.

On January 14, 1991, the headlines reflected Americans' shared apprehensions about the war. The country was split over whether to launch an attack. People prayed along with George Bush—for peace, for victory, for wisdom, for the soldiers, for all those "in harm's way." In the *New York Times*, Robert McFadden wrote, "And everywhere lurked undercurrents that were not easy to define—a sense that the crisis was moving inexorably out of control, that one's own voice had been lost in the rush of events. . . ."[6] Billy Graham called Bush at the White House and read to him a passage from the James Lowell poem, "The Present Crisis": "once to every man and nation comes the moment to decide and the choice goes by forever twixt that darkness and that light."[7] Americans (and Iraqis) were having to face death, real death, death outside the movie theater.

In Ann Arbor, Michigan, my housemates and I had constructed a half-dozen crude torches out of some branches wrapped with kerosene-soaked rags. On the night of the fifteenth, we joined the crowd of students and activists in a march around the campus of the University of Michigan. The crowd displayed mixed emotions—solemnity, apprehension, wild abandon. The march was an opportunity simply to do something, in a time when it felt for many like events were moving out of control. We walked through the night carrying the torches, unsure of what was coming, of our stance on it all, but palpably aware of the emotional disturbance to the normal rhythms of daily life.

The next night, hearing on CNN of the initial bombing of Baghdad, a Lebanese student turned in disgust and frustration and kicked a garbage can in the student union. It seemed to me that for him and many others, the bombs were falling on them. For those who did not identify with the U.S. government, the cruise missiles were aimed not by them, but at them. In various ways, we were all coming to terms with war, and a large portion of that involved coming to terms with death.

TALK ABOUT "THE TERMINATOR"

How was George Bush dealing with the situation? We will never know for certain what he did to "be at peace with war," but there are clues in various places—in writings and speeches, transcripts of National Security Council (NSC) meetings—and we can look at what he chose to do and who he chose to be with on the eve of the war. In these ante-bellum days, the president was visited by a Neo-Dickensian trinity of ghostly father, hypermasculine son, and evangelical minister. Prescott Bush, Arnold Schwarzenegger, and Billy Graham—respectively the ghosts of wars present (the world wars), wars future (postapocalyptic cyborg of Terminator), and wars past (the Crusades)—all sat with George as the specter of death in battle approached.

First, on Christmas Eve 1990, the ghost of his father returned, in a dream the president described in his journal. In the dream, Bush goes to visit his father at a golf course. The son George is now playing on his own fancy golf course, while his father is playing on a shabbier course. Patriarch Prescott's time is past, and now George is in the limelight. He goes to greet his father and they embrace. His father seems so real, so "big, strong, and highly respected."[8] Dad still looms large, but at last George has one-upped him. He is now president, he holds in his hand the power over life and death, while his father is dead. The son is both supported and embraced by his father, the representative of the midcentury Establishment, of the "good war." Poppy can now be satisfied to have bettered him. But is there not also in this encounter the "kiss of death"? Is not George also aware that he is on his way to join his father, and that hundreds of thousands of soldiers in the Persian Gulf will soon be as well? Perhaps there is need of the advice and consent of other archetypal figures.

On the weekend of January 12–13, 1991, while waiting to hear of Saddam Hussein's response to the ultimatum, George and Barbara Bush decided to go to Camp David. The First Family had to decide how to spend their weekend. I imagine they wanted to relax, to reduce the antacid intake, to be with people with whom they would be comfortable, while the prospect of a major bloodletting hung over their heads. Who did they invite to Camp David? Some close friends, people who will make this worrisome time a little easier. They decide that it might be nice to have Arnold Schwarzenegger and Maria Schriver.

We can imagine that on Friday evening they lift off from the White House lawn in the big helicopter and fly off into the night. Speeding toward the Maryland hills, the prospect of a visit from Arnold Schwarzenegger is perhaps a little comforting. Arnold is solid as a rock; he will have no doubts about what to do with Saddam Hussein. In the meantime, troops ready themselves for combat, the Iraqi forces continue to dig in to the Kuwaiti dessert, and the crews of the American battleships in the Persian Gulf ready the cruise missiles for launch.

Arnold Schwarzenegger had been a steady companion to the president since the 1988 campaign, and was frequently mentioned in speeches by Bush. The president liked being able to call Arnold his friend. He is also a source of laughter for the president, the humor being of the following sort:

> As you may know, Arnold—Arnold Schwarzenegger—spent a day with us up at Camp David, and competing with Barbara in tobogganing, she broke her leg. [Laughter] Then, Arnold spent a day with us at the White House promoting fitness, and I ended up in the hospital with arterial fibrillation, or something like that. [Laughter] You'll never eat lunch in my town again, Arnold. [Laughter] But I'm delighted to see you. Come to think of it, you could be my special emissary to Congress. [Laughter] Talk about "The Terminator."[9]

This is a humor of power—Arnold the cyborg is a symbol of raw power, and to think of him as on "their side" makes George Bush and his audiences laugh. As such a powerful icon, Schwarzenegger the symbol works in a number of ways. Bush stressed that Schwarzenegger's power was being used for the public good. The chairman of the President's Council on Physical Fitness, Bush repeatedly noted, was serving his country selflessly.[10] But the former Mr. Universe was also reassuring as the personification of pure physical and destructive power—the unfeeling, unthinking, remorseless cyborg. As cyborg Terminator, he is the embodiment of the fusion of human physical and technological power, which in the first *Terminator* movie is portrayed as the enemy of humanity but, in the second, has been "reprogrammed" to help and protect.[11] As his cyborg self would be described in *Terminator*, "It can't be bargained with, it can't be reasoned with, it doesn't feel pity or remorse, or fear, and it absolutely will not stop until you are dead." This, one can suppose, was akin to the message George Bush was trying to send to Saddam Hussein, in January 1991. The cyborg is the modern nightmare, "the Machine" of modernity, come to life as the man/machine. To have him on your side is, perhaps, to be friends with Death itself. The symbolic Schwarzenegger inhabits the simple Manichean dramas of Hollywood, in which good battles evil and everything is clear and neatly resolved. And Arnold represents the "beautiful body"—the body that is powerful, fit, and healthy. His is the body that does not betray any signs of mortality, while simultaneously containing within it the power to kill the Other. In various ways he represents both hegemonic masculinity, the fantasy of immortality, and the power to kill.

Perhaps this is all irrelevant to George Bush, and he likes having Arnold there for the stimulating conversation on current events, or because Arnold likes hearing George tell war stories or tales of high political intrigue; but maybe Arnold as symbol is important as well. In any case Arnold is there; that is the important thing.

On that Sunday, Arnold and Maria and the kids have fun sledding, except that Barbara has an accident and suffers what the *New York Times* reports as a "nondisplaced fracture of the left fibula bone." Anna Perez, her press secretary states the next day, "She doesn't know why she didn't bail out. She just held on and the next thing she knew, there was the tree."[12] Barbara is with the kids, they are laughing and enjoying themselves. She is a good sport, joining in even though she is in her seventies. She sits on the round plastic disk of the sled, poised at the crest of the hill. The kids push her over, and she starts her descent, the controlled fall, bouncing along, slowing rotating one way and then another. She hears the shouts of the children telling her to let go; but she is lost. She doesn't bail out, and she says she doesn't know why. She has to hold on, hang on to something.

Back in the White House, Barbara in a wheelchair, the wait continues. On January 15, 1991, the deadline passes with no sign of movement from the Iraqi troops. On January 16, Billy Graham (who had played golf with George Bush's father Prescott, and with every president since Eisenhower) receives an "urgent" request to join the Bushes for lunch or dinner at the White House. He had supported Johnson and Nixon throughout the Vietnam War, delivered the sermon at Johnson's funeral, and supported Reagan throughout his prosecution of the Cold War. And now he had been reassuring Bush that Saddam Hussein was in fact the anti-Christ.[13] Graham again agrees to come, and ends up staying the night in the now infamous Lincoln bedroom the night that the Gulf War starts. That evening, sitting in "the Blue Room, which was made cozy with family pictures and personal mementos," they heard the news on CNN that the bombing of Baghdad had commenced.[14] Graham reports that on hearing the news, and at the president's request, Graham led them in prayer that night; and he did so again the next morning when he delivered a sermon on the "peace of God." Bush, after his speech, told Graham, "I know in my heart I've done right." It helps to say that to Billy Graham and have him affirm that sentiment. Pity the men who have made these decisions. Pity those who will die as a result. Pity George Bush, who needed his father and Arnold Schwarzenegger and Billy Graham there to make it through the night. The trigger had been pulled and the bullet sped through the Persian night and certain young and old people were torn asunder and ushered into oblivion. And George Bush needed something to hang onto as well.

EQUATIONS OF WAR

Much has been written about war within the social sciences under the general heading of "war studies." Little of that writing captures the mix of humanness, profundity, absurdity, and emotional power of that moment, to which the above examples allude. The emphasis in the field of security studies has been on causal explanations of war—finding quantifiable variables that, when analyzed uniformly, explain variation in international violence. Within political science, one of the more highly regarded treatments of the subject has been the rigorous, quantified, operationalized studies of international conflict. It is an approach with roots in the Clauswitzean attempt to develop a science of war, and the classical Enlightenment faith in the application of science to social problems. This approach treats war largely as a matter of economics—as a process of exchange in which things of value are traded or land is bought for a cost—those costs including most centrally the deaths of human beings. Despite the horrific destructiveness of war, more often than not, it is represented simply as another political phenomenon not unlike an election.[15] In this body of work, war is turned into equations about power and expected utility, is described as a game, and death in battle is simply another cost figured into a utility function.[16] In this view, humans are seen as disembodied, rational utility maximizers, and war as arising from processes such as diffusion, power shifts, and the calculation of expected utility.[17] In the academic realm, there has been a trend toward the greater use of these approaches, evidenced by the rise of the behavioral school within the social sciences after World War II, and, more recently, in the popularity of rational choice theory, formal modeling, and statistical analysis in the study of war.[18]

This is not to say that this trend has necessarily been for the worse. We have gained useful information from these studies—both about war and about how we like to think about war. These studies reveal pieces of the causal puzzle; but at the same time they are revealing in terms of what they leave out. These studies operate within a set of brackets, as it were, outside of which lies all that is horribly sad, wild, and uncontrolled. In the field of statistics, the term "stochastic" signifies the random or unexplained "residue" in an analysis of correlation of variables. It is that which remains unquantifiable and therefore, within the frame of statistics, unknowable. The work in this book, however, locates itself squarely within the "realm of the stochastic." By definition, these positivist approaches must exclude all that cannot be operationalized and formalized. This self-limitation within the field of war studies means that it by and large leaves out, among other things, the art of politics—the tradition, ritual, and tragedy that remain an integral part of the process of making foreign policy, particularly when people are dying as a result of that policy. It is from this residue—the realm of the stochastic, or what Daniel Pick calls the "friction" of war—that I draw the material for my study.[19]

For all the analytic rigor and deductive logic of the theories, there is something missing; in large part, it is their seductive clarity and antiseptic aura, as these differ so radically from their subject of study, that prompt me to offer the alternative view developed in this book. These theories present a view of war that avoids directly confronting the nauseating horror of the event, and I think it is important to stay focused on what Kurtz in Conrad's *Heart of Darkness* and Coppola's *Apocalypse Now* would melodramatically refer to as "the horror, the horror." There is some important theoretical leverage to be gained by not averting our gaze, and not being above using a few clichés.

There is further reason to be wary of the objectivity of such approaches, in that there is a psychological incentive to adopt them. The danger of bias and partiality, against which the scientific method is supposed to guard, is part and parcel of the social scientific approach to studying war. The social scientific approach reflects an aesthetics of order and cleanliness, a will to render the insanity of war in controllable and rational terms, which indicates that for all its methodological precautions against bias, it provides us with at best a highly circumscribed view of warfare. There is a great appeal to that approach. It has the ability to imbue one with a sense of control over war, and such a sense of control is highly valued, especially in the nuclear age. While striving for objectivity and "realism" in its account of war, these approaches likewise still make use of highly subjective and figurative language; they employ certain metaphors for war—as an economic exchange, as a conscious choice, as "deterrence failure"—while avoiding speaking of war as involving the tearing of flesh and bone.

The rational choice and game theoretical approaches to international security have come under scrutiny from a variety of critics. In economics, Amartya Sen has pointed out how the idea of revealed preferences assumes both too little and too much. Humans, he points out, act on the basis of a variety of concerns, including what Sen refers to as commitment and other ethical concerns.[20] The same can certainly be said of soldiers choosing to risk their lives in battle. Social constructionist literature also questions the ontological status of the actors, values, and conceptions of "anarchy," "threat," or "crisis" that rational choice models take for granted.[21] But there are other reasons to be careful not to get too caught up in the intricacies of these models.

Take two examples from prominent works in the field of international relations which might be said to share the above aesthetic sensibility—the diagram from Robert Axelrod's *The Evolution of Cooperation* (Figure 1) and the equation from Bruce Bueno de Mesquita's *The War Trap* (Figure 2).[22] Robert Axelrod's diagram is the product of a computer simulation in which each "X" represents what he calls "nice" actors who have adopted a tit-for-tat bargaining strategy in their interactions with their neighbors. These interactions are modeled as a series of "prisoner's dilemma games," which involve what amounts to either total war (leading to the destruction of one of the actors) or peace. Depending on the outcome of these interactions, the chances of an actor surviving to the next round either increase or decrease. In this computer-generated evolutionary scenario, Axelrod demonstrates with reassuring optimism that, given certain assumptions, good will triumph over evil. This is good news for those concerned with global war and peace; the model appears to offer a way out of the trap of the security dilemma and arms racing that has characterized much of the sad history of international politics. Moreover, it will do so with geometric regularity and symmetry; this is one of the things that makes a work such as this so appealing. Here is history as a lab experiment in which peace spreads like a crystal forming in solution, and the bloody realities of the interactions this simulation is supposed to represent are completely absent. This is a "fun" and "neat" study of war, but perhaps a little too neat.

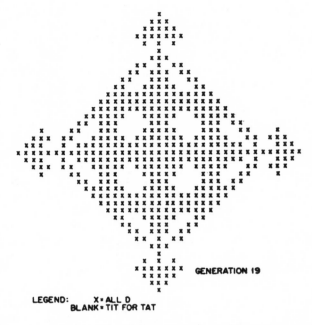

GENERATION 19

LEGEND: X = ALL D
BLANK = TIT FOR TAT

Figure 1   The mix of "nice" and "mean" units in a simulation experiment, in Robert Axelrod's *The Evolution of Cooperation.*

Similarly, Bruce Bueno de Mesquita's equation is a work of mathematical art, a paean to Newtonian mechanics applied to human affairs (he opens his chapter on the expected utility theory of war by quoting Galileo: "The book of Nature is written in mathematical characters."). Here our thoughts are drawn to figuring out how the formula was derived and what all the subscripts and subsubscripts refer to. We are in a land of "i's" and "j's" and "k's," notable for its abstraction. It is also admirable in its complexity, and that complexity works wonderfully to avert the mind's eye from the subject of study. It turns war into a math problem (the formula being the result of "substituting, multiplying through and rearranging terms"). It draws students in graduate seminars into questions of operationalization and measurement. (Has he used good measures of military power? Has he used the appropriate statistical analysis?) It offers the hope that warfare might be understood in some technical sense and eventually be prevented by the application of some technical fix.

$$\sum_{l=1}^{5} E(U_i)_{k_l} = \sum_{l=1}^{5} \left(P_{ik_{t_0}} \left[U_{iki_{t_0}} - U_{ikj_{t_0}} + \Delta U_{iki_{t_0} - t_n} - \Delta U_{ikj_{t_0} - t_n} \right] \right.$$

$$+ P_{jk_{t_0}} \left[U_{iki_{t_0}} - U_{ikj_{t_0}} + \Delta U_{iki_{t_0} - t_n} - \Delta U_{ikj_{t_0} - t_n} \right]$$

$$\left. - 1 \left[U_{iki_{t_0}} - U_{ikj_{t_0}} + \Delta U_{iki_{t_0} - t_n} - \Delta U_{ikj_{t_0} - t_n} \right] \right)$$

$$= \sum_{l=1}^{5} \left((P_{ik_{t_0}} + P_{jk_{t_0}} - 1) \left[U_{iki_{t_0}} - U_{ikj_{t_0}} + \right. \right.$$

$$\left. \left. \Delta U_{iki_{t_0} - t_n} - \Delta U_{ikj_{t_0} - t_n} \right] \right) \tag{5}$$

Figure 2   The mathematical formula for figuring the expected utility of war, from Bruce Bueno de Mesquita's *The War Trap*.

In *War and Reason*, a follow-on to *The War Trap*, Bueno de Mesquita and coauthor Bruce Lalman begin with a discussion of a few Goya prints depicting the gruesomeness of war.[23] These are used to pose the question of the book: Is war the result of a rational process or not? And does it necessarily improve the general welfare? (To which, not surprisingly, they answer in the affirmative to the first and negative to the second.) But once the bloody reality of war is acknowledged, it is again set aside, and perhaps inspires the descent into the antiseptic nether world of formulae. In neither work is the gruesomeness used as a theoretical tool, as an avenue for understanding war. In both books, Bueno de Mesquita offers us an arcane and highly abstract language, and for all its predictive power, it pulls us away from the experience that follows this supposed calculation—an experience so powerful as to inspire awe, terror, abject sadness, and insanity. In the calculus of *The War Trap*, the more than 50 million dead in World War II result from the expected utility calculations of Nazi Germany and Poland in 1939, which turn out to be .306 and -.306, respectively. The equation correctly predicts that Germany, rather than Poland, will initiate the war, but incorrectly predicts the winner. And it leaves something out.

THE COMPOST PILE OF WAR

My critique of these works stems in large part from the fact that the aim of my work differs from that of the rational choice scholars. I do not critique them on their own terms, because I have found those terms unsatisfactory. They seek, among other things, causal explanations of war, while I am pursuing the somewhat more amorphous goal of an "understanding" of war in human terms. It is understandable, then, that Axelrod and Bueno de Mesquita leave certain aspects of war out (every perspective leaves something out), and that I focus on those very elements—namely, on the "results" of these calculations. We find an example of these results in a memoir of the experiences of E. B. Sledge in World War II during the battle between American and Japanese forces on Okinawa. There are any number of accounts of this sort, from people who have been through war or genocide, but Sledge's account serves our purposes here. In it, he offers a strikingly literal picture of the physical nature of warfare, of the body, and of what happens to it when it is dead.[24] It can serve as a tangible, visceral, pungent starting point to an analysis of war that takes the body, the stench, and the insanity of warfare into account. It is a realism of a different sort (paleorealist?) from that employed by Hans Morgenthau or Kenneth Waltz, but one that I think can be equally useful. Paul Fussell summarizes Sledge's account as follows:

> . . . the worst of all was a week-long stay in rain-soaked foxholes on a muddy ridge facing the Japanese, a site strewn with decomposing corpses turning various colors, nauseating with the stench of death, "an environment so degrading I believed we had been flung into hell's own cesspool." Because there were no latrines and because there was no moving in daylight, the men relieved themselves in their holes and flung the excrement out into the already foul mud. It was a latterday Verdun, the Marine occupation of that ridge, where the artillery shelling uncovered scores of half-buried Marine and Japanese bodies, making the position "a stinking compost pile."
>
> If a Marine slipped and slid down the back slope of the muddy ridge, he was apt to reach the bottom vomiting. I saw more than one man lose his footing and slip and slide all the way to the bottom only to stand up horror-stricken as he watched in disbelief while fat maggots tumbled out of his muddy dungaree pockets, cartridge belt, legging lacings, and the like. . . .

There is a certain incongruence between this picture of war and conceptions of it as some sort of geopolitical election or attempt at utility maximization—an incongruence that points to the importance of coming up with an account of war that incorporates how those making decisions about war came to terms with the death of the body. This is not a clean or pleasant way to think about war, but then again war is neither pleasant nor clean.

It is my understanding that getting a country to spend on the order of $300 billion annually during peacetime, and much more during times of full mobilization, and to march by the thousands into battle requires something more than what is captured in calculations of expected utility. To make such sacrifices requires tapping into some kind of powerful human motivations. People may be willing to put in long hours at the office in order to achieve an expected profit of $306,000, but they will not march off to war for an expected utility of .306 ("My fellow Americans, our expected utility in the battle we are about to face is a whopping .822. Charge!"). Those responsible for the deaths of these soldiers must have something more powerful than numbers to allow them to justify and sell those decisions; and the citizens who support these decisions in various ways must have some experiences and motivations that resonate more powerfully with the purported aims of war. There are a whole range of powerful human desires that could be drawn on—desires for control, for fame and glory, for wealth, stability, meaning in life, and so on. Sexual desire and the particularly male preoccupation with sexual possession or control is certainly a candidate, and this basic drive has been drawn on extensively in constructing the motivational basis for the support of war. But for this study, I focus on another powerful human experience: on terror, on fear, and particularly the fear of death. Although, on the surface, one would think that this would provide a powerful motivation not to go to war (see Chapter 6), my argument here is that this fear was turned back on itself, so that going to war, even for those on the battlefield itself, could be construed as a way to address fears about death—fears elicited by the very deaths caused in war. For soldiers, the motivations and training are of a particular sort. On the field of battle, soldiers are driven by the dictates of survival, by exhaustion, by mindless obedience, camaraderie, and Freud's *thanatos* or bloodlust.[25] But for the citizens and politicians, the dynamics are different, and I focus here instead on the whole complex social, cultural, and psychological structure constructed within élite discourse on the home front to make sense of, justify, and even glorify death in battle.

Terry Eagleton argues that, "[i]t is in the significant silences of a text, in its gaps and absences that the presence of ideology can be most positively felt."[26] Taking Eagleton's cue to look for "what is not there," perhaps the most significant void in social scientific studies of war is the lack of discussion of death. As the death of the body is so painfully present in the field of battle, it is equally lacking from the field of study. This silence provides a particularly useful point of entry into the study of the political discourse on war in that it constitutes a paradoxical void; what is missing is actually itself an "absence"—the absence of the voices and lives of those killed in war. This "absence-like" quality of death is found in the absolute stillness and silence of the corpse, in the fact that the person killed in war is no longer present as a physical actor within society.[27] This lack of a lack, as it were, has thus resulted in a view in studies of war that is too complete, too neat; it is devoid of corpses. All of war is instead said to be captured in an equation.

This act of "bringing death back in" to the field of war studies is part of a project of humanizing the study of war.[28] In part, this involves taking seriously the study of politics within the humanities. I use the term "human" here in the sense of contrasted either with the divine or the machine—encompassing such aspects of our existence as the body, pain, sorrow, sadness, fear, desire. It is not dissimilar to the term as used by Jack Valenti in describing Lyndon Johnson as a "very human" president and George Stephanapoulos's account of his "all too human" boss.[29] It can be taken in this case as virtually a synonym for the condition of mortality, as that word connotes fallibility and limitation. I attempt this reintroduction by focusing on the cultural and psychological responses to mortality, the fate of the body in battle, and the fears and pain that accompany these facets of war. The research examines the views of a group—the foreign policy élite in Washington—which was generally far removed from these horrors of war, but it attempts to keep these aspects of war in mind nonetheless. That they were not too removed from those horrors was reflected in part by a certain discursive excess, complementing the absence of direct reference to death.

THE METAPHORICAL EXCESS

Although the purpose of theory is to explain rather than describe, we still expect theory to have some plausibility in the face of our immediate observations about a particular phenomenon. The picture painted by rational choice frameworks is of political élite engaged in utility maximization based on a predetermined set of preferences. Decisions are supposed to be reached by gathering information until the marginal utility for the information search is negative, assigning probabilities and values to each of the various available options, and choosing the one option that would maximize expected utility over a reasonable timeframe. Although rational choice theorists are quick to point out that they are only assuming that decisions are made "as if" they were the result of a rational calculation, the "picture in the head" of what this rational decision maker is doing is of fully self-aware, controlled, instrumentally rational political accountant, tabulating cost, benefits, and probabilities. The goals pursued, and the costs and benefits associated with various outcomes, can certainly be quite varied, but at its root this view has a sense of decision-makers who know who they are, where they want to go, and how to get there. Although not impossible, it is certainly difficult to derive much of the actual behavior of the élite from such a model.

The rational choice framework is certainly more parsimonious and rigorous than the one developed here, but it fails to take account of a wide range of élite behaviors—behaviors that can in various ways be seen as symbolic, superstitious, or ritualistic. Although the list of such behaviors that follows does not invalidate the logic of the rational choice models, I hope it at least points to the need to pursue other avenues of investigation into the nature of warfare. The absence of death in war studies and in the political discourse of the élite is mirrored by and can be contrasted with an excess, of symbolism, ritual, and pageantry, which is hard to account for in strictly rational terms, and that I will argue is in part a response to the troubling fact of human mortality. Politics, as some have argued, is in part a realm of symbolism in which the participants form identities and views of the world, a realm that "sustains broader social visions."[30] The foreign policy élite, in their words and acts, create and make decisions within symbolic worlds, realms that are "socially constructed" and within which utility functions and policy options may be as much a product of fantasy as raw empiricism.

For an explicit statement of the symbolic nature of political discourse, we turn to an unlikely occasion: a 1885 speech given at the dedication of a library by one member of the foreign policy élite, John Long (later Secretary of the Navy under McKinley and Roosevelt). The public library, he claimed, was composed of

> symbols, noble and exquisite in themselves but faint and fleeting in comparison with that deeper reality,—that *reality of ideality*, inexpressible in human language or architectural material,—the reality of the love of the human heart, of the charity of human brotherhood, of the eternal progress of the human mind. . . .[31]

The library building Long describes is a concrete entity, built using all the skills of the engineer and contractor to serve specific needs. But, as Long describes it, the building is much more than this. Through Long's words, this public works project—the building of a library—comes to stand for a whole view of human nature and history, a window into the unseen recesses of the soul. A whole new reality of "ideality" is conjured up by the speaker for his audience—a world of love and charity and progress. These concepts, as they constitute Long's beatific twilight zone, point to the set of human concerns and strategies with which this book deals.

If we find such rich symbolism at the solemn, but fairly mundane, occasion of the library dedications, we certainly find them when life and death are at stake. During wartime, the citizens and leaders of nations must define what their core values are—those for which they are willing to die. As George Bush put it prior to the Gulf War, "In the life of a nation, we're called upon to define who we are and what we believe."[32] Although war can be understood in part as a rational decision, it as well takes part in the process of self-definition and the search for meaning in the face of the deaths of individuals and the lives of nations.

In that search for self-definition and meaning, George Bush was not the first to seek religious council in prayer before sending the United States off to war. William McKinley, when asked by a group of ministers to explain his decision to conquer the Philippines, replied that it was the result of divine inspiration, received after falling to his knees in prayer. In the debate over whether the United States should take the Philippines, senators supported their arguments with reference to political deities as much as they did with strategic rationales. Henry Cabot Lodge claimed that the revered statesmen, John Marshall, Thomas Jefferson, and William Seward, would all have approved of taking the Philippines. George Hoar literally recreated a vote of the political demigods on the Philippine issue, and found, not surprisingly, that only the buccaneering Aaron Burr (the Loki of the pantheon) would have approved of the venture. Hoar, in his opposition to that conquest, equated it with the temptation of Christ by the devil.[33]

John Hay, in his eulogy for William McKinley, spoke of the United States as a newly metamorphosed being that now had wings and could fly; and he described America's leaders themselves as being prophets. On the occasion of McKinley's inauguration, Hay gave the incoming president a ring containing a hair from George Washington's head; to Theodore Roosevelt, Hay gave one containing a hair of Lincoln. While fighting in Cuba, Teddy Roosevelt shot a Spanish soldier with a pistol salvaged from the sunken U.S.S. Maine, and went into battle with a saber and on horseback, even though he was fighting in dense jungle against a force armed with rifles. Similarly, Secretary of War Robert Patterson made a point of wearing the belt of a German he had killed in World War I.[34] A large part of Roosevelt's recreation consisted of killing dangerous animals and filling his home with their preserved remains. Is there some way of accounting for the symbolism of these acts? What might they tell us about how these men thought about mortality and death in battle?

Near the end of his life, the first Secretary of Defense, James Forrestal, began scratching his head unconsciously, so hard that he wore a bare spot in his scalp; he impulsively dipped his fingers in water and wet his lips; and he came to fear that communists were everywhere and were "going to get" him. While in the hospital with a diagnosis of schizophrenia resulting from excessive stress, he copied out a passage from Sophocles' *Ajax* and leapt to his death from the fourteenth floor of the hospital. During the Vietnam War, George Ball, in a memo to Lyndon Johnson, argued for deescalation by quoting from Ralph Waldo Emerson: "Things are in the saddle and ride mankind." One of Forrestal's protégés, Robert McNamara—who prided himself on his emotional detachment and strove for the ideal of fully quantified cost-benefit decision making—found himself, as he calculated how much ammunition would be necessary for the next phase of the Vietnam War, collapsing in tears. During the war, Lyndon Johnson had recurring nightmares of drowning in a river or being paralyzed, and would rise at night and go touch the portrait of the invalid Woodrow Wilson, reassuring himself that although Wilson had been an invalid, he himself was still alive and powerful. After leaving office, he would speak of Vietnam and Nixon as having ruined his Great Society Program, which he described as like a once-beautiful woman who was now old and ugly. The maverick Senator Wayne Morse would declare in the Senate chambers that the "skeleton symbol of death" hung over the battle in Vietnam, while John McNaughton (an assistant to McNamara) would argue that the United States should try to emerge from the war "looking like the good doctor."[35]

The list could go on, but the point, I hope, is clear: While the élite were engaged in debating the costs and benefits of different options in pursuit of the national interest, they also were involved in the creation and perpetuation of a world in which horses, "things," dangerous animals, taxidermy, beautiful women, floods, winged creatures, bodily remains, dead men's pistols, God, and Jesus were all elements. Although it would be easy to dismiss these words and behaviors as pure rhetoric or distracting epiphenomena, they need to be explained somehow. These were not random acts, but occurred for a reason. The use of such highly symbolic language, the strange dreams, the odd habits, and even insanity—all indicate the extent to which the worldviews and coping mechanisms of the élite were not rational in the way we usually think of that term or derived solely from direct reference to the empirical world. They could not be, for deriving their worldviews from the profusion of experiences alone cannot produce a coherent, satisfying picture. The élite, as with anyone else, had to construct an artificial view, a mythology of foreign affairs that was part of their particular cosmologies.

These words and actions both pose a challenge to rational choice theories of decision making and provide a source of information for an investigation of the symbolic world of the foreign policy élite. Although not necessarily contradicting rational choice theories, these behaviors are difficult to reconcile with them. The approach developed here is devoted to giving some account of this behavior and language used by the élite. The account offered is centered in the unavoidable reality of the human body, a reality that is all too vivid for those actually in battle.

BODIES AND BULLETS

These processes of humanizing and "embodying" the study of war entail crossing boundaries between disciplines and aspects of human existence. The body is itself an interface between the interior of the self and the myriad external conditions of existence, and humans are both isolated individuals and inextricably linked to and part of the society within which they exist. Likewise, this work, in a style and strategy that will be unsatisfying for purists of a particular discipline or approach, moves back and forth between political theory and political science, the psychology of individuals and the culture of groups, and the material realities of physical existence and the way those realities are interpreted and shaped by our ideas. In so doing, this work attempts to occupy the site of liminality (on the threshold between in and out), and transgress the boundaries that have inhibited such interdisciplinarity. Rather than reduce my explanation to a purely materialist or idealist set of factors, I make what seems the rather obvious assumption that both sets of factors are important and that it is in the tensions and contradictions between them that the most interesting explanations of political behavior lie.

Both rational choice and cognitive psychological frameworks treat values and beliefs as fixed characteristics of individual decision makers. Here I emphasize the contingent and constructed nature of these views. At the same time, I have not found it useful to leave the discussion of foreign policy dangling in midair, and instead ground it in the material realities of which the body so powerfully reminds us. I attempt to show that these constructions are shaped by the élite's attempts at coming to terms with mortality and the limits imposed on them because of their existence as embodied beings. We need to be sensitive to both the material constraints on human action and the malleability of reality. There are undeniable limits to our ability to change the world by thinking about it differently (we cannot wish away the knowledge of how to build nuclear weapons, the presence of aggressive states, or age-old injustices), but such "new thinking" is by no means insignificant.

This framework seeks as well to avoid the shortcomings of realism and idealism in their pure form by looking at the interaction between the material world and human interpretations of it. Thus, this approach looks at the role of words, bodies, and bullets—words as a conveyor of symbols, bodies (sensory organs, brains, hands, mouths, vocal chords) as the threshold or interface between the symbolic and material worlds, and bullets as part of that material world that sometimes cannot be denied. Realist interpretations discount the fact that much of our reality is interpreted in highly subjective manner within idiosyncratic cultural and institutional settings. My aim is to ground this investigation in the human body—to occupy that often uncomfortable site on the borders between fact and fiction, good and evil, self and other, material and ideal. The condition of mortality, that physical existence of human beings, is itself liminal—an existence always on the threshold between life and death—and, as such, provides us with a basis for existing "in between."[36] This chapter, and the analysis that follows, moves back and forth from the material to the ideal, from culture and artifice to body and desire, from word to bullet, attempting to show the interaction between the two realms.

We can use the body as a vantage point from which to construct a view of the world that lapses neither into dogmatic materialism nor doctrinaire idealism. Again, the place to begin is on the battlefield, with an account from one of the few political élite who actually experienced war firsthand. We find, in an account of death in battle written by Theodore Roosevelt, how the body—and particularly the mouth—stands as that boundary between the depths of the soul and the wide world outside.[37] The account, taken from Roosevelt's *The Rough Riders,* describes one of Roosevelt's favorite comrades-in-arms, Captain Bucky O'Neil, a former sheriff and mayor who had fought Apaches and outlaws in Arizona. Roosevelt describes O'Neil as a born leader, fearless and ambitious.[38] Each day he would join with his fellow soldiers in the toast of the regiment: "The officers: may the war last until each is killed, wounded, or promoted." Before the charge up San Juan Hill, O'Neil, who held to the philosophy that officers should expose themselves to fire in order to encourage their men, was strolling cavalierly in the line of fire, smoking a cigarette. As Roosevelt describes the scene:

> As O'Neil moved to and fro, his men begged him to lie down, and one of the sergeants said: "Captain, a bullet is sure to hit you." O'Neil took his cigarette out of his mouth, and blowing out a cloud of smoke laughed and said: "Sergeant, the Spanish bullet isn't made that will kill me." . . . As he

turned on his heel a bullet struck him in the mouth and came out at the back of his head; so that even before he fell his wild and gallant soul had gone out into the darkness."[39]

The story illustrates some of the shortcomings of attempting to take account of O'Neil's behavior and death only in terms of the words uttered, the body from which they came, or the bullet that contradicted his claim about the world. The words, body, and bullet all interact in a dialogue between the ideal and material, as mediated through O'Neil's body. They form two kinds of reality—one that came out of his mouth and one that entered it. One is a reality shaped by a set of expectations and socializations within which this soldier lived—John Long's "reality of ideality." Like the smoke so nonchalantly blown from O'Neil's mouth, it is a bit of cultural smoke and mirrors.[40] This reality is constituted by the words he utters, and the actions he takes. He created for himself and for his audience an image of himself as bold, fearless, and confident. The words he utters are part of this process of self-creation. In speaking them and performing that act, he in part creates himself as someone who *is* fearless and knows his death will not come there. It is conceivable that he might have risked his life in that way even if he had not uttered those words (Roosevelt apparently displayed similar bravado without making any claims about Spanish bullets), but these words add something to his act—an air of reassurance, a sense of destiny, of control over his fate—that make it easier to perform and, further, are potentially emboldening for his men.[41] They do so by constructing a notion of agency and destiny that engenders a sense of control. O'Neil asserts that he has a destiny and that the cosmos is ordered in minute detail, such that each American soldier is somehow matched or not matched with a particular bullet manufactured somewhere in Spain. He asserts that no such bullet has been made for him, and, therefore, that he is not in danger. These words transform a situation of danger and uncertainty into one of security and knowledge. These illusions created by O'Neil are part of what enables him to stand in the open as the bullets fly, and they demonstrate the importance of the social construction of identity and the world.

We should note here as well the importance of the social context within which O'Neil performs this act. A key element of the concreteness of the identity and worldview constructed by these acts is their inherently social nature. These myths and religions are not the "Promethean vision of the solitary individual" but are formed through an inherently social process.[42] Although, in general, I examine the worldviews of individual élite, these views should not be seen as reified psychological entities that exists in isolation from the social context. As poststructuralists have pointed out, the very idea of the authorship of texts is problematic. In simple terms, given the extent to which the expressions used by particular individuals are drawn from the broader social discourse, it becomes difficult to consider them one's own. In Roosevelt's account, the words written are not Roosevelt's but a quote of O'Neil's, and, furthermore, the phrase, "The bullet isn't made . . ." was not O'Neil's either, but part of long military tradition, dating back to at least the sixteenth century, that embodied a notion of personal destiny in battle. The phrase had been attributed to Napoleon and would later be used by Douglas MacArthur as he engaged in his own cavalier behavior in battle. These words, which were part of the vocabulary available to these élite, then helped them to adopt a particular stance toward death.

But to look at the words and social context is only half the story. O'Neil's identity and constructed view of the world—the world that we know from what comes out of his mouth—constitute one kind of reality that shapes his life. There is the contrasting reality that enters his mouth—a "Spanish Mauser bullet" traveling very fast, which contradicts the statement he had just made. It is now clear that "he" (a person capable of uttering words) will not be leading or inspiring his troops by strolling about under fire, that in fact there was a Spanish bullet made that would kill him, that he is mortal. Thus, we must recognize, while realizing the great and amazing human ability to construct reality, that there are limits to the malleability of reality. His denial of death has been shown to be "problematic" to the extent that he can no longer voice that denial, his ideas about knowing his destiny shown to lack congruence with the event just witnessed by Roosevelt and the other soldiers.

The scene thus illustrates the interrelationship of what is referred to in empiricist terms as experienced or felt reality and what is referred to in cultural terms as the social construction of reality.[43] This distinction between experienced and constructed reality is obviously problematic—there is no clear line between these two kinds of realities. As the social theorist Anthony Giddens has pointed out, society is formed and changes as a result of the social constructions of the members of that society.[44] We can only know and make sense of O'Neil's death through words or other representations. Human identity and the norms and institutions that order society are part of the reality that constitutes our world, and, yet, they are socially constructed. The attempt to study humanity scientifically is complicated by this very fact, that humanity and society are malleable and the result of an ongoing process of creation and transformation—ideas turn into institutions, dreams into reality. As social constructions become real, so physical entities and felt experiences are often vague and subject to various interpretations.[45] But despite the fact that these two realities sometimes blend into each other, they do not completely collapse into one—the distinction between words and bullets remains. The powers of the mind to create the world are limited by the intransigence of the material world and the condition of mortality, our existence as embodied, physical beings. Changing the social constructions of reality will not erase certain, often painful, realities—human mortality, the ratio of U.S. to Philippine GNPs, the destructive effect of high explosives or napalm.

The view from the body thus incorporates aspects of culture and physicality, of human creative powers and of their limits, that can be used to develop an alternative to the conception of humans as "economic men." This alternative focuses on the condition of mortality, on desire, creativity and limitation. It is to that framework that I now turn.

CHAPTER 2

DEATH AND THE STATESMEN

What we make of life is shaped by what we make of death; for we live in the presence of the inevitability of death and we dedicate our lives to the proof of the proposition that death is not what it seems to be: the irrevocable end of our existence. We search for immortality, and the kind of immortality we seek determines the kind of life we lead.

—Hans Morgenthau[1]

The deaths occurring during wartime have a deep and varied impact on everyone involved—most obviously, the soldiers and civilians caught in the fire and the soldiers' families and, less directly, the citizens who are implicated by the war. National leaders have the unique responsibility, however, for making the decisions about who will live and die. The leaders of the modern state possess, in Weber's terms, the monopoly on the legitimate use of force; as politicians and powerseekers they can take this as a great accomplishment, but as humans they must somehow come to terms with this fact. They may openly or secretly revel in that grim power, they may dread it, and they may, in time, become callous to that fact. But they must in some way come to terms with these deaths. To any but the most pathological or hardened, death, especially death of the young, is troubling. The worldviews developed by those making these life-and-death decisions then can in part be accounted for by looking at their attempts at coming to terms with their own mortality. After all, the death of soldiers was not a fate that these élite would themselves escape. They too would be dying, and, thus, while coming to terms with the soldiers' deaths, men such as

Theodore Roosevelt, John F. Kennedy, and Lyndon Johnson likewise had to come to terms with their own.

John Hay—personal secretary to Abraham Lincoln, Secretary of State under McKinley and Roosevelt, author of the "Open Door Notes," and the man who termed the Spanish-American conflict, a "splendid, little war"—was as well someone who frequently dwelt on the prospect of his own demise. As with a few other American foreign policy officials (including Jimmy Carter and the recent secretary of defense, William Cohen) he was a published poet in his day, and much of his poetry dealt with the theme of death and the quest for immortality. Perhaps the best example is his 1881 poem, "The Stirrup Cup." It portrays death as an ever-present "Pale Horse" that has come to "carry me to unknown lands."[2]

> His whinny shrill, his pawing hoof,
> Sound dreadful as a gathering storm;
> And I must leave this sheltering roof,
> And joys of life so soft and warm.

The possibility of death is always present, always waiting outside the door. We cannot say to what extent, as Morgenthau puts it, the search for immortality determined the life Hay led, but concerns about this horse waiting outside his door seemed to have played some role in his life. He certainly did not appear sanguine about the prospect of taking that ride.

His concern with death, and the influence of Romanticism (in which he immersed himself as a student at Brown University), was evident in the writings of his early adulthood. "I sometimes think I am unhappy in my morbid delicacy of spiritual perception," he would write with gleeful pathos to his college friend Hannah Angell. He claimed to have suffered "sad strange glimpses of apocalyptic vision . . . joined in mysterious sympathy with cloudy premonitions of an early doom." More mundane concerns about the passage of time, about whether he would be able to "make it" in the world, and about aging were also found in his letters and private conversations. As an adult, he was plagued by exhaustion, insomnia, and depression, with no clear diagnosis. Hay also had his share of run-ins with the deaths of people he knew, was a bit of a hypochondriac, and seemed to expect his own death at any moment. On one occasion, after returning to the United States from Europe, he actually thought he had died. To his old friend John Nicolay, he wrote, "The other day I had the most ridiculous attack I have ever had—*thought I was dead for half an hour.* The Doctor said it was nothing at all serious—simply the effect of the cold." That he would imagine himself dead is at least a little odd. On what did he base this conclusion? Clearly he was preoccupied with his death, as he thought it such a distinct possibility that—on the basis of apparently slim, and patently false, evidence—he believed it had already occurred.

The event reflects as well a desire to know what death is like and to believe that one would still be around after the death of the body. As frightening as the experience might have been to Hay, it must likewise have been reassuring, for it implied an afterlife of some sort, a time when Hay could in fact realize that he was dead, which would be preferable to the alternative of infinite nonexistence. But Hay still lived in utter dread of dying. This "false alarm" was not a pleasant experience for him but an "attack," and it seems not unreasonable to expect that he would try to arrange his life both so as to avoid having to think about the prospect of death and to achieve some sense of immortality.[3]

Reflecting similar concerns, John Long, the other poet-politician of the McKinley administration, would write in his journal, as his heart condition worsened a few days before he died, "Pain from the hardening of my arteries suddenly became more intense last night. . . . Dread the coming night." This dread, however, was manifest throughout his life—reflected most saliently in his infatuation with the unstoppable flow of time. Long's writings are full of a bittersweet nostalgia, a concern with the tenuousness of existence, and a pronounced preoccupation with the irretrievability of the past. As early as his sixteenth birthday, he remarked that he was "growing older every day. How quickly, if I live, shall I be an old gray headed man of experience." While secretary of the navy, he expressed his desire to be 20 years younger, that his mind was fine, but regretfully declared, "If only the body kept pace!" After the death of his parents and brother, he regretted that, "[T]he family is scattered, the old home is gone, the hearth is cold. There are strangers in the sacred places. And we drift on like straws upon a torrent, always vainly looking back and trying to cheat ourselves into the belief that it is not all gone—all past—never, never to return." After suffering the losses of his daughter and close friend William McKinley in 1901, Long wrote that he was acting and appearing the same as ever, "And yet I am conscious all the time of a sense of indefinite loss; of being broken, if that is not too strong a word."[4] Although Long and Hay, in being poets, were unusual among political leaders, the experiences they expressed were by no means unique to them.

Among the politicians of Vietnam era, the "very human" President Johnson appeared to have been particularly troubled by mortality and concerned about his own fate after death. He held a not uncommon aversion to funerals and, according to biographer Doris Kearns Goodwin, was actually "apt to become physically ill in the presence of death." According to Billy Graham, Johnson, "thought a great deal about death, and he talked to me about it several times." Johnson would describe his mortality, in appropriately figurative language, as "a goddamn raven hovering over my shoulder." Part of this concern stemmed from the fact that Johnson came from a family in which the men had often died young, and in 1955 he suffered a severe heart attack; from that time on, the threat of another attack remained with him as a constant reminder of how tenuous his existence was and of the vagaries of the body. He was terrified as a young boy by both his aged and paralyzed grandmother and by the frequently flooding river near his house, and had repeated nightmares of either being paralyzed or of drowning in a swollen river. He often used the metaphors of paralysis and raging rivers in his discussion of policy.[5]

Although it remains difficult to plumb the depths or shallows of Ronald Reagan's mind, his deep religiosity and emotional devastation when encountering death reflected a similar fear and loathing. For instance, at the funeral of his father (an alcoholic and lapsed Catholic), he felt "greater despair than ever before in his life," and claimed to have heard his father speak to him, saying, "I'm OK." He felt sure that his father was fine and happy wherever he was. In 1947, just at the time when Reagan began his career as an active anti-Communist, he had also almost died from acute viral pneumonia and lost his first daughter shortly after her birth. His divorce from Jane Wyman shortly thereafter likewise "left him dead inside for several years." This triple blow apparently provided some fuel to his desire to enter the realm of politics. Once he had reached the highest office in the land, his second close scrape with death—after being shot by John Hinckley, Jr.—likewise reinforced his awareness of mortality and deepened his sense of religiosity. After coming out of surgery following the shooting he would scribble, "I am aren't alive aren't I [sic]," and on returning to office offered that "Whatever happens now I owe my life to God and will try to serve him every way I can."[6]

With no one was this concern with death more evident than Theodore Roosevelt. His youth included a series of fairly nightmarish physical ailments and frequent encounters with death that, by all accounts, left a deep imprint on his view of the world. As Roosevelt put it in his *Autobiography,* he was "a sickly, delicate boy." Beginning at age three and continuing through his early adulthood, Roosevelt had recurrent attacks of asthma and "cholera morbus" (a chronic form of diarrhea). His sense of physical limitations was heightened by the fact that Roosevelt had terrible eyesight and in college was diagnosed as having a bad heart. Shortly before this diagnosis, Roosevelt's father died, at the age of 46. The death of his father, whom Roosevelt virtually worshipped, devastated the young man. In his diary, he wrote, "When I fully realize my loss, I feel as if I should go wild"; he described the time to his friend as "like a hideous dream." A few years later, both his first wife Alice and his mother died within 12 hours of each other. As the biographer David McCullough puts it, Roosevelt "learned at an early age what a precarious, unpredictable thing life is."[7]

Unlike Reagan, however, the trouble Roosevelt had with his body was not compensated by any faith that he might die a "good death." The biographer Edward Wagenknecht argues that, despite his Protestant upbringing, Roosevelt was not sustained by a belief in the immortality of the soul, and there is little evidence in Roosevelt's writings of faith in an afterlife. His thoughts on the nature of human existence were summed up in the phrase, "We have but one life here, and what comes after it we cannot with certainty tell." On the few occasions when he did discuss death or mortality, he referred to it simply as an "everlasting darkness."[8] Death remained for Roosevelt something that was unknowable and inexpressible. As such, his own mortality became that much more terrifying, and he had to try proportionately harder to overcome his sense of physical limits. Much of his life can be seen as an attempt to regain some sense of control over the contingency and mortality of his body.

DREAD THE COMING NIGHT

Death in battle is only a specific instance of a general phenomenon of some relevance to any mortal. Furthermore, in the context of a study of death in battle, an examination of the élite's responses to mortality is relevant because there are similarities between how the élite view their own deaths and how they view the deaths of the soldiers in battle. The dominant response to mortality among the élite takes the form of a symbolic "battle with death." The élite used the soldiers as a model for their own lives and deaths. The condition of mortality entails a tension between our aspirations and abilities, between the material and ideal aspects of existence, and it is to this tension that the immortality projects respond.

This response to mortality is carried out largely through the use of symbols, metaphors, and rituals—artificial constructs that are distinct from the natural world. Although a number of scholars have emphasized the importance of symbolism and rhetoric in politics, they often are vague on why this is the case.[9] The main thrust of much of the social constructionist, linguistic, and cultural literature is that these constructions are a prerequisite for social functioning of any sort.[10] The symbols and symbolic acts used by members of a society facilitate the ordering of social interactions and allow us to navigate through our lives successfully. To understand what makes rhetoric persuasive and able to motivate people to go to war, we need to understand not just the structure of the language but also what drives humans. Many explanations of the persuasiveness of ideology and propaganda draw on some account of psychology, pointing to how the symbols and rituals tap into deeply held emotions and concerns.[11] Like these Freudian accounts, the explanation given here is rooted in the realm of human limitations and physical desires. They are part of the human project to construct and maintain and defend an artificial world in which one has a sense of control and from which things that cannot be controlled are excluded.[12]

To understand war requires an account of some immense motivations. We cannot explain events on the order of world wars as the result simply of positive net expected utility. Something very powerful must account for the act of wholesale slaughter and suicide. Motivation is, of course, a notoriously complex and illusive quality.[13] But to exclude it would be like trying to explain the movement of a locomotive without any reference to its engine, instead just simply assuming that it moves and leaving it at that. People do not march off to war without something very powerful motivating that behavior.

Along these lines, the sociologists Peter Berger and Thomas Luckmann have argued that the state and society together serve the function of constructing a coherent vision of social reality through integrating the vast array of social institutions—from kinship to religion to economic relations—and argue that death poses the greatest threat to that social order.[14]

> The experience of the death of others and, subsequently, the anticipation of one's own death posit the marginal situation par excellence for the individual. Needless to elaborate, death also posits the most terrifying threat to the taken-for-granted realities of everyday life. The integration of death within the paramount reality of social existence is, therefore, of the greatest importance for any institutional order.[15]

In other words, not only must the state (as part of the larger "institutional order") protect its citizens from untimely death, but it must also make sense of death within the symbolic social order. This making sense of death is part of the general project of coming to terms with the gap between what we want and what we get, and what Benedict Anderson refers to as the "contingency of life . . . [and] . . . the overwhelming burden of human suffering—disease, mutilation, grief, age, and death."[16]

Much of the symbolic content of language is derived from this tension between human aspirations and abilities.[17] Humans are willful creatures, exercising power in a struggle against chaos, entropy, and decay. "Are we to believe," Senator Henry Cabot Lodge would ask in 1900, "that the races of men go stumbling blindly through the centuries, the playthings of chance, the helpless victims of their own passions?"[18] The chaotic, help-less view of human history implied by Lodge's rhetorical question was clearly meant to be (and may actually have been) disturbing to his audi-ence, and Lodge uses this language to tar his opponents' policies. He of-fers instead policies (seizure of the Philippines, for instance) that he claims will provide the order and control that are such central concerns for most humans, or at least most senators.

The need or requirement for a coherent view of the world is a tenet of both psychological theories about cognitive economy and anthropological and sociological theories about the ways in which societies order their worlds.[19] For goal seekers, a sense of power or control over the ability to achieve these ends is also crucial. As Senator Gallinger would put it in 1897, "I have wished sometimes, not irreverently, I hope, that I might pos-sess the power of omnipotence."[20] Although he might have been some-what less subtle than other politicians in his will to power, Gallinger certainly was not alone in this desire.

But in Gallinger's statement there is, of course, a tacit acknowledg-ment of the futility of his wish; these human aspirations are at various times and to varying degrees frustrated by the fact that we are mortal and are neither omniscient nor omnipotent. Freud placed the empha-sis on the limitations placed on human drives by social norms. William Connolly refers to the problems of evil and suffering as the beginning of his discussion of identity and difference. And Benedict Anderson uses the problem of mortality and contingency as the starting point for his discussion of nationalism. Similarly, Clifford Geertz argues that the origins of religion lie in three such limits derived from the finite nature of existence—to human endurance, moral reasoning, and analytic abil-ities.[21] On one level, this aspect of the human condition is obvious, and supposed thus to be academically uninteresting; but it is also an aspect of existence about which we diligently avoid thinking, and, thus, one of which we should be wary. We desire life but will all die; we desire meaning yet rarely find it; we seek a sense of control but often feel pow-erless; we seek knowledge yet are always faced with new unanswerable questions.[22]

To a certain extent, these goals can be pursued in a rational manner. We can try to increase our power, for instance, by getting richer, and thereby gain some sense of control over such things as our health and per-sonal safety. We can gather more information and use more sophisticated analyses to gain a greater understanding of how nature and society oper-ate, thereby increasing our ability to control them. But, to varying de-grees, human aspirations for power, knowledge, and meaning will be frustrated by the ineluctable fact that we are finite creatures existing in an infinite universe. As John Long would put it more concretely in his speech about libraries, this is the problem of the "vicissitudes of fortune, the fluctuations of business, the rise and fall of stocks and prices, the successions of good times and hard times, the inequalities of material lot. . . ." The fact of mortality (and the various other more mundane limitations listed by Long) stands as the limit to, and in death the ultimate negation of, our rational pursuit of the satisfaction of our varied desires.

Because of our limitations as mortals, the gap between aspirations and abilities can never be completely closed, and, thus, the problem is never completely resolved.[23] Some may develop more or less successful means of coping with the human condition of mortality, but simply because they have developed these coping mechanisms does not mean that the problem has disappeared. The presence of those mechanisms is in fact one piece of evidence that the problem remains, as the source of that mechanism. This fact is a potential source of internal pain, or sorrow and rage, which we seek to avoid or heal. For the sake of argument, I will make the fairly safe assumption that people do not want to die. It seems that if this were not the case, we would be killing ourselves much more frequently than we do now. In any case, those, like Forrestal, who do want to die select themselves out by killing themselves. Even the one instance of suicide among this group did so under great duress, and after leaving office and suffering a nervous breakdown. This general aversion to the inevitability of death I term the "problem of mortality."[24] Although we certainly will all die, it is difficult to say to what extent all human behavior is shaped by this problem. But it still seems to be a powerful force shaping our lives, even as we try to ignore it and get on with our lives.

This is not the same as saying simply that death is bad. Although the inevitable cessation of the functioning of the body is undeniable and generally regarded as unfortunate, there are a whole variety of conceptions or "social constructions" within which death is conceived as unproblematic, even pleasant. The vision of death as simply a transition of the self "from this world to that which is to come"[25] is generally not seen as one to be dreaded or feared, and for certain religious faithful a transition that they welcome and sometimes even hasten. Such a view, for instance, is found in the language of John Long, who, early in life, would espouse the optimism of his Unitarian Universalism, arguing that "death makes no change in our moral nature . . . in the next world we shall go on from that point to which we have arrived in this."[26] In typical late-nineteenth-century fashion, when Long personified death, he turned it into a sweet female companion or a more pleasant version of sleep. He would say that when his colleague Senator Pike died,

The angel, who is even tenderer and gentler than her sister Sleep, had indeed walked at his side so long that he recognized her as the blessed angel of man's succor and peace. She had waited till their walk that bright day, over the pleasant fields and under the blue sky, gave the opportunity happiest for her and for him. Then she gathered her arms about him. His head fell upon her shoulder even as he went. And lo! he was at rest in the mansions of his Father's house.[27]

People of different faiths and persuasions have constructed views of dying that make it a welcome transition. For some the prospect of eternal life in heaven might be as terrifying as the prospect of eternal nonexistence, or, as David Byrne puts it, that it would just be really boring, but most people seem to find the idea more reassuring than frightening.

The "problem" with mortality is the prospect of a cessation of the self—that possibility that there is no immortal soul and the undeniable fact that when we die our bodies cease to function and are no longer able to interact with the living. Whatever hopes and faith one might have about the existence of an immortal soul, the death of the body—its loss of powers of expression, its decomposition—is a potent reminder that *something* ends with death. There has always been the suspicion, expressed in Hamlet's "perchance to dream," that death is simply an end, and it is in this aspect of mortality that lies the rub. The idea of the complete obliteration of the self, one's memories, experiences, passions, and knowledge—forever, without end—is fairly troubling. We are creatures who generally have some attachment to the "self" and would like to see it continue, and, as such, the prospect of cessation is a source of tension that we may seek to resolve in various ways.

The self can be conceived of in a variety of ways, and some of these self-conceptions are more susceptible to problematic constructions of death than others. In particular, the conceptions of self that are tied to the weak and fallible body (as opposed to a vision of the body as "ageless" or the self as some extracorporeal entity such as "mind" or soul) and to the individual (as opposed to some larger social whole) are susceptible to these concerns about eternal nonexistence. For it is the body that undeniably goes away, is no longer capable of interaction with those who remain, and does not come back. The creations, thoughts, soul, or social identity of that person may to varying degrees survive the death of the body and, as such, constitute bases for different ways of coming to terms with the problem of mortality.

Thus, we need to examine not how the élite related to death in general but to the "bad death," the death of the body, to the reminders of that doubt that haunted the élite. The agenda promulgated by the problem of mortality consists of the need to create a sense of immortality (or at least nonmortality or denial of death), and, when this no longer possible, to die some form of "good death," one dependent on the construction of an identity as not simply an isolated physical being. A new identity, one distanced from the self as physical being and grounded in society and culture, must be developed, and the élite's attempt to do that both for themselves and for the soldiers in battle constitutes the main focus of this book.

RESPONSES TO MORTALITY

Although some apprehension about dying may be common, there is, nonetheless, a great variety of responses to that fear. In the face of those tensions arising from human limits, people can seek distraction (Heidegger's notion of "fallenness"), use drugs or ways to deny or "not think" about one's troubles, vent their frustrations by finding some thing weaker than themselves to manipulate, employ humor, lower their expectations, or create or find a fantasy world in which these frustrations do not exist. These various responses are rooted both in psychological dynamics of denial, projection, or catharsis, and cultural mechanisms of ritual and shared faith.

Here I distinguish between two responses to the condition of mortality—an acceptance of death and an active denial of it. These are not mutually exclusive responses—we generally engage in both, but to varying degrees, or fluctuate back and forth between the two. The categories in part reflect differences in the degree to which the condition of mortality has been successfully integrated into one's identity and worldview. Some people may develop ways of coming to terms with death, such that both tensions concerning it and its effect on behavior are reduced. One such approach, more common in non-Western cultures, involves a resigned recognition of mortality and/or the expression of those emotions associated with that recognition—sorrow and anger. The acceptance of and active engagement with the fact of mortality, however painful this may be, is certainly within the scope of our psychological and emotion abilities. But the dominant response in contemporary Western culture—according to Ernest Becker, Philippe Aries, and Octavio Paz—is that of denial, or what James Farrell calls the "dying of death."[28] In this view, mortality and powerlessness remain a source of pain and anguish that we seek to avoid, that we refuse to accept because such an acceptance is painful. This approach stands in contrast to the stance in which death, both literal and figurative, is an integral and accepted part of life. As the anthropologists Huntington and Metcalf point out in *Celebrations of Death*, this Western approach to death also stands in stark contrast to funerary practices in a variety of the world's cultures in which the relationship to death in much more intimate—so much so that, in some cases, mourners sit with the dead for prolonged periods or even eat or smear the remains on the body.

These two responses are also gendered in that the acceptant stance is one more commonly found in and socially sanctioned for women, while denial and stoicism are deemed more appropriate for men. That this is so is not biologically determined nor universal—there are certainly stoic women and emotional men. But these are roles into which males and females are generally socialized. Given that virtually all the people making foreign policy are men—and "real men" at that—it is not surprising then that the dominant form of their response to death was one of denial.

This account of élite culture is largely a story about boys trying to live up to the standards established for them, and of the typically male concerns that the dominant forms of masculinity engender.[29] On a more superficial level, gender is important because of the obvious fact that the people doing the ordering and the people dying were virtually all men. Women generally were excluded from the activity of war, except insofar as they were victims of and resisters against its violence.[30] But gender is important because of the way that those engaged in making foreign policy formed their identity and values. For Jeanne Kirkpatrick and Madeleine Albright, as well as all their male colleagues, there was a certain set of expectations. This sense of self, and corresponding stance toward mortality, were characteristically male, and, thus, defined by socially constructed conceptions of gender. The point is not that having women making foreign policy will change wartime decision-making, but that these typically male values have shaped how the foreign policy élite viewed the world and thought about war.

This characteristically Western and male denial is not simply a negative project or a running away; it also involves the creation of a transcendent identity. As the realist Hans Morgenthau puts it, death is

> the very negation of all man experiences as specifically human in his existence: the consciousness of himself and of his world, the remembrance of things past and the anticipation of things to come, a creativeness in thought and action which aspires to, and approximates, the eternal. Thus man has been compelled, for the sake of his existence as man, to bridge the gap between death and his specifically human attributes by transcending death.[31]

I term these responses "immortality projects," which involve an attempt symbolically to overcome death and can take a variety of religious and secular forms.[32] To the extent that these projects are successful, they may, depending on the type of project used, make death a less devastating prospect.

The acceptant stance, by contrast, is typified by the words of the Roman emperor Marcus Aurelius, who urged his fellow citizens to be, "neither superficial, nor impatient, nor yet contemptuous in [their] attitude toward death, but to await it as one of the operations of Nature which [one] will have to undergo."[33] Because ultimately there is nothing that can be done about death, from this perspective we are released from any responsibility and therefore any concern about it. This acceptance can take various forms as well, including that exemplified by existentialists such as Sartre, which seeks to face a truth about our existence, no matter how painful it might be, and takes strength and solace from that truthfulness. An example of this honesty is the phenomenon of terminally ill patients who turn away from the world and literally "face the wall" in their hospital rooms, often to the dismay of the medical staff bent on avoiding this sense of resignation.[34] In part, this acceptance involves a lowering of expectations—in fully facing mortality, one must needs give up at least some hopes of continued existence of the embodied self. This acceptance, however, remains a second-best solution. One accepts mortality only after having given up on the preferred goal of immortality.

The acceptance of death need not be completely passive. Humans are constituted with certain capabilities for responding psychologically to situations of powerlessness, including the expression of emotions such as sorrow and anger. One of the most common aspects across cultures of funeral ritual is emotional expression, which helps to relieve some of the tension caused by this sense of powerlessness. It does not resolve the situation or create illusions about it. Instead, this expressiveness involves directly experiencing the pain caused by the contemplation of mortality; and this expression can serve as a catharsis for the psychological tension.[35] It involves an embrace of that pain, rather than a suppression of it. This response to death and mortality, although common in a variety of cultures, is largely absent from that of the foreign policy élite. The typically male response to death contained a norm of nonemotionalism, exemplified by Dean Rusk's dictum that the word "feel" not be used in any State Department memoranda.[36] The open expression of sorrow was taboo within those circles, as the recognition of powerlessness was anathema to the culture of power. Much more common were the responses of denial and of the symbolic immortality projects.

THE IMMORTALITY PROJECT

If those who have traditionally been denied power have tended to use emotional expressiveness as one way of coming to terms with their frustrations, an alternative approach, fostered by the illusion of power, attempts to avoid whatever painful emotions might be associated with death, and instead tries to create and sustain some vision of a transcendent self. In response to their fears of death, political leaders such as Lyndon Johnson and John Hay sought immortality. Having left office knowing that he had not gained the popularity of his political idol FDR, Johnson would express regret that he had not sought immortality in other ways than political fame. "There's no chance the ordinary person in the future will ever remember me. No chance. I'd have been better off *looking for immortality* through my wife and children and their children instead of seeking all that love and affection from the American people. They're just too fickle." Johnson thus summed up his political activities as a search for immortality; and his political failures signified a failure of his attempt to live on after death. Woodrow Wilson likewise spoke of his great desire to do "immortal deeds" as president. John Hay, on nearing the end of his life, would write, "I know death is the common lot, and what is universal ought not to be deemed a misfortune; and yet—instead of confronting it with dignity and philosophy, I cling instinctively to life and the things of life, as eagerly as if I had not had my chance at happiness and gained nearly all the great prizes."[37] As Johnson and Wilson sought immortality through their search for a place in history, Hay likewise sought to win "all the great prizes" as part of his immortality project.

Although most people seek to construct an identity that will transcend the death of the body—whether through the family, fame, or the product of one's work—politicians seem to value the pursuit of immortality particularly highly. High office offers a powerful form of immortality (a phenomenon discussed more in Chapter 4), and it is likely that those who are drawn to that office are particularly interested in the issue of mortality. In his psychological study of Abraham Lincoln, Dwight G. Anderson argues that "Ultimately, what Lincoln sought through political action was to transcend the finitude of the human condition, to triumph over death, by identifying his personal transcendence with the immortality of the Union." He describes Lincoln as someone infatuated with death and mortality, and determined to make a name for himself by associating himself with the Union.[38] Lincoln, Hay, and Johnson were not the only politicians concerned with their "legacy," and it seems fair to say that lurking in the back of most presidents' minds is a concern with their place in history.

Whereas Ernest Becker emphasizes the psychological dilemmas of the modern age and the failures of modern attempts at achieving symbolic mortality, other scholars, such as Robert Lifton and Alfred Killelea, have pointed to the viability and success of both religious and secular attempts at coming to terms with mortality. Although the task may have become more difficult in the age of rationalism and science, this does not mean that it has been abandoned—science has often simply been employed in the task. The questions and dilemmas of the human condition remain and people still seek answers to them. In a sense, the search for immortality has only gained a greater sense of urgency in a time when the traditional heroic projects and religious faiths are being eroded. Religion remains a vital and integral aspect of modern life (especially in the United States), despite the challenges of positivism, Darwinism, and the anomie of late modernity.

There are number of common elements to this immortality project. In general, it entails an attempt to control the material world and one's life and death. Rather than accepting death, one *does* something about it. As whatever actions might be taken to control death will ultimately be frustrated, this move is accomplished through the construction of a symbolic world or cosmology in which death is represented in ways that make it more manageable, thereby making our experience of death easier to bear. The problem of mortality is then addressed by the construction of a transcendent identity and by seeking control over symbols of death. The fear of death as an unknown can be reduced by naming it, representing it by familiar objects or experiences. Death also can be made contingent on a particular kind of behavior rather than an essential characteristic of the human condition, as is the case in Pauline theology.

These constructed views, as part of an immortality project, involve constructing an identity and cosmology that allows for a continuation of the self after the death of the body. A "project" in this sense is some basic, life-long task or set of life goals—for example, the search for financial security, for the perfect lover, the search for meaning and self-esteem, the raising of a healthy and loving family. Although the behaviors resulting from this project may not always be readily apparent in one's daily actions, the project shapes and defines some of the broad parameters of our choices. The immortality project is such an undertaking, in this case directed toward creating a good death.

The problem of mortality and of limited knowledge and power can in part be addressed rationally, but where the material capabilities of the human mind and body leave off—when gaining more data or money no longer suffice—other means must be used to attempt to come to terms with our mortality and limits. As Ernest Becker argues, in the face of death, humans engage in the heroic project of constructing a symbolic world in which they have a sense of meaning, power, order, and even immortality. These nonrational responses lie in the human ability to intuit, imagine, and construct pictures or fantasies of the world.

This creation of illusion is rooted in the human ability, even the necessity, of thinking metaphorically—to have faith and believe, to hope, to imagine, and in numerous ways to manipulate experiences so as to create a world in which one has a sense of power, meaning, and immortality.[39] Another way to think of these constructions is in terms of what Jacques Lacan and his contemporary champion Slavoj Žižek calls "fantasy space," or that realm in which the unspoken and ultimately unsatisfiable drives, as shaped by society into particular desires, find an illusory and temporary satisfaction. The metaphors and symbols used by the élite were drawn from the myths and religions that contain narrative and symbolic structures, which create a coherent and integrated picture of the world and humanity's place in it.[40]

To get a sense of this project of transcending the limits of material existence and constructing a symbolic world in which anxieties about mortality are made more manageable, we can turn once again to the grandiloquent prose of John Long in his library dedication speech. In large part, the speech can be read as a paean to the powers of discourse and the ability of the mind to control and shape matter. His answer to the "vicissitudes of fortune" is to be found in the "inexhaustible riches of the ideal." In the world of the library, the soul moves through "the transcendent ranges of an upper world,—the world of aspiring imagination— . . . in which all the good and wise and lovely are our society." Gone are the ups and downs of the market. In their place is the realm of power and mastery, in which

> the soul is supreme master of the realm, and man recognizes that he is a god. It is more than a school,—more than education; it is *absolute possession*. . . . The soul inherits the earth. No devil tempts him, yet his are all the kingdoms of the world, and all the glory of them.[41]

Here the problems of entropy and transience of the material world are gone. Humans have become goddesses and gods, achieving that Lockean ideal of the "absolute possession" of the objects of their desire.

In addition to the creation of a symbolic world that addresses some of the concerns about mortality, the immortality project involves creating a transcendent identity. If death is a problem, one needs to remove it not just from the world around oneself but, most importantly, from one's own self. The transcendent sense of self is one in which the body is either controlled by the spirit, or in which the self is removed from the body and placed in some social entity (family, office, nation) that transcends the individual. In either case, the goal is to create a sense of self in which that self does not die. As the body is that aspect of the self that most certainly undergoes a radical turn for the worse in death, the transcendent identity generally involved distancing oneself from the body, or identifying oneself with a youthful, vigorous body rather than a sick and decaying one. The goal of identity formation is to determine what one *is* and what one is *not*, and the transcendent identity involves establishing an identity as a being that will not die.

William Connolly and Richard Ashley argue that the process of identity formation is based on the construction of difference—one's identity is defined largely in terms of what one is not.[42] The maintenance of identity requires a reduction of ambiguity, the maintenance of the boundaries between self and other. Part of this is accomplished through the division of the world into hierarchical dichotomies based on the self/other distinction, such as the sovereignty/anarchy dichotomy in international politics. These distinctions can correspond directly to that between life and death. As but one example of this basis for identity, we have Hitler's declaration of his identity, stated, according to a friend of his, while visiting his mother's grave when he was 26: " 'I am not like that yet.' He then gripped his riding whip tightly in his hands and said, 'I would like you to call me Wolf.' "[43] Facing the prospect of the grave, Hitler resolved to construct a new identity for himself. In struggling to determine who he was, he asserted that he was not dead, and instead that he was a beast, someone who would send others to their graves. Given the trauma of combat experience in the trenches of World War I, we can understand why that project would have been so pressing for Hitler.

Identity is formed in part as a differentiation of the self from the cosmos, a differentiation that is at least partially negated in death. The maintenance of identity requires the maintenance of life *qua* differentiation from the cosmos. Just as the boundaries between self and other must be maintained, so must the separation of life and death. The identity of self as "not-the-body" requires then that death be an "Other." The Other in international politics was, likewise, frequently equated with death.

Thomas Berger and Peter Luckmann describe a similar process arising from the "dialectic between identity and its biological substratum." They argue that socialized humans have a socially constructed symbolic view of themselves but also cannot ignore the experience of oneself "as an organism." This internal split is hierarchical—"this dialectic is apprehended as a struggle between a 'higher' and a 'lower' self, respectively equated with social identity and pre-social, possibly anti-social animality. The 'higher' self must repeatedly assert itself over the 'lower,' sometimes in critical tests of strength. For example, a man must overcome his instinctive fear of death by courage in battle."[44] Thus, identity formation generally takes the form of this struggle between a higher self (which will not die) and a lower self (which will).

As the problem of death is rooted in the fragile vessel of the body, the transcendent identity is one that is separate from this unreliable vehicle and associated with some entity that will survive the body. One can form an identity with some larger social entity such as the family, ethnic group, or nation, or emphasize the disembodied elements of oneself, such as the writing or art produced by oneself. This transcendent identity generally involves the mind mastering the body, a practice trumpeted as well in John Long's speech. The library, he claims, is

> but poetry and religion,—the tribute of the creature to God,—the obeisance of matter to mind, of toil to rest, of the hard, practical forces to their master, the spirit of thought and vision,—the recognition of that spiritual, that *mental and moral sovereignty* which is the divine equality of all the children of God and to which all lower life with its inequalities of circumstance, its dross of riches, and its grime of toil, is the shell of the chambered nautilus![45]

Here the contrasts between the material and ideal, in their various manifestations—force and vision, mind and body, children of God and other, rest and toil—are clear. And it is through this "mental and moral sovereignty" that one gains life; for in the library, Long continues, one can drink "the waters of life."[46] By claiming and asserting these divine powers, one becomes a creature of God, the library becomes a church, and reading a means to commune with the eternal.

This immortality project was formed within the context of a society profoundly influenced by Christian theology. There is an ongoing debate as to the relative importance of religion in American political culture, but there are a number of indications that its role should not be underestimated. Despite the deeply held values of separation of church and state and aversion to any doctrine of the divine right of kings, Americans and their politicians still hold a consistent faith in God as well as country. As Richard Hutcheson puts it, while there has been an "institutional separation" between church and state, there has been a "cultural linkage" between religion and politics.[47] What de Tocqueville pointed out in the 1840s—that religion, rather than ideology, constitutes the bedrock of American political culture—seems to be even more so today than it was then.[48] Michael Hunt, Ron Hirschbein, and Stephen Twing all emphasize the Puritan and millennialist elements of American political culture.[49]

The continuing importance of religion in American culture is seen in opinion polls which show 94 percent to 98 percent of Americas expressing a belief in God, and only a slightly lower percentage believing they will meet their maker when they die. In one poll, 80 percent of the respondents said that they expected to stand before God on Judgment Day, and another showed that 73 percent believe in life after death. Roughly 96 percent of Americans associate themselves with some religion, and this number rose steadily over the course of the twentieth century.[50] Despite claims or questions about the "death of God" and increased secularization of American society, church membership increased steadily from an estimated 17 percent in 1776 to 62 percent in 1980.[51]

A visit to any U.S. military cemetery reveals immediately the prominence of Christianity in the cultural response to death in battle. On the vast majority of the graves are crosses, marking each of the dead as someone who died "in Christ," and who mimicked, in their sacrifice on the altar of the nation, Christ's martyrdom on the cross. As Benedict Anderson and George Mosse argue, the nation did not replace religion as a source of transcendent identities but exists along side it, and emerges out of these religious roots.[52] The strong linkage between faith and foreign policy, exemplified by the crusade, stems largely from the fact that, at their roots, both are centrally concerned with death. As Bronislaw Malinowski argues, "Of all the sources of religion, the supreme and final crisis of life—death—is of the greatest importance."[53] As the sociologist Robert Bellah writes, "The separation of church and state has not denied the political realm a religious dimension. Although matters of personal religious belief, worship, and association are considered to be strictly private affairs, there are, at the same time, certain common elements of religious orientation that the great majority of Americans share."[54] One of those elements is a religious orientation toward death and dying. Thus, it is worth exploring this "civil religious" dimension to nationalism and the culture of U.S. foreign policy officials.

We should not be surprised then to find that George Bush had Billy Graham at his side as the Gulf War commenced, just as Lyndon Johnson sought solace from that evangelist during the Vietnam War; or that William McKinley would offer his justification for taking the Philippines as a tale of divine revelation told to the visiting ministers; or that Ronald Reagan, after ordering his first execution as California governor, would invite another evangelical minister (and former football star) to his home to seek absolution.[55] In the face of these grave responsibilities, most American leaders have placed those deaths in a religious context.[56]

CHRISTIAN IMMORTALITY

> Life is short
> Death is sure
> Sin the cause
> Christ the cure[57]

As with any religion, Christianity contains within it many complex ideas and beliefs about mortality and the human soul. Likewise, the religious fabric of America is richly varied and evolving. While acknowledging this diversity, the focus here is on one strand of the Christian faith that appears to have helped many members of the American foreign policy establishment make sense of death. It involves two basic biblical claims about human nature. One is the idea that mortality is a contingent rather than inherent or necessary aspect of human existence. The possibility of an afterlife is premised on the basic Christian theological assertion of a soul separate from the body. These two basic assumptions open up the possibility for that characteristically male response to painful emotions—*doing* something about the discomfort, rather than just accepting the fact and expressing those emotions.

Within Christian ontology, one way in which death is made manageable is by making the counterintuitive claim that mortality is not a necessary aspect of human existence but, rather, came about because of certain choices and particular mistakes. In the Old Testament, we learn that death was not originally an aspect of the human lot but instead a punishment for disobeying God's instructions to remain ignorant (that is, not eat of the tree of knowledge of good and evil).[58] As troubling as the expulsion from Eden might be, it is reassuring to the extent that rather than being part of human nature—and therefore inescapable—death is seen as having come about because of man's fall (which would naturally be blamed on an identifiable, female culprit); as such, it was something that could be undone, as it was through Christ's self-sacrifice on the cross.[59]

This "denaturalized" view of death opened up the possibility for Christians to overcome death by adopting a faith, giving oneself up to God, and so on. Thus, although all around us we see people and animals dying (what could be *more* natural?), this article of Christian faith allowed at least the human deaths to be given a new meaning as a transition to eternal life for the faithful. This provides an ontological basis for an activist strategy for dealing with death, which the foreign policy élite drew on in constructing war as a battle against death.

In the face of all the evidence that our bodies do die, the possibility of this transition and the reformulation of death requires the construction of a bipartite identity. The tension between finite and infinite, body and mind, good and evil, are reconciled in Christian and Puritan theology through the separation of self into a sinful, desirous body and (at least potentially) a transcendent, virtuous soul. This creates the tension between body and soul—what William James would characterize as the "divided self." A key element of the élite discourse is the construction of the self as a hierarchical opposition of body and soul, and a corresponding global hierarchy of the virtuous ruling the sinful. This fundamental distinction can be overlaid on various other constructed dichotomies—between reason and passion, strength and weakness, bravery and fear, selfishness and self-lessness. In élite discourse, each of these qualities was associated with life or death, virtue or sin, soul or body.

Within this framework, the problem of the body's mortality is translated into the problem of sin. As Paul would write in Romans 6:23, "The wages of sin is death," and gaining immortality entailed somehow overcoming this sinfulness. Although humans after Eden had "fallen" and were sinful, still they could do something about this: take up the faith, repent, and follow the path of God. In this worldview, the body was one, if not the primary, source of sin and evil. To overcome death, one had to overcome the body with its desires, which served as constant reminders of the physical nature, needs, and weaknesses of human beings. Because death became contingent on one's behavior and was rooted in the attributes of desire and knowledge, the problem of mortality then was translated into that of virtue and sin.

This religious notion of the self as the product of a battle between the body and the soul was paralleled by the conception of the nation as the product of war. The policy of imperialism overseas had its analogue in the individual as composed of a symbolic empire of the mind ruling over the body. Anderson in *Imagined Communities* and David Campbell in *Writing Security* discuss how nationalism was mobilized and created by means of new mass media and in élite discourse, but they do not tie this directly to the issue of mortality and the motivation that immortality projects provide; as such, their accounts leave out a crucial part of the picture. Many of the élite showed some signs of being engaged in an attempt to assert the dominance of the soul over the body, just as they asserted the dominance of Anglo-Saxon, Christian, and republican government over the Asiatic, pagan, and communist realms. This framework was a nearly universal aspect of foreign policy discourse, shared by the most belligerent and most pacifist advocates alike.

In this discourse, the survival of the soul after death was portrayed as dependent on the victory of the soul over the body. The project entailed by this conception was one of the assertion and proof of this triumph. The élite construed all deaths—but especially those in battle—in terms of this struggle. Within this framework, if deaths were to result from human actions, they had to be seen as playing a role in the triumph of the spirit over the flesh, as this remained the most basic means of gaining immortality. As long as this was the case, then the deaths were acceptable, because they were part of this larger scheme within which death itself was rendered acceptable through the creation of an identity that transcended the flesh. This was the symbolic and ritualistic maneuver that made possible that reversal, captured in the passage from Matthew 10:39 of gaining life by losing it on the field of battle.

RITUAL AND THE AFFIRMATION OF FAITH

Believing in immortality—although it may be fun and nice—unfortunately is difficult if one pays any attention to the most readily available information. As Vera Brittain experienced when she lost both her lover and brother in World War I, there were no immediately available signs of an afterlife:

> Edward, like Roland, had promised me that if a life existed beyond the grave, he would somehow come back and make me know of it. I had thought that, of the two, Roland, with his reckless determination, would be the more likely to trespass from the infinite across the boundaries of the tangible, and incur any penalties that might be imposed. But he had sent no sign and Edward sent none; nor did I expect one. I knew now that death was the end and that I was quite alone. There was no hereafter, no Easter morning, no meeting again; I walked in a darkness, a dumbness, a silence, which no beloved voice would penetrate, no fond hope illumine.[60]

And if such silence were not enough, the grim spectacle of physical decay, the gross mechanical nature of our bodies (all those strange organs and parts and sinews and so on), in conjunction with the intimate intertwining of our physical and mental/spiritual existence, make it all the more difficult to believe that something of the self-conscious self remains after the body ceases to function. As Ernest Becker points out, the project of attempting to achieve symbolic immortality is periodically repudiated by our encounters with the aging, unreliable human body. It is only our lack of omniscience that allows us the luxury of speculating that there may be some existence of the self after death.

Unless one is blessed with divine revelation, the maintenance of this belief in immortality takes work. We must make ourselves believe these things, and a great deal of what we do can be understood as involving this process of self-creation, which is driven by all the sadness and pain and despair that accompanies the loss of loved ones and the contemplation of our own demise. The precariousness of our identities, happiness, and beliefs require that they be shored up and reinforced in various ways. The immortality projects must address the concerns about mortality, power, and meaning in a way that is convincing. The success of these illusions depends on processes such as repetition; on the uniformity of views within the "community of faithful"; and on an illusive and variable mix of coherence, concreteness, and complexity that renders it both intelligible and imbues these beliefs with a sense of authority.[61]

Part of this plausibility is achieved through acting out the symbolic dramas and in actualizing the ideals embodied in these world views. Words alone are often not enough to create convincing illusion. They must be supplemented by ritual acts.[62] These rituals involve an acting out of that symbolic world that is constructed in the symbolic structures of a culture. As such, they serve a parallel function to that of metaphors in language—they stand for other events and render them manageable and integrate them into the social order. They are a way of increasing the power and plausibility of the illusions contained within the mythologies of a culture.

Many of the "performances" of the political élite lack the order and complexity typically associated with ritual. In addition to the usual holiday rituals or perfunctory attendance at Sunday services, each member of the élite had personal rituals—the hunting trips, the writing of books, the trips to Europe—that took on cosmological and transformative value for these men and can be analyzed in terms of their symbolic content. In general, these rituals entail some kind of empowerment. They are a response to frustrations that cannot be directly addressed. The response to this situation of powerlessness is to create a new situation in which one has power, by finding a surrogate for that thing that cannot be controlled in reality, and then acting out a drama in which one controls that thing and, thus, feels powerful. As death is one "thing" we cannot control, many of these rituals involve finding some symbolic equivalent to death which can then be symbolically mastered.

To avoid the fate of Jonathan Edwards's helpless sinners, dangled by an angry God over the pits of hell, many seek to find something less powerful than themselves and dangle it instead over some metaphorical inferno. Foreign policy officials, as well, have been known to engage in this sort of symbolic retribution. Sports often involve elements of this ritual empowerment, as in the following example from the life of one man charged with making foreign policy decisions. Paul Nitze recounts that after leaving the Department of State he felt bitter and frustrated by his absence from the places of power. He recalled "not quite feeling right until he had ridden in a steeplechase . . . and looked back, as he crossed the finish line in first place, to see mud splattered all over the also-rans."[63] In the aftermath of his removal from power, which was an unpleasant reminder of life's limitations (of which mortality was the purest example), the race was a way of achieving that elusive state of "feeling right." For Nitze, that power that he was unable to possess in reality was ritually recreated within the context of a sporting event. Although we cannot know for certain why he found the event so pleasurable, the structure of the race lent itself to creating a convincing illusion—riding the horse (time-honored symbol of martial glory) could convey a sense of power, and the mud splattered on the losers signified their inferiority, even mortality. Evidently, the ritual was powerful enough that the sting of political defeat was assuaged by the salve of his athletic accomplishment.

Similarly, Dwight Eisenhower recounts a form of ritual empowerment in which he engaged during World War II. When he felt mad at someone but could not express that anger or do anything about whatever it was that was making him mad, he would write that person's name on a scrap of paper and stick it in the bottom drawer of his desk. In this way, he could control the object of his anger and frustration symbolically by first transforming the person into a rather unimaginative voodoo doll, and then, rather than sticking pins in it, hiding the person away. The act clearly did not change the outside world in such a way as to resolve the problem that made Ike mad, but it created a fantasy world in which he was able to experience a sense of power in a situation of powerlessness. This empowerment is one of the principal functions of ritual.

In World War II, Eisenhower's ritual was reenacted on a much more horrific scale. Eisenhower wrote that "there was no question of the deep-seated hatred I felt for Hitler and all that he stood for. But there were ways to deal with him other than the drawer."[64] In this case, his well-founded anger could be expressed, if indirectly, through the socially sanctioned act of war. War represented for Eisenhower a chance to do something about the things that made him angry. Unlike the drawer ritual in which the "real" problem could not be addressed, during war, the real problem—in this case the military offensives of Nazi Germany—could be addressed. But on another level, Hitler was but a specific instance of the general problem of the vagaries of existence, and the war was a way to ritually address a whole set of concerns besides the manifest problem of Germany and Japan's attacks. It was paradoxically one of the oldest and most powerful ways of addressing the problem of mortality.

WAR AS RITUAL

If much of the symbolic and ritual content of our lives is informed and shaped by concerns about mortality, warfare, in which humans exercise the greatest amount of raw power, can be seen as in part addressing these same concerns. This is partially the case because world politics remains one of the few arenas in which the participants are relatively free of the constraints imposed by civil society, and in which the actors wield enormous power. As officeholders, they had at their disposal a staggering array of resources to exert control over the outside world. They could facilitate their own, the soldiers', and the nation's sense of transcendence by employing those tools to control things in the world (e.g., driving Iraqi troops out of Kuwait) and thereby gain a sense of power over all those things that could not be controlled.

In her book *Blood Rites*, Barbara Ehrenreich examines the ritual nature of warfare, arguing that war evolved as a response to the early human experience of being preyed on by dangerous animals. For Ehrenreich, war enables participants to symbolically reenact the hunt in order to address deep-rooted concerns about being killed and eaten. In this scheme, war constitutes a form of empowerment similar to that described above. To expand on Ehrenreich's thesis, there are three related ritual forms of warfare that contribute to the creation of a sense of power in relationship to death—one a ritual of affirming nationalist articles of faith, another a ritual of renewal, and, third, an empowering ritual of symbolically doing battle with death. Where Ehrenreich looks back to the origins of the human species to find the anxiety underlying warfare, I see it existing in the ongoing fears of death. Although our fear of being preyed on by vicious carnivores may stem from our early hominid experiences, the fear of death is still very much with us. Although we may still harbor some ancient, visceral fear of fang and claw, one need look no further than the daily paper to find a fine array of contemporary dangers, be they infectious diseases, atom bombs, reckless drivers, or enemy soldiers. We still strive to have power over death because death is something we share with the hominid.

This ritual of gaining power over death has several elements. First, death has to be known; the vague, diffuse thing "death" has to be made tangible and immediately understandable, so that it can then be battled. The "truth" of immortality then has to be proven through human action, particularly soldiers sacrificing themselves for the nation. Within the context of international politics, this affirmation of a faith in a transcendent self is linked to a faith in the nation and the timeless principles embodied in it. This is tied to a conception of the nation that would allow it to follow the path of virtue and life (rather than sin and death), and that would in turn allow for the rejuvenation and continued health of the "body politic."

How can war function to affirm faith in a transcendent self? Rituals render articles of faith more believable by enacting in symbolic form the dynamics and values espoused within a particular belief system. As social reality is itself partially the product of what we choose to do, we constantly attempt to bring social reality in line with our ideals and wishes by acting out those wishes. Although religious beliefs have always relied heavily on faith, there has always been a need for some substantiation of the tenets of religion and cosmology. In questions concerning the nature of one's own existence and identity, and whether one could truly transcend the physical realm, that proof is found in one's own behavior and in history. As part of this history and behavior, war itself can be evaluated as evidence of the nature of humanity. As a human artifice and a manifestation of human will, war is a way of "making real" the myths and worldviews. As Senator Platt put it in 1898, the war with Spain was a way of affirming America's faith in itself, in its essential goodness and righteousness. America, he argued, should be bid "godspeed in its mission to relieve the oppressed, to right every wrong, and to extend the institutions of free government." "Let us have faith," he continued,

> in the Government, faith in its future. Stilled be the voice of timidity and distrust, stilled be the utterance of captious and carping criticism. Let us have faith that the powers of government will never be unrighteously exercised. Like Lincoln, when he met the contention that the Government had no power adequate to its self-preservation, let us turn from disputatious subtleties and "have faith that right makes might, and in that faith dare to do our duty as we understand it." In that faith the mountains of doubt will be removed and the way of duty become straight and plain.[65]

By going to war with Spain, Platt argued, America would affirm its faith in itself as a benevolent, righteous nation going to battle with "God on its side." War would allow Americans to remove the "mountains of doubt," because it would provide tangible proof of the selfless principles for which the Americans were fighting and dying. War, in Platt's words, was then part of a self-fulfilling belief system, in which one proved the belief in a set of ideals by dying for them. The deaths then stand as proof of those beliefs. After all, what better proof could there be of a belief than a person's willingness to die for it? And, as the power of ritual is in large part dependent on the unanimous belief in its reality, dissent weakened the illusion and therefore was anathema to the ritual functions of warfare.

One of the oldest and more powerful forms of religious ritual is human sacrifice. Although no longer part of religious practice, it is still central to the secular rituals of the nation. As ritual, war partakes of the same logic as that used in sacrifice. In Western mythology and religion, deaths in battle, like those in sacrifice, are said to serve a purpose, to maintain the proper balance in the cosmos or appease the gods.[66] As Douglas MacArthur said, in praise of fallen soldiers,

> The soldier, above all other men, is required to perform the highest act of religious teaching—sacrifice. In battle and in the face of danger he discloses

those divine attributes which his Maker gave when He created man in his own image. No physical courage and no brute instincts can take the place of the divine annunciation and spiritual uplift which will alone sustain him. However horrible the incidents of war may be, the solider who is called upon to offer and to give his life for his country is the noblest development of mankind.

The dead soldiers, MacArthur claimed, would no longer be burdened by this toilsome and weary life but, now had

gone beyond the mists that blind us here and become part of that beautiful thing we call the Spirit of the Unknown Soldier. In chambered temples of silence the dust of their dauntless valor sleeps, waiting. Waiting in the chancery of Heaven the final reckoning of Judgment Day: "Only those are fit to live who are not afraid to die."[67]

MacArthur's words nicely capture the ritual of war as a form of religious salvation. Their deaths affirmed a religious article of faith—that the soldiers were masters of the flesh and worldly desires and had the "divine attributes" mentioned by MacArthur. But it was also a way of transforming the disembodied principles and national values that were supposedly guiding these men into the reality of flesh and blood. That death in war could come to take on such a transcendent quality in part stemmed from its ability to confer a sense of reality onto otherwise fragile beliefs.

War is in part the most literal, the most "real" of events, in that it involves the body in its most undeniable form: dismembered, bloodied, lifeless. It is this pressing reality of war, these inescapable reminders of the problem of mortality that make the creation of the ritual elements of war such a pressing task. If anything does, the terror and horror of the scenes of war demand some rationalization and legitimization. As Johnson would put it after Vietnam, when asked if the war might have been avoided, "I will not let you take me backward in time on Vietnam. 50,000 American boys are dead. Nothing we say can change that fact."[68] The undeniable, irreversible losses of war elicit a desire to see them as legitimate, as necessary; and Johnson would not relinquish his claim that those deaths had been necessary, as he saw it, to avoid World War III. Because the fact of those deaths could not be changed by what was said, the words then had to be put to the service of rendering that irreversibility more acceptable and understandable.

But it was the bodies themselves that were used to make the words real. Elaine Scarry, in *The Body in Pain*, argues that war, as it operates in the realm of symbolism and national mythology, is as profoundly constructive of social order as it was destructive of bodies, buildings, and landscapes. Scarry argues that war is in part a "reality affirming" activity, in the sense that the corpses that result from it affirm in very tangible, visible form the national affiliation and cherished principles of citizens whose identities are otherwise often difficult to determine. As she puts it, the destruction of bodies in war is part of a "process by which a made world of culture acquires the characteristics of "reality," the process of perception that allows invented ideas, beliefs, and made objects to be accepted and entered into as though they had the same ontological status as the naturally given world."[69]

As well, it is a means by which the "national identity" can be formed, uncovered, or affirmed. John Hay, for instance, would speak of the Revolutionary and Civil wars as times of "spiritual awakening," each an apocalypse in which the nation was "revealed to itself."[70] War, thus, became a way in which identity—which during peacetime would remain hidden under a veil of materialism and superfluities—was revealed by the acts of those who sacrificed all for the principles and values that made up that identity.

The justifications offered by the élite for these wars were principles—words and abstract phrases such as "freedom," "union," and "democracy." But faith in these abstract and often unsubstantiated concepts needed to be bolstered by ritual acts, by some proof of the genuineness of these beliefs and the reality of those concepts, regardless of their substantive meaning or reality within daily social life. Whether or not "freedom" or "democracy," however defined, actually could be said to exist within American society, if 20-year-old men were dying for those principles, then, by God, those principles were real—real because people were dying for them.

Scarry speaks of this "reality confirmation" in one form: the substantiation of otherwise abstract and unverifiable issues by the bodies of the dead soldiers. This substantiation is found not just in the corpses, however, but also in the *acts of the soldiers choosing to risk their lives*. It is not simply in the dead body of the soldier but in the knowledge that the soldier on some level chose to risk death for those abstract principles that one can find substantiation of the principles said to be embodied in a nation.

This ritual function of the soldiers' sacrifices is reflected in the first Memorial Day ceremonies at Arlington Cemetery in 1868. There General (later President) Garfield spoke of how war rendered death meaningful and was a means of establishing identity and a certain personal truth. Sacrifice, he argued, was a genuine act, nearly impossible to conceive of as self-interested. With words the soldiers could lie or be false, Garfield asserted, but in their actions they had proved themselves as true patriots. Words are used to make promises that may not be kept: "We do not know

one promise the men made, . . . but we do know they summed up and per-
fected, by one supreme act, the highest virtues of men and citizens. For
love of country, they accepted death, and thus *resolved all doubts,* and
made immortal their patriotism and their virtue."[71] Their act of sacrifice
then reaffirmed an overarching order, embodied in the state. They had
now "resolved all doubts" about the virtue and patriotism of those Americans. As such, these deaths became reassuring. As Lincoln had put it a
few years earlier, the soldiers' sacrifices had created a "living history . . .
bearing the indubitable testimonies of its own *authenticity,* in the limbs
mangled, in the scars of wounds received."[72] Echoing these sentiments,
Oliver Wendell Holmes wrote:

> I do not know what is true. I do not know the meaning of the universe. But
> in the midst of doubt, in the collapse of creeds, there is one thing I *do not
> doubt,* that no man who lives in the same world with most of us can doubt,
> and that is that the faith is true and adorable which leads a soldier to throw
> away his life in obedience to a blindly accepted duty, in a cause which he
> little understands, in a plan of campaign of which he has no notion under
> tactics of which he does not see the use.[73]

Garfield, Lincoln, and Holmes were each concerned about doubt and authenticity and found reassurance in the acts of the soldiers. In choosing
to die, the soldiers affirmed the belief that humans could somehow transcend death.

The deaths of the soldiers in battle were one way of rendering death—
the ultimate challenge to meaning and self—meaningful. For the foreign
policy élite, who had much of the power over whether to go to war or not,
war also was a way of taking control of death. As horrible as death in battle might be, in ways it can be more reassuring than some deaths during
peacetime. For it is an intelligible death, at least to the extent that it takes
place within a framework of goals, ideals, principles, honor, and the vast
array of social institutions that create order out of chaos. Although war
itself may be chaos for those in the midst of fighting it, for the élite who
directed the fighting, it still remained *their* chaos, a chaos contained
within a framework of strategies, flags, maps, and concerns about national
security. The foreign policy leaders, and their supporters among the general population, could see those deaths in war as deaths they were controlling, since they resulted from the country's decisions to send those
young men into battle. As such these deaths were preferable to death
within the chaos of nature and fate—to dying simply as part of what
Theodore Roosevelt would refer to as the "fecund torrent" of life in nature, in which humans are ultimately helpless.

The ritual of war is also reality confirming in that it provides one with a clearly identifiable "other"—someone dangerous, yet still susceptible to the destructive power of the bullets and explosives at one's disposal. In battle one is able to answer the question instinctually asked whenever someone dies—how and why did it happen? We ask these questions because we want to know the cause of death, to understand it, to avoid it, to control it; and in the case of war, there is a ready answer: They were killed by the enemy while defending their country's interests and honor. We may wonder what caused the war itself, but the immediate cause of death for the individual soldiers is relatively clear and tangible. Furthermore, once the deaths have occurred, there is a ready target for the pain and anger of the survivors—the killers can now receive the full brunt of the fury of the mourners, and the brothers, sisters, sons, and daughters of the dead can repeat the cycle by going out to kill the source of death: the enemy soldier. We see this dynamic acted out with saddening persistence in those areas of the world in which warfare is ever smoldering—the Balkans, Northern Ireland, the Middle East. The deaths in battle are in that sense preferable to those deaths that occur because of chance accident, by incurable disease, or the steady working of time, for with each of these there is no easy answer, no clear target, and often little that can be done to destroy the source of that death.

This act of psychologically projecting mortality onto the enemy functions as one of the main forms of legitimizing wars or political violence.[74] By framing the just war as a response to a prior violence that has struck innocent victims, the aggressor is associated with death itself. The collective response to this tragic death then is to destroy the source of this death. By associating this enemy with images of death, the war against them is transformed into a battle with mortality. As James Aho puts it, once we view "the enemy as a metaphor and conflict as a ceremonial rite," war can be formulated syllogistically as "The enemy represents evil; the ultimate evil is death. *Ergo* to expulse the enemy is to 'kill death.'"[75] This was the central conception of the foreign policy élite's response to mortality.

One of the usual reasons given for the tragic nature of warfare is that the deaths in battle were preventable or "untimely." Because they are seen as arising from human choices, choices that could have been different, there is a sense in which these deaths need not have occurred. For those who do not identify with the country or who see its policies as insane or misguided, these deaths seem doubly wasteful. For them, the source of death is the foreign policy officials who dragged the country into war. Yet, at the same time—and especially for those who identify with the nation and state—it is the fact of this choice that in part renders the deaths meaningful. For those who feel the choice has been made wrongly, the decision to go to war stands only as another representation of those forces beyond their control that may lead to death. But, for the élite, and those soldiers and citizens who believe in the legitimacy of the élite and values reflected in their decisions, war can take on ritual value as a means of controlling death by the paradoxical means of state-sanctioned mass murder/suicide.

War is a particularly powerful form of ritually dealing with death, in that it combines both the ritual of scapegoating and self-sacrifice. In battle, one both battles a tangible and readily identifiable manifestation of death and asserts the primacy of soul over body through being willing to die for the principles embodied in the nation. It is precisely the horror and insanity of warfare that stands at the basis of its symbolic logic. Death is overcome in the only way it can be overcome, by joining it, by becoming a tool of death, by dying. This is, of course, no victory over death literally, but a victory of death itself; but for those determined to control and fight death symbolically, this was a very powerful ritual.

Reflecting the value that the ritual of war held for the élite, Theodore Roosevelt wrote to his close friend Henry Cabot Lodge that, as long as the deaths of those under his command served a purpose, he would spill his troops' blood like water. Even the generally pacific John Long would claim that the deaths in battle "count as nothing" once a just cause for the war had been determined.[76] The particular standards by which the élite moved war from the realm of gross literalism into ethereal ritual varied in the specifics, but once those standards were met, war became a transcendent and paradoxically life-affirming activity. As long as the élite and soldiers felt the decision was "theirs" in some sense, could identify it as part of the process that they called civilization—involving the battle to keep out or destroy all that represented the mortal body, nature, and death—then what was for others the tragedy of war became for them its necessity and sanctity, if not its glory.[77] The ritual power of warfare in part accounts for why, throughout this country's history, enthusiasm for war has been so ardent and opposition to war among American élite has been so muted.[78] Those opposed to war could be branded as heretics within the patriotic faith, while those supporting the troops would contribute to the project of affirming faith in a transcendent self.

The act of war itself has many ritual elements, but the symbolic struggle with mortality took place during peacetime as well. The élite, even when not involved in affairs of state, engaged in other rituals that gave them a sense of power over death. These men drew from the masculine elements of Christian heritage and on their unique position and power within society to undergo a ritual transformation by means of a symbolic pilgrimage, the goal of which was a form of imperial control of the feminized mortal body by the masculinized immortal soul.

The following three chapters offer an idealized and simplified characterization of the dominant form of the culture of American foreign policy as it related to the human condition. The symbolic crusader battling the evil other is a "representative character" that we can use to understand this élite culture.[79] It is a culture richer and more varied than the one portrayed here, but the elements catalogued in the following chapters were surprisingly common and powerful. Although discussion of some of the alternative voices among the élite might be helpful earlier, that discussion is reserved for the concluding chapter. To understand how the discourse on war and the social construction vary and are changing, we must first understand their earlier, predominant form.

CHAPTER 3

THE PILGRIMAGE TO EMPIRE

O wretched man that I am! Who shall deliver me from the body of this death?

—Romans 7:24

Concern about the death of the body is common, if generally unconscious, and a human problem with particular relevance during wartime. The political élite's responses to this dilemma involved the use of a ritual that had elements of a pilgrimage. It involved a transformative journey that facilitated a sense of control over the body, over sinfulness, and over other people whom the élite concluded had not achieved that kind of control. To get a sense of these transformational rituals, we can turn again to the lives of a few prominent foreign policy officials who sought deliverance from the body of this death.

In 1909, right after leaving the presidency, Theodore Roosevelt and his son Kermit traveled to British East Africa (present-day Kenya) to participate in a massive safari and specimen-gathering expedition. This celebration of gunfire and taxidermy, carried out in the name of science, was a tonic to a man who loved being in places of power, and who was for the moment resigned to leaving the White House. That journey, like so many others undertaken by Roosevelt, was not unlike a pilgrimage, the goal of which was to achieve a state of proprietary nirvana, an empire in which the Self reaffirmed its identity as "not-Other," while also controlling the Other. Whereas John Long found "absolute possession" in the New England public library, Roosevelt found it in the "library" of the jungle and the veldt. Nature was Roosevelt's book, and he was a voracious reader.

Roosevelt with one of the elephants he shot, 1909. Photograph courtesy of the Theodore Roosevelt Collection, Harvard College Library.

Roosevelt, like many other high-ranking statesmen, was a literary man, a writer and avid reader, and his sojourn in Africa involved a curious elision of reading and killing. On the trip, besides personally shooting a grand total of 512 animals, he took along a leather-bound collection of 37 volumes, including the Bible, *Pilgrim's Progress,* Shakespeare, Homer, the *Nibelungenlied,* and *Huckleberry Finn.* He would later write that he nearly always had some book with him, and that "Often my reading would be done while resting under a tree at noon, perhaps besides the carcass of a beast I killed."[1] We unfortunately do not have a picture of that moment, although other photographs from the safari capture aspects of the scene described by Roosevelt.

We can imagine Mr. Roosevelt reclining in the shade of the tree, protected from the fierceness of the equatorial sun. Beside him lies the motionless carcass of a wildebeest or lion he has slain, destined to be skinned and stuffed and placed in his living room or before a painted diorama in New York or Washington or Chicago, to contribute to the edification of a public in need of absorbing the harsh lessons of the natural world. What was wild and dark would soon become frozen in time—a known quantity, subject now to Roosevelt's "moral and mental sovereignty." We can imagine the flies buzzing around the blood that has thickened around the bullet

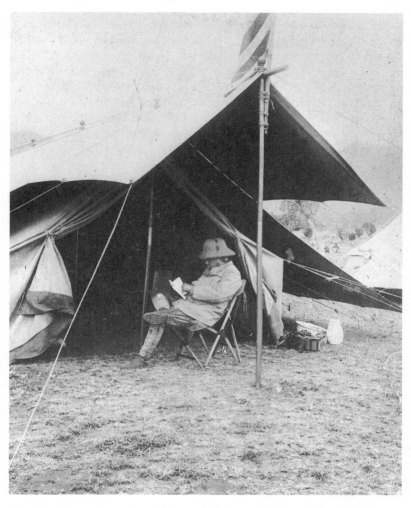

Theodore Roosevelt reading while on safari in British East Africa, 1909. Photograph courtesy of the Theodore Roosevelt Collection, Harvard College Library.

wounds inflicted by Teddy's Mauser rifle. From his saddlebag, he pulls out the *Nibelungenlied*, and begins to read of the heroic exploits of Siegfried.

Roosevelt reenacted a ritual that had begun in his early teens and continued throughout his life. This was the symbolic assertion of his difference from and superiority over the animal, physical world. Like Scarry's corpses that embodied national principles, there was the undeniable, empirical proof—the animal was dead, he was alive. He had power over the animal, over fear, and over his body. The words he read were like bullets, and the bullets he fired like words. (He would describe his rifle as "speaking" when he shot a lion, and he spoke of his words as additions to the personal arsenal he employed in the great battle of life.[2]) In reading, Roosevelt was participating in a culture that stretched back in time and could contemplate the future. The animal—once dumb, now dead—had only known the moment. Now it had returned to the "shadow" of death. The animal could have been the agent of Roosevelt's death, but instead Roosevelt, with his rifle and his steady nerves, had killed it. In the most tangible of ways, Roosevelt did battle with death, and in so doing reenacted the symbolic mastery of soul over the body. Although TR no longer ruled over the American empire, there in the British colonies he had arrived at that personal empire in which he ruled over his body, his emotions, and the natural world. By asserting that he was more than mortal flesh, he kept alive the notion that he had transcended his merely physical existence. For a moment, he could feel that he was in control. When the feeling faded, he would rise and go out again in search of another foe.

This ritual was reenacted with careful attention to the practices of the first safari, by TR's grandson Kermit Roosevelt, Jr. (whose father, Kermit Sr., had been killed in World War II). Following in his grandfather's footsteps, Kermit, Jr. and his two sons (one of whom also was named Kermit), went on their own "Sentimental Safari" in Kenya.[3] They brought their own reading, played with their own guns, hired their own native labor, killed their own animals, and experienced the same "golden joys" of which Theodore Roosevelt had written, thereby carrying on the tradition and asserting the same control over nature that the patriarch had sought. Like his grandfather, Kermit, Jr. also enjoyed hunting expeditions in the realm of international politics, and helped orchestrate the overthrow of Mossedegh in Iran in 1954.[4]

This ritual mastering of nature was echoed in somewhat milder form in the life of Lyndon Johnson. As with Roosevelt, the ritual was part of an assertion of masculinity, but with Johnson it reflected more of an infatuation with technological power than with personal prowess. Lyndon Johnson's father had forced him to go hunting as a young man, as a way of proving his manhood, but, whereas Roosevelt may have reveled in the hunt, Johnson's reaction, after killing a rabbit, was to vomit.[5] Johnson would later take up hunting as a pastime, and embrace the battle against nature. To Johnson, nature was an opponent with which humans did battle and over which technology allowed humans to triumph. This battle with nature was a common theme in Johnson's political speeches, the two principal fronts in this battle against disease and floods.[6]

Billy Graham would recount the story of visiting the Johnson ranch where LBJ had retired after leaving office. It was a hard time for Johnson, a man who, like Roosevelt, thrived on being in positions of power; and he brooded about his death, which he knew with his bad heart was not far off. Graham served as a companion and a minister for Johnson, and Johnson asked Graham if he would speak at Johnson's funeral. But when not talking about death and funerals, they engaged in a form of recreation that partook of some of the same ritual used by Roosevelt—with the difference that the technology used was a V-8 engine. Graham recounts the story of how, as a way of relaxing and having some fun, Johnson would take him out to chase deer across the prairie in a big Cadillac. We can imagine in the scene the power of the car, which served as an artificial body and as a means of having cyborg power over animals, even if they were not the man-eating lions that Roosevelt hunted. The thrill of seeing the frightened and powerless animals scatter apparently was another ritual of empowerment for Johnson. But as with other rituals, the effect was short-lived; Graham recounted that after having had their fun, they would stop, at Johnson's request pray for his soul, and sit silently in the car watching the sun set.[7]

FREE FALLING

George Bush shared some of Johnson's love of outdoor recreation and large internal combustion engines. His recreations included roaring across the waters off the coast of Maine in his cigarette boat; and he shared with Herbert Hoover and Jimmy Carter a fascination with the quieter but wonderfully symbolic activity of plumbing the watery depths in search of piscine prey. On leaving the presidency, like Roosevelt, he also engaged in a rather intriguing form of thrill-seeking. Instead of taking off for big game in Africa, Bush reenacted the most terrifying moment of his youth as a Navy pilot by jumping out of an airplane, first on March 25, 1997, and then again in June 1999, to mark his seventy-fifth birthday. As his career faded, death approached and Bush took to the skies to stand poised above the abyss and to take control. His account of the first jump is telling, in several ways.[8]

Once Bush got the idea in his head, the jump is something that he says he *must* do. It is a "matter of closure" for Bush, an obsession, and he refuses to be dissuaded by anyone, even though nearly everyone (at times even himself) views the jump as a bit of lunacy. He writes that the desire to take the jump stemmed from his thoughts about the day he was shot down over the Pacific and avoided capture by the "cannibalistic" Japanese on the island of Chichi Jima. This was understandably a terrifying, traumatic experience—a brush with death that he found, to say the least, unsatisfactory. He recounts the confusion of the moment when his plane is hit by Japanese anti-aircraft fire, his failed attempt to do all the right things in the course of parachuting out of the plane, and his eventual rescue. It was a moment when he was very close to death and forced to perform certain tasks on which his survival depended. In order to feel that he was not completely at the mercy of Death but in control of his body and fate, he had to feel like he had acted coolly and competently under pressure. But he was concerned that he made some mistakes—failed to take off his radio headset, did not get far enough out on the wing, did not properly release his chest strap. This apparently continued to bother him—it bothered him so much that, at the age of 71, he decided to try to get a second chance.

The jump also has to do with his sense of manhood, something with which George Bush seems to be fairly concerned. He must prove that he has the right stuff, and that stuff consists of a sense of both physical and sexual efficacy. In Bush's account, the parachute jump is equated with sexual potency, as when his son George W. chides him not to tell anyone "about your 18-year-old girlfriend"—as if the jump is akin to him being involved in a illicit affair with a younger woman. According to Bush, the major obstacle to the jump is overcoming the objection of his wife and daughter, who end up having little to say in the matter, but who still represent a response to the thrill-seeking that sees such activity as boyish foolishness. As when he first assumed the presidency, Bush was determined not to have to eat his broccoli, and to defy the dictates of maternal authority.

In the moment before dropping into thin air, we can see, in the video footage, both the look of terror and his effort to overcome it. In the end, he does "get it right," more or less, and as he floats peacefully to the ground, he concludes, "All was well with the world." Mission accomplished, empire achieved, cannibalistic Japanese once again escaped. By being able to reenact this death encounter in his youth, he was able to feel in control again, to feel like he had done the right thing when standing poised above the abyss, and to have mastered his fear. Once that sense of personal empire over fear and the "body of this death" had been achieved, his pilgrimage was over, and he could return to his golf and fishing and his impending demise, presumably feeling just a little bit better.

The projects of making sense of death in battle and making sense of mortality in general are closely intertwined. The élite's lives and the symbolism contained in their writings were rooted in a strategy—an immor-

George Bush skydiving with the U.S. Army Golden Knights, March 25, 1997, at age 72. Photograph courtesy of U.S. Army Photos, Ken Kassens.

tality project—for making the prospect of death less painful than it might otherwise have been and giving them a temporary sense of power over death. As we will see, the project engaged in by the élite had particular relevance to an understanding of death in battle, as the kind of death the élite strove to make for themselves was that of the soldier—the martyr-warrior who was sacrificed for a country that embodied the transcendent principles that were the primary affirmation of human immortality within the nationalist and Christian worldview of the élite. But to die like a soldier, one first had to become one, and to do that involved a transformation.

The ritual act of pilgrimage has a special place within the American Puritan tradition.[9] The pilgrimage, like the frontier, is embedded in the founding *mythos* of the United States, and it was a notion particularly alive among New Englanders at least up until the early twentieth century. In a country defined by its early European settlers, its westward movement and existence on the frontier, the pilgrimage was one symbolic act used to create a sense of transformation. The physical movement from the familiar to the strange, old and corrupt to new and pure, paralleled the symbolic shift from the realm of the body to that of the spirit. The changes involved and the hardship necessitated by the journey, functioned to reinforce and strengthen the experience of transformation and the creation of a new view of the self as separate from one's past as a helpless infant, a needy and crying child, a person born of the flesh, and raised within a biological family.[10]

The American pilgrimage was part of a historical movement that eventually led to a political empire that covered a large part of the North American continent, eventually extending out across the Pacific to Hawaii, Guam, and the Philippines. This geopolitical pilgrimage to empire took another, interior form, however, in which individuals engaged in a symbolic search for that "absolute possession" and "mental and moral sovereignty," of which John Long spoke, over the body of this death. The anthropologist Victor Turner has argued as well that the pilgrimage is a ritual with particular relevance to concerns about mortality, as, like dying, the pilgrimage is a liminal state of existence. In his research, Turner found that death motifs were common in the symbolism of pilgrimage.[11] The pilgrimage has special relevance to those preparing to die, and in many religious traditions to die on pilgrimage is taken to be particularly auspicious. Although the foreign policy élite did not engage in formal pilgrimages, their lives contained some frequently traveled paths. As children and young adults, nearly all the élite would journey to Europe to visit the holy cites of Western imperial civilization and "true culture"; and as their careers advanced, they nearly all strove to make their way, in one capacity or another, to the White House— that most sacred of shrines in American political religion and the mecca of political power.

For John Hay and Dean Rusk alike, these physical journeys facilitated symbolic transformations of identity. These transformations have two components—one at the level of the individual and locating in the physical body, the other at the level of the collectivity and located in the body politic. The first involves a taming of the body, of nature, and the painful emotions, all of which have associations with physical death. It amounts as well to a "masculinization" of the élite. The second involves the formation of an identity that transcends the body by associating the self with principles or institutions that outlive the body. Each amounts to a transformation in ways that allow them to transcend the "body of this death" and thereby avoid dying a "bad death." These worldviews and immortality projects served as a basis for the élite's construction of death in battle. As with the deaths of the élite themselves, these deaths in battle were justified as a form of transcendence of physical existence and as part of the symbolic battle with death.

To get some sense of how the élite came to terms with mortality, we can turn to their writings and speeches, occasional poetry, religious and philosophical views, and their lived experiences. From the following patchwork of glimpses into the world created in the élite's speeches and writings, we get some sense of the mental landscape—what George Kennan would call the "map of my cosmology"[12]—through which their individual pilgrimages progressed.

CREATING THE TRANSCENDENT SELF

The process of creating the purified, disembodied self was a matter of "self-creation" and self-control—a kind of basic training for the soul. One started out as a sinful, fallen creature—a helpless infant born of the flesh of woman—and had to become a "man," a "Christian," a "statesman," a "martyr." This is a process typified poignantly by the plight of Franklin Delano Roosevelt and his desire to transcend the limitations of polio, and by John Kennedy's back trouble and attempt to maintain the public aura of vitality and athleticism. Both were painfully aware of the frailties of the body and strove with heroic resolve to overcome those limitations and present to the world an image of vitality. But if the limitations of the body were so salient to these two men, they also are qualities found in less dramatic form in everyone.

The process of mastering the body—in pursuit of the masculinized body of Arnold Schwarzenegger—has both interior and exterior components, reflected in Lyndon Johnson's conception of history as a "record of man's conflict with nature and with himself."[13] The interior conflict involved overcoming one's own bodily weaknesses—desires, weaknesses, needs, fears, illnesses, and painful emotions. The exterior aspect bolstered this process of self-control by attributing these traits to entities such as dangerous animals, enemy soldiers, and Nature writ large, which could be controlled instead.

The term "self-mastery" implies a multiple identity, a sense in which one is composed of several distinct parts, one of which will master the other. The transformations undertaken by Hay, Roosevelt, and their successors in the foreign policy élite took place within a religious context that posited the separation of body and soul, evidenced in the writings of George Hoar and John Long. George Hoar's immortality project partook of the Puritan war between body and soul, holding to the view that the means to salvation was the "purifying of the soul from sin." He argued that the Senate needed to rise "above the tempests of human passion, the excitements of popular feeling."[14] As a Christian idealist, John Long likewise divided existence into the spiritual and material, and equated the material with death, the spiritual with life. "The material is nothing, and dies; but the soul sings on," he declared in a speech on the disastrous 1889 Johnstown flood. Long's writings express the notion that God was manifest in the heart and mind of humans, which he saw as the vehicle for human immortality. It was the workings of the mind—through science and writing—that brought about progress and carried out the work of God. In this same speech, Long noted that even though the people were killed, man was still "master of nature" because of the workings of the human heart that ties all people to each other and to the "heart of God himself."[15]

Self-mastery, in this scheme, meant mastery of the body by the soul/mind/reason. The complete separation of body and soul could only be accomplished in allegory, as in *Pilgrim's Progress,* in which Christian carries his sinfulness as a "burden" on his back;[16] in "real life," one could not get rid of the body, and this separation of body and soul could only be approximated by some form of rule of the soul over the body—of self-mastery. This entailed an aristocratic and hierarchical view of the "politics" within each individual, and supported a similar notion of the politics within the nation.

This self-abnegation, at its purest, took the form of self-sacrifice or martyrdom. The élite, when under attack or political pressure, often referred to themselves as being crucified, and the ideal of Christ was forwarded as part of the élite's immortality project.[17] In his poetry, John Hay glorified the sacrifice of Christ and equated the sacrifice of civic heroes with that of Jesus. In his poem "Mount Tabor," he spoke of St. Peter's loss of fear when inspired by the vision of Christ. In Hay's most famous poetic work, *Pike County Ballads,* he espoused a view of virtue and religiosity grounded not in piety and knowledge of the details of religious ceremony, but in doing one's duty and in self-sacrifice. In "Jim Bludso," the Parson is seen gambling away pledge money, while Jim Bludso, a drunk adulterer, is nonetheless a hero for having saved the passengers on the steamboat— and "Christ ain't a-going to be too hard / On a man that died for men." Golyer's Ben, another rough character, saves a young orphan from an Indian attack, and dies in the process, assuring himself a place in heaven.[18]

The assassinated presidents all were portrayed as martyrs, and it was common to speak of soldiers as having sacrificed themselves "on the altar of the nation." For the few élite who actually went off to battle (and for James Forrestal, who committed suicide), this ritual took on a particularly powerful form. Most of the élite, however, did not literally martyr themselves; instead, this project of self-mastery was manifest in the norm, widely touted among the élite, of selflessness. In taking on the responsibilities of national leadership, the élite made it necessary for themselves to set aside all other concerns—family, health, even sanity—for these overriding concerns of state. What mattered to them was not their bodies, but the principles for which they fought. It was a tradition epitomized by the founders of the modern foreign policy establishment—Theodore Roosevelt, Elihu Root, Henry Stimson—and carried on by disciples such as John McCloy, Paul Nitze, McGeorge Bundy, Dean Rusk, and Robert McNamara. They were part of the establishment culture that, as Nelson Aldrich describes them, attempted to make themselves artificially tough by going through the "ordeals" of boarding school, the rough life in the wilds, and battle.[19]

The Puritan project of making of oneself something different from what one was as a sinful child required formation of an identity separate from the body. For the politician and the statesman, this meant a separation from those aspects of the past that were grounded in biological existence—in particular, the private, feminized realm of family, reproduction, and sustenance. Part of this involved becoming a Christian, but it also meant becoming a participant in the public realm of disembodied ideas and principles. It was their profession, thoughts, words, and principles that became most important to the élite's self-conception. In *Pilgrim's Progress*, the protagonist Christian begins his pilgrimage by fleeing from the realm of the private physical existence in the family. His wife and children implore him to stay, "but the Man put his fingers in his Ears, and ran on crying, Life, Life, Eternal Life: so he looked not behind him."[20] Teddy Roosevelt would likewise flee his past, distancing himself from his childhood, with its profusion of physical ailments, to the extent that in his *Autobiography* he could write that his life as a youth was "not the present [me], individually, but an ancestor."[21]

In its most basic form, the project of transcending the body involved creating an artificial self—not just wearing a costume (formal diplomatic attire or suit with "power tie"), but playing a role of one's own creation and choosing. Theodore Roosevelt, as Richard Collins argues, was a "myth maker," someone who was adept at the political skill of creating an image of himself for public consumption. A number of Roosevelt's biographers have noted his forced optimism and how he worked to create a new image of himself. Similarly, Dean Acheson would praise Winston Churchill (another role model for the American élite) because of his "great art," which not only directed world affairs but, more importantly, excelled at the "creation and development of personality." This was the standard by which the greatness of world leaders was to be judged. Those, like Churchill, who succeeded in foreign affairs and thereby gained the immortality of historic fame, did so on the basis of their ability to shape themselves and others. As Harry Truman would comment as he embarked on his career in the U.S. Senate, "In reading the lives of great men, I have found that the first victory they won was over themselves and their carnal urges. Self-discipline with all of them came first."[22]

As indicated by Truman's perceived need to control his "carnal urges," the most important element of the élite's immortality project was, as stated in James 3:2, to be "able also to bridle the whole body." The body, like the emotions, was seen as like an animal that one rode, and that had to be controlled and tamed. For the élite, the pilgrimage to empire ideally was one undertaken on horseback, for the activity of riding an animal had particular compatibility with the élite's project of asserting their difference and superiority over the "animal" aspects of oneself.[23] The Book of James was one of Teddy Roosevelt's favorites, and among the élite he epitomized this project of "bridling" the body. He took from this religious upbringing a sense of the need to transcend the needs and desires of the flesh, and this project fit in neatly with his desire to overcome his physical handicaps.

The tension between the undeniable physical nature of existence and the attempt to overcome or master this physical nature is particularly pronounced in Roosevelt's writings. Despite his emphasis on the importance of ideals and "character," he still conceived of humans as animals—not simply animals, but animals nonetheless. His awareness of humanity's links to the presumably soulless creatures only heightened the urgency of his project to master the body. In 1910, he declared, "He who would fully treat of man must know at least something of biology, of the science that treats of living, breathing things." As well, he argued, there was a need to know about Darwin and evolution in order to understand history. He held that this animal nature, the "wolf rising in the heart," was an essential, not cultural, aspect of human nature. You could not get rid of these animal urges, only hope to channel or control them.[24] Thus, we see that Roosevelt both held a view of humans as biological creatures but also had an identity as a spiritual being who was able to overcome the body that so troubled him.

In line with his strong sense of physicality, his view of morality made both implicit and explicit connections between physical strength and moral purity.[25] TR's philosophy was one of "bodily vigor as a method of getting that vigor of the soul without which vigor of the body counts for nothing." He argued that to have yielded to the demands of Columbia concerning Panama would have been a "weakness which stands on the level of wickedness." He held a visceral hatred Woodrow Wilson, calling him "a timid man physically." He scorned the "arbitration types" who had "flabbiness of moral fiber as well as flabbiness of physique." He likewise equated pacifism with immorality, weakness, and race suicide.[26]

The psychological and material tools Roosevelt employed to come to terms with this keen sense of mortality had their roots in the religious beliefs of his family, and the belief of his father and some in the medical profession that his ailments could be overcome by strenuous physical exercise. At the age of 15, with the urging of his father, Roosevelt resolved to "make my body."[27] The reasoning seemed fairly clear. The young Roosevelt lived in a world he perceived to be a Darwinian struggle for survival, and he was what he called a "little monkey" who had been given a poor body with which to enter into this struggle. It was too small and too weak. Fortunately however, it was malleable, and so he began to shape his body so as to increase his chances of surviving both his boughts of asthma and his encounters with the larger animals he feared so much. In his diary he recorded his body size and physical feats, so as to track his progress along this pilgrimage toward the salvation of a good left jab, a steady trigger finger, and a healthy set of lungs. TR engaged in a strenuous regimen of self-discipline and exercise, taking up boxing and wrestling, and becoming fairly proficient at these skills.[28] By overcoming the weaknesses of his body, Roosevelt was able to participate in a very tangible way in the ritual of creating an identity as someone who had mastered the body.

The ritual of self-transformation is also clearly seen in the life of John Hay, who undertook a pilgrimage that shaped his identity from that of a romantic poet to one as a capitalist, an office seeker, and a statesman. Hay's embrace of Christian heroism and the search for historical immortality meant that he felt the need to become a hero. Tyler Dennett uses the theme of transformation as the central motif of his Pulitzer Prize-winning biography of Hay, subtitled "from poetry to politics." During Hay's years of relative idleness (1886–96), Dennett writes that, he "would have presented a suitable theme for John Bunyan." His life was a rather aimless pursuit of pleasure and gaiety, "which he found soon tarnished in his hand and long before the decade was finished he was numbering his days and waiting to die." His redemption, according to Dennett, began when he accepted the position as Secretary of State. Dennett writes, "Somewhere in him was a hero" like those Hay had written of in his *Pike County Ballads.* His sense of duty and aspirations to rise within the Republican Party, which had struggled with his love of ease, had at last triumphed. In conclusion, Dennett argues that Hay was a hero because he "overcame himself."[29]

This transformation, as with Roosevelt's, involved a distancing from the past and family. Hay was concerned that history would view him as a statesman and not as a poet from the backwoods of Illinois. He frequently instructed people to destroy letters in which he made harsh criticisms or was impolitic (i.e., in which he had "lost control"). Not wanting his experiences within the family to be part of the historic record of his life, near the end of his life Hay burned nearly all the letters written to his family.[30] What merited recording was his time in high office. In fact, we see in his life a general movement away from the world of his past, of his family, toward the world that he found in Washington. Hay went from being expressive, passive, indecisive, and contemplating the human condition, to busying himself with making money, and thoroughly immersed in power and politics.

Like Teddy Roosevelt, Lyndon Johnson was a mythmaker who tried to shape his life according to the ideals of the hero. In Johnson's case, this often involved a fair amount of creative fabrication. He would claim for instance that his great-grandfather had been a war hero, although this was not the case, and would habitually exaggerate the danger of his own wartime experiences. His teenage rites of passage involved a number of tests of his manhood, involving public humiliation and the demand that he overcome his fears. Throughout his life, he displayed incredible will power, overcoming exhaustion, extreme pain, and moments of doubt in his quest for political power. He would speak of the need to have heroes, as "[h]ero worship is a tremendous force in uplifting and strengthening" a person. It was through social and political ascent that Johnson sought salvation. "Ambition," he would write, "makes of a creature a real man." Johnson's self-transformation from a base "creature" into a "real man" involved overcoming his bodily limitations, his fears, and societal fetters. This upward movement was symbolized for Johnson by no one more than Charles Lindbergh, a man, according to Johnson, whose courage and self-mastery had led to a "spiritual independence." This use of technology and self-mastery to achieve freedom and transcendence has been at the heart of the American dream, and the élite of the twentieth century liked to dream that dream.[31]

Dean Rusk was described by his associates as brilliant, driven, hardworking, even "transcendent" and an "incredible stoic, durable beyond belief." Like Forrestal, he was a man who never stopped moving, never took a vacation, never complained, and, thus, had overcome himself as well. In Rusk's life, duty prevailed over fatigue, health concerns, and public ostracism. He was raised in a family with the values of what he would call "hard shell Protestantism," that advocated another form of overcoming the body—transforming it by shielding the soft interior from the harsh outside world. In Rusk's autobiography, we find the same trope of the need for self-control, manifest in civilization and rule of law, against the appetites and temptations of the body. He saw the problems facing the United States as stemming from original sin or a "primal drive"; they were to be solved by an overcoming of the flesh and its desires. Dean Rusk also was noted for the way he maintained a firm boundary between his public and private lives. He had a decided penchant for privacy, went to great lengths to make sure his conversations with the president were not overheard by others, and on leaving office destroyed all his old phone transcripts. He was described by his associates as inscrutable, "a man without a shadow" who always kept people at arm's length.[32]

In the technocratic world of Washington in the 1960s, this trope of self-control was wrapped in the language of management and computers. General Westmoreland, commenting on Robert McNamara's stamina and composure, would describe him as having "an unbelievable constitution."[33] We get some sense of the philosophy that supported this iron constitution in a 1967 commencement address delivered by McNamara. In it, he forwarded the notion that "[m]anagement is the gate through which social, political, economic, technological change, indeed change in every dimension, is rationally spread through society." "Management" was a central theme in McNamara's life, and it applied both to the administration of the huge Department of Defense and to the inner workings of the self. As he continued, "To undermanage reality is not to keep it free. It is simply to let some force other than reason shape reality. That force may be unbridled emotion; it may be greed; it may be aggressiveness; it may be hatred; it may be ignorance; it may be inertia; it may be *anything other than reason*. But whatever it is, if it is not reason that rules man, then man falls short of his potential." The ideal of "freedom" forwarded by McNamara, the ideal toward which humans should strive, amounted to a form of self-control and transformation whereby emotion—like a wild horse "unbridled"—and hatred and aggression would be ruled by reason and the higher powers of, what he called that "utterly incredible computer itself," the brain.[34]

As one last example of this project of self-transformation, we can examine a case in which that goal was so important that failure to attain it meant that life was not worth living. James Forrestal's life story, like that of the other élite, can be understood as a process of self-construction, and his suicide as both a logical result of and a failure of that project. He created an identity for himself as a man of action, driven to succeed and to be accepted into establishment circles. As with Theodore Roosevelt, James Forrestal was weak as a child and worked to overcome this through strenuous exercise and participation in sports, including boxing. At Princeton, he became what his biographers Hoopes and Brinkley term self-created—a "man without a past," for whom "escape and transcendence were categorical imperatives." His life was characterized by "terrific drive" and ambition to rise, matched by an equal desire for freedom and an aversion to private or marital commitments. Reflecting his distance from the private world of the family, he had numerous affairs and little involvement with his children, doing little more than encourage them to be self-reliant. At the investment firm of Dillon, Read, and Company, Forrestal strove to maintain a "posture of clear, hard, rational mastery of each situation based on total information." He could never relax and turned even his recreation into a form of business. One friend commented that Forrestal was so competitive that he succeeded in converting the usually genteel game of tennis into "a cult of violence." His biographers would write that he "had become addicted to the pace, the excitement, and the exercise of governmental power." The journalist Hanson Baldwin would describe him as a man who had "built around himself an armor of energy and a moat of intellectual activity; the man is obscured by the mind." His life, Hoopes and Brinkley conclude, was characterized by "the legendary hero's quest for the transcendent ideal."[35] This was the life worth living for Forrestal, a life in which he could make progress in his pilgrimage toward the land of power, self-control, and security.

With such an attachment to his professional life and the world of political power, when Forrestal was removed from that world by Truman in 1949, it is not too surprising that he found life after that time not worth living. Before leaping to his death from the thirteenth-floor window of the Bethesda Naval hospital where he was being treated for a nervous breakdown, Forrestal had transcribed a portion of the chorus from Sophocles' *Ajax,* and the passage and play nicely illustrate a number of elements of the élite's quest for a transcendent identity. The section of the play transcribed by Forrestal describes the sorrows of a son far from his native shores who can now find no comfort except in the grave. Although we cannot know for certain what the transcribed words meant to Forrestal, they clearly convey a picture of a life without hope. It is a poem of a warrior's separation from his home, addressed to those of his homeland. Like the soldiers who fought and died on Iwo Jima,[36] home is a place far away, a place of stability and stasis—"firm in the ocean set."

Throughout his life, Forrestal consciously worked to distance himself from his family, and it was in part this distance from the "private sphere" that made his departure from public life seem so hopeless. He could not return to private life because, in effect, he had none. Shortly before leaving office, when Forrestal's assistant suggested that his exhausted boss go home, Forrestal replied, "Go home? Home to what?"[37] His marriage was ruined, and he had never established any close rapport with his two sons. He wrote in his diary that he did not have "the faintest idea what I'm going to do when I get out of [office]."[38] He was hopeless because he was both so separated from his past, and had been shamed in his present role within the public sphere.

When he was no longer able to keep climbing the social ladder, when he had been rejected by the Establishment, and was no longer able to do anything about the threat of communism, his life was no longer worth living. His identity as a public figure was now shattered, and he was powerless in the face of his enemies and in pursuit of his goals. With neither honor nor family as solace, the ritual of the immortality project had to be forsaken and the ritual death undertaken instead. "Better to die," the selection concludes, than live when the "soul's life is gone." The "soul's life" here was the project in which Forrestal was so completely immersed—namely, the exercise of power to protect America from the Soviet and communist threat that he saw as so dire and so near. The chorus sings that "Reason's day" has ended and now "cold decay" has begun. The situation is "hopeless" now "save in the dark prospect of the yawning grave." Suicide came as a form of hope and comfort because it represented, if nothing else, the only way left for Forrestal to take control of his death by sacrificing his body.

THINKING ONLY OF VICTORY

Writing in 1899 to one Mr. Hall, Theodore Roosevelt argued that "Oversentimentality, oversoftness, in fact, washiness and mushiness are the great dangers of this age and of this people. Unless we keep the barbarian virtues, gaining the civilized ones will be of little avail." Emotionalism for TR meant sympathy, an excessive attachment to this life, an unwillingness to kill—qualities that Roosevelt rejected.[39] When his sister Corrinne's son Stewart died, he urged her to meet the "bitter sorrow . . . undaunted. . . . Grief in no way helps the dead [and] overindulgence in it is wrong." Instead, he advised his sister that one needed to keep active and strong. The emotional pain of mourning nearly surfaced at the end of his life, when he experienced the loss of his youngest son Quentin in World War I, but even then TR managed to maintain his self-control. Passing a group of weeping gold star mothers, Roosevelt "had to swallow in order to talk," but advised the women, "We must not weep. Though I too have lost a dear one, I think only of victory."[40]

One key element of the élite's self-transformation involved controlling the sorrow and fear associated with the problem of mortality. In the discourse of foreign policy, the "soft" emotions were associated with the body, disease, and with a loss of control; expression of these emotions was seen as a sign of weakness, and, by extension, of having been beaten by Death. This was particularly true during wartime, and the linkage between the emotions and death was evident in the élite's expression of the need to harden themselves during wartime. Politicians throughout this nation's history have spoken of the need for the nation and its leaders to "steel" themselves against fear, sadness, or despair. As Plato had advised, the rulers had to avoid all "lamentations and pitiful speeches" if they were to carry out their business as leaders during wartime.[41]

Not all emotion was prohibited, just those sentiments associated with mortality or a sense of powerlessness. As Hobbes describes the emotions, sorrow stemmed from a recognition of one's weakness, whereas anger was a form of "sudden Courage."[42] Among the élite, laughter, hatred and anger were permitted, though still only in moderate doses or veiled form. Eisenhower was famous for his temper, which, although he did his best to control it, still manifested itself in both public and private life. Acheson, known himself for his icy "coolness," would write approvingly of the angry passion of a number of his associates—of Henry Morgenthau's "passionate" hatred of Hitler, of Robert Lovett's anger, and how Ellsworth Bunker won respect because he was "icily cold, meticulously correct, hard as a rock in negotiation." Clark Clifford would likewise emphasize points he was arguing with the occasional outburst of righteous anger.[43] In other words, manly emotions were acceptable, but any emotional acknowledgment of weakness was relegated to the female private sphere.

This control of the emotions came to be seen as necessary for survival itself. As Goodwin puts it, Lyndon Johnson "was always afraid that he himself might give way to irrational emotions; control came to appear a requirement of survival of the self." He would write as a college student that when trouble came, the women could cry but the men had to grit their teeth and get down to business. When President Kennedy was assassinated, LBJ described the élite as "like a bunch of cattle caught in a swamp, . . . simply circling 'round and 'round,'" and Johnson resolved to lead them out of this emotional morass—"I could not allow the tide of grief to overwhelm me."[44]

The World War II icon, George Marshall, was revered in large part for his emotional control. Dean Acheson, who noted on several occasions Marshall's amazing emotional control, recounted an episode when Marshall was unmoved by news of the death of a close friend and quietly and calmly concluded the business at hand. His "self-control came," Acheson wrote, "as I suppose it always comes, from self-discipline." In describing the "stuff of command" possessed by Marshall, Acheson would note that "he had no feelings . . . except those which [he reserved] for Mrs. Marshall." The ideal public man then was one devoid of the public expression of emotion. The reticent Dean Rusk also would hold up Marshall as his role model: the man with the stiff upper lip, always very formal, a man of duty and self-control who required that everyone take care of their own morale. Marshall, who was particular about wording, avoided using the word "feel" in memos: "I think it. I don't feel it," he would tell Rusk. Rusk in turn followed this literary aesthetic, instructing his subordinates in the state department not to use the word "feel" in their memos.[45]

One common element in the life stories of the élite was that sorrow and fear were not permitted in the family. Such was the case in the home of Douglas MacArthur; and John Long's father would advise him to, "Command yourself. Keep cool. He that ruleth his spirit is better than he that taketh a city."[46] Eisenhower recounted a similar story from his youth—after he had fallen into a deep rage, first his father beat him and then his mother advised him that "[h]e that conquereth his own soul is greater than he who taketh a city." Later he would write of how he made it a "religion" not to get carried away by his anger.[47]

These norms of their childhood were repeated within their professional families. Forrestal, a man known for the "iron control of his emotions," also called repeatedly for "cold and objective thinking" about Russia and Communism. Part of this project involved an attempt to remove foreign policy decisions from the interests or emotions of partisan politics. Like Acheson, Forrestal would refer frequently to the need to keep "politics" out of decision making, especially in regard to the issue of Palestine. He would separate the world into two realms—one of emotion, selfish interest, partisanship, and atrophy; the other of rationality, cold objectivity, vitality, and national security.[48]

As Walt Rostow would put it in a memo to President Johnson, "There are dangerously strong feelings in your official family which tend to overwhelm the strictly military factors." Emotions, Rostow implied, might break up the family, and among the élite, there was a strictly held norm against being either soft or "wet." Robert McNamara likewise claimed that his administration was to be based on "analysis and logic, not on politics and emotion," and he admired what he called the "containment of emotion" among the RAND Corporation strategists. Like his predecessor Forrestal, McNamara when under stress was known to wear the "taut look" that betrayed the intensity with which he was trying to control his emotions and fears of losing control. According to Henry Trewhitt, while working at Ford, McNamara was described as "mature to the point that he eliminates his own feelings, and thereby automatically eliminates the feelings of others." At the Pentagon, "associates found him determined to exclude emotion from his official responsibilities—a characteristic which he freely acknowledged."[49] Thus, the strategic logic of containing Communism was mirrored by an internal logic of containing sorrow.

This masculinizing pilgrimage to empire is evidenced quite dramatically in the life of John Hay. His life and writings show a gradual but steady shift from a world of expression and emotion to one of action and reserve. At about the time he began his transformation from poet to politician, Hay wrote to a friend from his poetic college days that he felt a strange and sad self-pity. Yet there is no fire that can light again the decaying altar-flame. I feel like one who is drifting out upon an ebbing tide, hopelessly struggling with the sullen might of its waters, & gazing with wild longing on those he loves, wandering in quiet joy & plucking buttercups & daisies on the sunny shore that is lost to him forever.[50]

On entering the world of politics and feeling himself getting dragged away from the world of "buttercups and daisies," he would come to write, like so many of the élite, of the "battle of life" in which the bugle of God called the advances and martyrdom was the means to eternal life.[51]

At the age of 16, he clearly identified himself as an expressive poet. He wrote to his sister of the gifted poet (a title he aspired to at the time), who "can no more keep silent, and withhold from pouring out a flood of song, than can the songsters of the grove, refrain from warbling their notes of praise, or the rivulet refuse to flow."[52] As a young man, he wrote love poems, full of images of flowers and beautiful eyes that make life worth living and are compensation for all the tragedies. But this side became increasingly constrained by his identity as a politician and the norms within élite circles against emotional expressiveness.

The transformation seems to have begun after leaving college, when we see signs that the life of the poet is not for him. At the age of 20, he wrote that he had "always subjected my affections to my will. My head has always ruled my heart." In his young adulthood, he found that work was a welcome distraction from his poetic reflections on mortality. In one of his melancholy letters to his college friends, he noted the paradox that "In work I always find rest," and that "When my mind is employed I forget the *wasting atrophy of soul and feeling.*" This increase in work was accompanied by a decline in his emotional expressiveness. Dennett notes that Hay's depression and moodiness was reserved to a limited number of correspondents. In public, he maintained a facade of cheerfulness and resolve and an appearance of contentment and health. In his later poetry, we see an association between the emotions and mortality, as when a woman's passionate love brings her "down to death, and [from] death to hell." Sometime in midlife, he wrote the poem "Lagrimas," in which he prayed for tears that will not come:

> God send me tears!
> Loose the fierce band that binds my tired brain,
> Give me the melting heart of other years,
> And let me weep again!

Apparently, somewhere inside him was an expressive poet, but his public persona would not allow that heart to express itself.[53]

As seen in the example of George Bush's parachute jump, fear was another emotion the élite sought to control in their confrontation with death. Courage, as stated in the opening lines of Kennedy's *Profiles in Courage*, was "the most admirable of human virtues" within élite culture.[54] As in *Pilgrim's Progress*, where the only way to salvation was past the dreaded lions on the Hill of Difficulty, so the pilgrimage of the élite required some overcoming of fear of wild beasts and the pain and death those creatures might bring. This was the self-discipline found in élite such as Robert McNamara, who "had disciplined himself to nervelessness under conditions that caused other men to tremble."[55] This sense of needing to become "nerveless" and, hence, become partially disembodied, facilitated the transcendence of fear. In both foreign policy and personal ritual, the overcoming of fear was at the center of the élite's immortality project.

In the Theodore Roosevelt Memorial in the atrium to the American Museum of Natural History, a quote of Roosevelt's sums up this attitude toward life and fear: "Only those are fit to live who do not fear to die; and none are fit to die who have shrunk from the joy of life. Both life and death are part of the same great adventure."[56] But fearlessness was not something one was born with—again, a transformation was required. As a boy, Roosevelt experienced himself as "nervous and timid," while at the same time the models held up for his emulation were those of fearless men—the heroes of the adventure stories, his Confederate relatives, and his father. The means of resolving this clash between his experience of who he was and who he ought to be was resolved through invoking a greater fear and practice.

Of this greater fear, Soren Kierkegaard wrote that the Christian "acquires as a Christian a courage which the natural man does not know—this courage he acquires by learning fear for the still more dreadful. Such is the way a man always acquires courage; when one fears a greater danger."[57] For Theodore Roosevelt, these greater fears were of his father and of God. In the title to his call to arms during World War I, he called on America to "Fear God and Take your own Part." That fear of God had come to the young TR in the form of a father who read the Bible to his children every Sunday.[58] Roosevelt had a very close relationship with his father, writing to him as "his best and most intimate friend," but also writing that he was "the only man of whom I was ever afraid."[59] It was in his father's arms that TR was nursed through many of his asthma attacks, and it appears that he came to feel completely dependent on the ministrations of this stern and usually gentle man. According to TR, his father only beat him once; but coming from a figure that loomed so large in the mind of the young Roosevelt, that was all that was necessary to elicit the total respect of the son. This fear of the disapproval of his father haunted

Roosevelt throughout his life, and it appears to have been sufficient to enable him to overcome his fears and brashly risk his life (or political career) in the campaigns on Cuba and in the jungles of Brazil.

When the wrath of God or father were insufficient, however, practice was needed. He was impressed as a boy by a passage in one of the adventure stories he liked to read about how fearlessness was a quality that one could develop through hard work. In a discussion of hunting, TR wrote of the "buck fever" that struck beginners. This was a "state of intense nervous excitement" that could strike anyone who was addressing a large audience, going into battle, or trying to shoot a male deer for the first time. The solution to this was to get one's "nerves thoroughly under control," which, Roosevelt advised, was "largely a matter of habit." TR overcame his buck fever through conscious effort and "deliberate determination." The trick was to shape oneself so as to separate and distinguish the self from the body and its nerves. The other crucial aspect of this project was to become proficient in firearms. If you became powerful enough, you could simply eliminate the source of fear. Roosevelt admitted he was scared of grizzly bears, mean horses, and gunfighters, but proudly reported that he was eventually able to overcome these fears. His experience in the North Dakota Badlands, where he lived on and off for three years in an unsuccessful attempt at ranching, served as a proving ground. Life there was somewhat precarious, and Roosevelt described the men in the Dakotas as "reckless riders who unmoved looked in the eyes of life and death."[60] During his time there Roosevelt partially succeeded in proving to himself that, like those reckless riders, he was not afraid to die.

Although much less extreme than Roosevelt's transformation, part of John Long's transformation also required overcoming fear. Long's early experience with fear was not—as it was for Roosevelt and later with Eisenhower, Acheson, and Nitze[61]—a personal encounter with some powerful antagonist who threatened him physically, but with the fear of public speaking. It was in the face of the audience in the Hebron Academy (the school he attended in Maine) that he experienced his sense of weakness, and it was through his eloquence that he came to have a sense of power. The transformation involved overcoming his fear—after succeeding as a speaker at Harvard, Long felt he had become "a man with no fear." As with the other élite, manhood required overcoming fear, but the means to doing so was not on the battlefield but at the podium.

We get some sense of the urgency felt by the élite to overcome their fear of death, and the prestige derived from demonstrating such transcendence, in Henry Stimson's account of his combat experience in World War I. In 1917, Henry Stimson—the man who was to serve as Secretary of War during World War II and the intellectual godfather of the postwar realists such as Acheson, McGeorge Bundy, and Forrestal—was 48 years old. Although he was much older than the average recruit, he enlisted in the Army, served as a Colonel of the Seventy-seventh Field Artillery Regiment, and fought for a short time in the trenches in France. In his memoirs, he gave two quite different reasons for fighting, which shed some light on what it was that made men such as Stimson volunteer to go off to battle. Stimson did not explain his service in terms of a desire to avenge the German attack on Belgium and France or the need to make the world safe for democracy. His reasons seem to have had more to do with how he thought others would view him and his personal need to face his own fears. As Stimson described it to his biographer McGeorge Bundy (who was to serve as National Security Advisor during the Vietnam War), during the three weeks when he was in command and in battle "he was wonderfully happy," because "the only thing worse than the fear that fills all battlefields is *the fear of fear* that fills the hearts of men who have not fought."[62]

Stimson acknowledges his fear of death—this is the "fear that fills all battlefields"—but claims that there is something worse—namely, not being able to face this fear, to face mortality, or rather not *knowing* whether he would be able to overcome that fear or not. Viewed within the framework of the élite immortality project this uncertainty is troubling, because it leaves open the possibility that the flesh (and its fears) will triumph over the mind and spirit. Stimson needed to prove to himself and to others that he was not afraid of dying. As part of the ritual of war, fighting in battle then became a way of overcoming death, not letting it have the better of you. It was a triumph of the human will over the limitations of the body.

Stimson's father and many of Stimson's superiors in Washington had fought in the Civil War. Stimson envied their battle experience and found they enjoyed a prestige he felt he could never have without a similar personal history. After his military service, he finally felt their equal and recounted his battle stories with great relish. He felt he needed the "prestige of having been shot at,"[63] because he had for a number of years been advocating general mobilization and American involvement in World War I. The only way he felt he could ask others to go off and die was if he knew he was willing to do so himself, and the only way for him to do so was actually to fight. So the fear of death was something Stimson felt he had to overcome both for himself and to gain the authority needed to ask others to die. This authority could only come from proving that he was not afraid himself of risking his life in battle.

Battle not only provides an opportunity for proving oneself fearless; it is as well a setting in which one faces an enemy. Whereas the enemy is a threat to oneself, it is also a convenient symbolic receptacle for all those unpleasant inner characteristics that the élite tried to battle within themselves.

HUNTING THE SINFUL OTHER

The strains and inner conflicts of this dualistic identity, which reflected the tensions of the human condition, could in part be lessened by attempting to turn them into a battle between a good self and an evil Other. Just as an identity of immortal soul and mortal body could be created, so could a worldview divided into the realms of life, immortality, and goodness on one side, and death, mortality, and evil on the other. One way to facilitate the construction of an identity purged of reminders of mortality was to construct an image of the "other" as composed of exactly those characteristics. To the extent that the American élite defined themselves as different from the other, they could escape their mortality or at least ease the tensions that stemmed from the human condition by projecting mortality onto something external. This allowed the élite to construct an image of themselves as "reborn," and thus feel uplifted.

Thus we see the various troubling inner attributes—pain, sadness, disease, aging—associated with external entities, particularly animals.[64] If art, language, and "the Word" were what distinguished humans from animals, it was the body that tied the élite to the natural world, and, thus, the project of overcoming the body was symbolically carried out by overcoming nature. John Foster Dulles would take the battle against "the elements that he couldn't control" as "an allegory of life itself."[65] To Roosevelt, death was an aspect of man's animal nature, and nature itself was a place of death. In nature, he wrote, the "fecund stream of life, especially life on the lower levels, flows like an immense torrent out of nonexistence for but the briefest moment before the enormous majority of the beings composing it are engulfed in the jaws of death, and again go out into the shadow."[66] Life in nature, in Roosevelt's view, was pure transience and raw meaninglessness. A large part of the ritual journey of his life involved symbolically stopping this flow in nature. His association between death, oblivion, and animal predators is seen in a poem he quoted in a letter to Oliver Wendell Holmes:

> Over the infinite prairie of level eternity,
>   Flying as flies the deer,
> Time is pursued by a pitiless, cruel oblivion,
>   Following fast and near.
>
> Ever and ever the famished coyote is following
>   Patiently in the rear;
> Trifling the interval, yet we are calling it "History"—
>   Distance from wolf to deer.[67]

The living room at Theodore Roosevelt's home on Long Island. Photo courtesy of the Theodore Roosevelt Collection, Harvard College Library.

If oblivion took the form of wolves, or bears, or men with guns, Roosevelt attempted to gain some sense of control in relations to that impending death by facing those predators with gun in hand. Roosevelt was never happier than when he was engaged in the process of dominating, destroying, or preserving the denizens of that "fecund torrent" of animal life.[68]

The principal way in which he attempted to control nature was by transforming the wild animal into his property—to use Long's words once again, to make it his "absolute possession." At the age of 12, TR became fascinated with identifying, killing, and preserving animals.[69] On his family's second trip to Europe, the young Roosevelt had begun his avid pursuit of specimens to add to his collection. From the age of 14 until he left Harvard for law school, he went through a sometimes daily ritual of killing animals, skinning them, preserving, and then stuffing them. The house he later built on Long Island became a repository for preserved specimens.[70] As Donna Haraway argues, the practice of taxidermy that flourished around the turn of the century embodied an attempt to own and preserve these creatures. Taxidermy stopped the flow of time, because, like the camera, it captured a moment and gave to these creatures a form of immortality.[71] As such it addressed symbolically Roosevelt's concerns about the effects of time on the body. As a friend of Roosevelt's put it, "He wants to be killing something all the time."[72]

The object of projection or domination was not always found in nature—other humans often provided the most compatible target for projections, as seen in the writings of John Hay.[73] The moral geography of Hay's semiautobiographical novel, *The Bread-winners*, divided the world into the clean Anglo-Saxons heroes and the dirty, licentious, dark, Irish, drunk, and misguided villains. *The Bread-winners* centers around criticism of the character of Offitt, a populist labor leader, whom Hay describes as a ferret, snake, dog, and tiger.[74] Dean Acheson would refer to his critics in Congress as the "animals" or "enraged bulls," which he would prod into "bellowing and earth-pawing" with his sharp wit and cutting remarks. He would equate his opponents with the forces of nature—a "storm that blew itself out"—or as a "poison" that has a "toxic effect" on the people. When Acheson's NATO policy came under heavy criticism during Senate hearings, he reported that the room was "steamed up with animal lust." Acheson's Others were uniformly associated with emotionalism, arbitrary death, and loss of control.[75]

In transforming themselves, the élite transformed their view of the world. As they sought to overcome themselves, they conceived of their enemies as those who had failed in this task. They created an image of the world in which the self was good and in which there existed some Other that was imbued with characteristics associated with death and mortality—existence in nature, lack of a soul, lack of self control. Roosevelt would battle animals, Hay would demonize the labor movement, Johnson chase deer in his Cadillac, and Acheson imbue his opponents in Congress with all those characteristics from which the élite culture sought to distance itself. By dividing the world into these two groups, the élite culture was not surprisingly one that viewed life as a battle against this Other.

THE GREAT BATTLEFIELD OF LIFE

Whereas history is a mix of peace and conflict, our common perception of it is as a series of wars. History and the news (and cinema) focus on the dramatic and bloody, because there is a fascination with and an audience for it. But for the vast majority of people, the norm consists of the blessedly mundane activities of simply getting through the day. It is impossible to say whether the "essential character" of international relations is one of peace or war: It is simply a fluctuating mix of the two. Given the grand scope of global politics and world history, it is possible to interpret that history in myriad ways.

For the foreign policy élite, the maneuver of projecting characteristics associated with mortality out into the world tends to color that world blood red. This particular characterization of the world serves various purposes—to legitimate the need for a strong executive branch and high military spending, to distract attention away from the domestic dilemma *du jour*, but also to symbolically purge any evil or guilt from within the national sanctum. To gain some sense of control over death, whoever or whatever was associated with the body and death could be battled, controlled, or destroyed. It was a view that drew frequently on Chapter 10 of Matthew, as in Douglas MacArthur's 1931 response to the clergy's opposition to war: "In all modesty may I not say to the opponents of national defense that our Lord, who preached the Sermon on the Mount, later in his career declared: 'Think not that I am come to send peace on earth. I came not to send peace, but a sword.' " Dean Acheson similarly spoke of his liking for the "rugged militancy of St. Paul's words to the Ephesians . . . 'Wherefore take unto you the whole armor of God, that ye may be able to stand in the evil day.'"[76] When forced to come to terms with the deaths of those close to them, the élite resorted to the language of battle.

This sense of life as a battle or competition is also seen in the élite's characterizations of the lives of their families and associates. Rufus Dawes, the son of Charles Dawes (a close associate of William McKinley's, Coolidge's vice president, and Hoover's Ambassador to Britain), died after falling from a window, either drunken or suicidal, but the young man's life was still construed as heroic. To deal with the awful sorrow and tragedy of that death, Dawes would portray his son's life as both a race and a battlefield. In the race, Dawes claimed his son had ignored any natural handicaps, considering them a "self-confession of inferiority"; instead he had kept his "eyes only on the runners in front, and not on the multitude behind." This, Dawes claimed, had led him to a "moral victory," which he had earned, not achieved by accident. In the *great battlefield of life,* with its fine victories to be won," Dawes portrayed his son as willing to face death "without complaint, clear eyed, unafraid, in simple, unquestioning faith, with hope and trust in his Lord."[77] By structuring life as a contest or battle, the élite were able to allow for the transcendence of those who died, as long as they showed themselves to have "fought the good fight," which showed that they had overcome the weaknesses of the flesh.

This Christian dualism provided the basis for the use of martial language in many of the speeches and writings of John Long, John Hay,

Dean Rusk, Robert McNamara, and Dean Acheson, who spoke of the
Bible as a guide "to endure hardship, struggle with nature, battle with
enemies, or face one's journey through life to death." The "omnipresent
battle in every life every day," Acheson asserted, "was the struggle between good and evil."[78] Teddy Roosevelt saw life not simply as full of
conflict but as a full-blown battle for survival. His writings are full of
swords ringing and shots being fired, as in the 1912 presidential campaign. "My hat is in the ring," he proclaimed. "The fight is on and I am
stripped to the buff." He asserted in self-righteous hyperbole that the Bull
Moose party would triumph in the end, for "We stand at Armageddon,
and we battle for the Lord!"[79]

With a view of the self as composed of mutually incompatible and con-
flicting components, the élite tended to see the world in the same way—
as composed of different groups, some of which had succeeded in
controlling their desires and bodies and others who had not and, therefore, had to be controlled by those who had. Like Christian's journey to
heaven in *Pilgrim's Progress*, the ritual pilgrimage engaged in by the élite
involved frequent battles against opponents who embodied all those characteristics associated with the "bad" death—sin, the body, and disease. As
such their battles became battles against Death itself. This ritual made it
possible to render death as a concrete, known entity, with which one
could grapple, and that hopefully could be overcome. This same structure
was mirrored in the nation, in which the principles which it embodied
served as a basis for what Anthony Giddens would refer to as the process
whereby the "limitations of individual 'presence' are transcended by the
'stretching' of social relations across time and space."[80]

CHAPTER 4

THE IMMORTAL BODY POLITIC

The King has two Capacities, for he has two Bodies, the one whereof is a Body natural, consisting of natural Members as every other Man has, and in this he is subject to Passions and Death as other Men are; the other is a Body politic, and the Members thereof are his Subjects . . . and this Body is not subject to Passions as the other is, nor to Death. . . .

—Justice Southcote in *Willion v. Berkley*[1]

. . . Saddam Hussein has given us a whole plateful of clarity, because today, in the Persian Gulf, what we are looking at is good and evil, right and wrong. And day after day, shocking new horrors reveal the true nature of the reign of terror in Kuwait. In one hospital, dialysis patients were ripped from their machines and the machines shipped from Kuwait to Baghdad. Iraqi soldiers pulled the plug on incubators supporting 22 premature babies. All twenty-two died. The hospital employees were shot, and the plundered machines were shipped off to Baghdad. But you cannot pull the plug on a nation.

—George Bush, November 11, 1990[2]

Innocent babies, whether apocryphal or real, can be killed, but the nation cannot die.[3] "We," or the babies with whom we identify, may die, but there is something we can do—drop lots of bombs on the baby killers. Those bombs often kill innocents too, and the cycle continues. The mutually reinforcing hatreds and sorrows elicited by these most awful of deaths, reenacted and manipulated by wartime leaders throughout history, find their analogue in the medieval political theology described in

Ernst Kantorowicz's *The King's Two Bodies.* Reflecting the ongoing human need for ritual and the creation of symbolic order, Kantorowicz's account captures how the state, whether ancient or modern, can come to embody what is spiritual, deathless (even "unpluggable") in a political community.[4] The issues raised by Kantorowicz's work were central to political and philosophical concerns prior to the modern age, but although these seemingly superstitious and naive practices have increasingly been replaced by the *Weltenshauung* of rational science, the needs met by these superstitions remain. Kantorowicz's discussion of the bipartite nature of the king as both mortal body and deathless body politic may not exist in so clear and explicit a form in contemporary office holders, but remnants and residue of that medieval past remain in modern conceptions of statesmen and the nation-state.[5] This can be seen in the way the foreign policy officials used the state as a vehicle for their pilgrimage, and formed an identity firmly rooted in the notion of an immortal body politic. The nation as a political institution, whether in Iraq, Kuwait, or the United States, was spoken of as sacred, an entity that would not die.

Most foreign policy decision makers did not share Theodore Roosevelt's enthusiasm for battling the embodiments of Death and Nature in the form of lions and bears; rather, as statesmen, they carried out their immortality projects in their capacity as office holders, using the powers of the state at their disposal to battle beast-like foreigners. They were, of course, state's men (and more recently women), whose identity was thoroughly enmeshed with that of the nation and its government. It was not just that, as Graham Allison put it in his encapsulation of organizational politics, where they stood on the issues depended on where they sat, but that *who and what they were* depended on what office they occupied. Benedict Anderson and Ernest Gellner explore how nationalism arose out of such developments as print capitalism and industrialization; little attention, however, has been paid to how that sense of nationalism infused the identities of national leaders—how it shaped their daily routines, and their worldviews, and how that identity imbued those men with a sense of immortality that helped address the subterranean fears of death. It is in the interaction of historical developments like nationalism and the personal lives of idiosyncratic individuals that the particularities of foreign policy take place.

Around the time of the Spanish-American War, George Hoar wrote that he admired Everett Hale's *Man Without a Country* for its depiction of the "infinite desolation" of anyone devoid of citizenship.[6] This desolation derived in part from the fact that much of the consolation that the élite took in the face of individual mortality was based in their identity as official representatives of the United States of America. This nationalistic aspect of the élite's immortality project contained the following mutually re-inforcing elements. First, the nation was construed as constituting a body that was potentially immortal. Nationalist discourse relegated the physi-cal human body to the background and spoke instead of the nation as a single transcendent being, à la Kantorowicz's body politic. The bases for its immortality were the principles, values, and shared history carried on by the ephemeral individuals within it. The life and the strength of this body politic were constantly in danger and, thus, had to be protected and maintained by the élite through what is generally referred to as foreign policy. In this light, the quest for "national security" can be interpreted as part of this ontological goal to maintain the immortality both of the self and of the nation. As long as the nation lived on, so did the élite, for their identities were firmly wrapped up in the nation-state. The national offices they occupied were the vehicles for exercising great power and gaining further immortality of the historical variety. The élite attempted to create a "name" for themselves, to write history, and to get themselves into the history books. They helped define the standards of historical greatness, and, not surprisingly, the standards they forwarded were primarily nation-alistic and martial. The greatest statesmen were those who had triumphed in battle and, thus, helped preserve the life of the body politic. The ideal kind of death for the élite then was that of the soldier, and they engaged in constructing views of their deaths as having occurred while battling for the transcendent principles that were the basis for the nation's, and there-fore in part their own, immortality.

A DEATHLESS THING

At least since Hobbes's depiction of the nation as a "leviathan," it has been common to describe social collectivities, whether nations or armies, as single bodies. Among American political élite, John Hay, for one, would describe modern society as "a superhuman composition through all of which beats the pulse of an abounding and ever-growing life, the rhythm of a swelling song, whose leading motives are democracy, freedom and light." In Hay's language, the collectivity was a living, breathing being, imbued with magical powers and a form of immortality—an "ever-growing life." The principle on which this immortality was based was that the state, and the offices of state, embodied certain values and customs that outlived the individuals who comprised the nation. As Douglas MacArthur put it after World War I, death in battle hallows a place, but there is a "deathless thing, the honor of a nation." Whereas individual bodies had a fixed life span, the body politic could be kept alive as long as its citizens were willing and able to keep those values strong and healthy.

This meant that the death of a president's physical body did not threaten the life of the body politic. In language strikingly reminiscent of that marking royal succession, Hay would claim that the genius of a republic was in part that it provided a replacement for the assassinated McKinley, so like him that it were as though there was no change at all (even though it would be hard to imagine two presidents less alike than the flamboyant Roosevelt and the staid and sober McKinley). George Hoar would likewise point out the immortality of the body of people that comprised the nation: "The anarchist must slay 75,000,000 Americans before he can slay the Republic." Thus, the nation, as long as it held to its principles and maintained institutions such as the presidency, would endure in "perennial life."[7]

This sense of identity was clearly separated from and contrasted with one's identity as part of a biological family. The family, within the domestic realm, is the most basic means by which humans collectively transcend the limitations of individual existence. But the élite, as part of the nationalist project, promoted and formed identities separate from the biological family. Although almost all were "family men," and some of them enthusiastically participated in family life, the general tendency was for them to place their highest priority on the demands of office and to center their identity around their profession. One did not make it high office by spending lots of time with one's children or supporting a spouse. The family, as much as the soldiers' bodies, were sacrificed on the national altar. If possible, public and private continuity could be combined through the modernized practice of primogeniture—as seen in such families as the Adams, Roosevelts, Lodges, Gores, and Bushes. At a minimum, the sense of notoriety and transcendence gained in their public life became a powerful supplement to the sense of immortality or continuity found in the family.

The family and nation were both important to Teddy Roosevelt because these functioned as conduits for the transmission of physical characteristics and values from the present to the future—a means for genetic continuance as well as the transfer of the values and principles he held dear. As he put it in a letter to his close friend Cecil Spring Rice, "Death is the one thing certain for the nation as for the man, though from the loins of the one as from the loins of the other descendants may spring to carry on through the ages the work done by the dead."[8] Reflecting a similar sentiment, Dean Acheson wrote that "a nation is no more than a constantly changing stream of persons, who, having experienced and decided, give way to strangers to both the experience and the decision. Constancy is the result of continued relearning and faith."[9] The nation, the lessons, the faith were constant, while the individuals were part of the great flux of nature. Like Roosevelt's "fecund torrent" of life in nature, the lives of individuals within the nation were a constant flux, preserved and fixed by the learning and civilizing carried on by them.

These social body metaphors served as another site on which the moral aspects of the élite discourse were played out. This nationalism existed within the same cultural framework of Christian dualism, and the immortality project involved transposing onto the nation the same dynamics played out within the physical body. As the body and disease were to be overcome by the spirit and rational science, so the enemies of the state would be overcome by the rational leadership of an enlightened élite.

The élite adopted the Hegelian notion of the nation-state as the embodiment of spirit in history. Theodore Roosevelt argued that nations were fundamentally cultural collectives, held together by the "things of the spirit" rather than those of the body.[10] Although he frequently referred to the various physical differences between peoples, he insisted that these were not what defined groups—rather it was language and the ideals embodied in a society. Using a similar analogy of the artificial body, Acheson would write of society as composed of "thinking cells, actions cells, emotion cells, and so on. The society operates best, improves its chances of survival most, in which the thinking cells work out a fairly long-range course of conduct before the others take over."[11] As in Plato's *Republic* (the work of political philosophy most frequently mentioned by the élite in their writings), Acheson called for a rule of philosopher kings as they embodied the rule of the rational mind over the body and emotions.

This nationalism manifests itself in foreign policy as the protection of national interest. Those protecting the national interest were seen as rising above the particular self-interests or passions of individuals or groups within the country. The national interest then was a manifestation of this same form of control and selflessness that was so central to the immortality project of the élite. There is repeated reference in élite discourse to their attempts at lifting foreign policy out of the morass of emotionalism and partisan politics and basing it solely on their conception of the soberly determined national interest. As the nation stood as the emblem of the rule of the spirit over body and passions and the president as the "head of state," so the national interest was imbued with a sense of being guided by transcendent principles in which passion or selfishness should have no role. Within the framework of Christian conceptions of life and death, the immortality of the nation was contingent on the same virtue and transcendence necessary at the level of the individual.

The immortality of the nation was not automatic but, like salvation, was something that had to be achieved. The body politic was potentially immortal, but not automatically so. As became apparent during World War II, the autonomy, if not the "life," of nations (such as France, Poland,

and the Soviet Union) could be gravely threatened, and in describing the tumult during and after the war, the élite often resorted to metaphors of physical birth and death. Acheson would describe the Marshall Plan as a "revivification" of Europe that was on the verge of being "submerged." Likewise, he would write that "the French in Indochina and North Africa had opened their veins and were bleeding to death." Both Rusk and Kennedy would speak of the United States being the "midwife of Indonesian independence" when the French left.[12]

The contingency of the nation was manifest in the élite's concerns about national decline or the problem of decadence, which had been given a new sense of urgency by the application of Darwinism to geopolitics. In the thinking of Social Darwinists, if species could become extinct, so could nations or peoples. Even the anti-Imperialist Hoar argued that the United States needed to be brave or it would "lose all" in the struggle for survival among states, and expressed a concern about the "disease and decline of states." States, Hoar argued, needed to grow or they would die.[13] Teddy Roosevelt, Henry Cabot Lodge, and Albert Beveridge all saw national survival as a matter of strength in battle, derived from economic power that could be translated into large navies. In opposition to the idealists, Lodge argued that what was important in international affairs was America's wealth and power more than the principles to which it adhered. The very survival of the United States was at stake, Lodge argued, and "our evolution would be retarded," if the marines did not take the Philippines. He argued that the "laws of our being" dictated that the United States expand, and thus the taking of the Philippines was inevitable. According to Lodge, these laws were the laws of the same God who "governs the movements of the uncounted stars in space, tints the wings of the moth so that his keen-eyed enemy can not distinguish him from the dead leaf . . . and paints the little sand spider so cunningly that unless he move his most virulent pursuer would not know that he was" there.[14] Lodge's imagery evoked fears that if the United States did not arm itself and adapt to its hostile environment, it would suffer the same fate as the tiny moth or spiders that did not protect themselves through camouflage.

This Darwinian view is clearly seen in a speech Theodore Roosevelt delivered at Oxford in 1910, entitled, "Biological Analogies in History." Although he began the speech by noting that "there is no exact parallelism between the birth, growth, and death of species" and of societies, he went on to argue, "Yet there is a certain parallelism. There are strange analogies."[15] What Roosevelt found most troubling about these parallels between extinct species and endangered nations was the fact that some of the extinctions of ancient species were inexplicable. In Roosevelt's view, hidden forces were at work, the effects of which could not be known. The central problem then became the analogous instability of nations—"Are we as nations soon to come under the rule of that great law of death which is itself part of the great law of life?"

Roosevelt would note elsewhere that all the great empires of the past had fallen, and the British Empire was beginning to show some signs of fraying around the edges. This potential transience of nations was particularly troubling, given Roosevelt's view that the United States was naturally a pacific country, and given what he saw as the rise of materialism and flabbiness in the wealthy nations generally. He saw that "ultimate decay . . . must inevitably come to all nations," but the timing and rate of that decay was still something national leaders could influence. The existence of nations was contingent on their continued strength and retention of the "barbaric virtues." Therefore military preparedness was always needed to avert "military disaster."[16] The puzzle for Roosevelt was how nations, like species, could disappear or die out. He hoped that with sufficient military strength the day of America's demise could be prolonged as long as possible.

These concerns with national weakness and lack of moral fiber were carried on by Roosevelt's protégés and fans. Roosevelt was part of a circle that met in places such as New York's Union League Club, whose members saw war as serving to purge the nation of materialism and the "growth of soft luxury."[17] Douglas MacArthur would cite the fallen empires of the past as a reason for the United States to eradicate emotionalism from its policies and increase its military capabilities. James Forrestal was reading Gibbon's *Decline and Fall* (a favorite among the élite) as the Cold War was beginning. After the war, Forrestal worried that the country was "going back to bed"—a path, he argued, that would likely lead to World War III. Isolationism would bring on "atrophy"; and military weakness, Forrestal claimed, was akin to "suicide." For Eisenhower, the rapid demobilization after World War II was an example of the country having let "its heart run away with its head." When, in 1968, riots broke out in Washington, DC, Dean Acheson would write that it reminded him of something out of Gibbon; the riots, he wrote, were a sign that America was succumbing to the forces of decline and would soon go the way of empires of the past.[18]

For the foreign policy élite, the problem in Vietnam also became part of the overarching goal of maintaining the vigor of the free, civilized world against the dangers of decadence and complacence. The Kennedy team conceived of themselves as reviving a country that had grown too materialistic, an America with "flabby waistlines." Johnson would warn that "[t]he complacent, the self-indulgent, the soft societies are about to be swept away with the debris of history." Dean Rusk worried about the unwillingness of a people in democracies to sacrifice, becoming too soft, as the British and Americans had been before World War II. He worried that the danger for America after Vietnam was getting into worse trouble because of "inadvertence, inattention, laziness" or isolationism. Europe in the 1960s, he claimed, was "comfortable and fat" and "lazy."[19] By taking an active role in shoring up European defense, America was setting an example for those countries that had slipped into the Slough of Despond, thereby rendering themselves vulnerable to attack from the Soviet Union.

As John Long and George Hoar had spoken of war as a means of clearing the "miasmatic air" of a sick society, so the élite in general framed war as the answer to the "sickness" of decadence. The future greatness of America, Roosevelt would assert, depended on it having a "fighting edge and the virile virtues." In 1895, he wrote that "the clamor of the peace faction has convinced me that this country needs a war." He noted troubling trends in the West—the decreased birth rate, and France's "gross sensuality and licentiousness." TR worried that the Eastern peoples with their faster population increases were winning the "warfare of the cradle." And, without an ability to defend itself, a nation faced "not danger, but death, death of the soul even more than the death of the body."[20] The nation always faced the death of the bodies that composed it, but if it lost its "character" that would entail the death of its soul as well.

THE WAR CURE

The ritual of war served as a means of substantiating the principles embodied in the nation; it also served as a means of national rejuvenation, a conceptualization of war paralleled by the function of ritual sacrifice in Indo-European mythic traditions. As Bruce Lincoln points out, a common theme in Indo-European myth and religion is that creation requires a prior destruction.[21] Although the influence or relevance of these early myths to contemporary understandings of foreign policy is limited, they help us to understand some of the basic and relatively timeless elements of warfare and humanity's attempts at symbolically making sense of the universe. A common element of creation myths is that some sort of prior dismemberment or sacrifice is necessary for the formation of society. From the parts of the original being, the various components of the cosmos are formed. A similar myth accompanies the formation of states, which are formed from the sacrifice of the original founder, such as Romulus in the case of Rome. This idea that the cosmos was created through destruction is symbolically reenacted through the soldier's sacrifice on the altar of the nation. War could function as a means of purifying the nation and restoring the proper order, in which the Ideal was shown to triumph over the Material. As James Aho argues, war is one way in which societies restore a sense of order in response to threats to that order.[22]

The regenerative function of violence for the nation was expressed early in the nation's history in Jefferson's well-known philosophy about the revivifying effects of revolution on the health of the republic.[23] Waging war required a transcendence of whatever attachment to the flesh there might have been, a repression of what the nineteenth-century American historian and statesman George Bancroft would call *"the vile thought that life is the greatest of blessings."*[24] In the case of the Spanish-American and Filipino-American wars, there was a widespread view that the wars were necessary because of their salutary effect on the health of an American society grown soft in its material prosperity. These wars took place in the shadow of the Civil War, which had been construed as a cleansing experience for the nation.

John Long's faith in progress, in combination with a world history full of bloodshed, required that he see warfare, a force he generally associated with chaos, as in accord with God's will. In a Memorial Day address he would state,

> I know not why it is that, if the future is always progress, the past is always sacrifice, unless it be that in the nation as *in the man sacrifice is the soil and seed of progress.* I know not why it is in the providence of God that through blood . . . the great gains of human freedom have had their impulse, unless it be that in the laws of growth, as in the laws of light, it is the red rays that are strongest and that first shine through and flash the dawn, foretelling the pure white fire of the uprising sun.[25]

In Long's speech, war is portrayed as God's way of bringing about the progress of humanity. The example of the Civil War, which Long clearly saw as facilitating progress, provided the evidence that God might indeed sanction war. So, despite his misgivings about the war in the Philippines, as long as he saw it as in accord with this same agenda, he would support it.

George Hoar also supported war as an activity through which the spirit would triumph over the body. If war was guided by spiritual principles, it was glorious and a source of salvation. The destruction wreaked on the bodies of the soldiers did not matter to Hoar, for in fighting for a noble cause their souls were safe. Given his view of mortality, war itself was not the worst evil; rather, it was the sacrifice of sacred principles, particularly liberty or self-government, which troubled Hoar. "I know and dread the horrors of war," he wrote to a friend, but added that "the loss of life and health to soldiers is by no means the larger part." He regretted the deaths in the Philippines, but declared, "what is far worse than all [is] the trampling under foot of [America's] cherished ideals." It was the soul of the nation and the souls of the young soldiers, not their bodies, that he saw as being in danger in the tropical jungles.[26] For with the individual bodies as with the body politic, what mattered most was the maintenance of the symbolic structure on which the élite based their notions of immortality.

When it came to the Philippines, Hoar saw these principles as being in danger and so opposed the war. But many of the younger, realist Senators argued that the very existence of the Anglo-Saxon people was at stake in that conflict. Taking the Philippines, they claimed, was a road to racial salvation rather than spiritual decline. Throughout Senator Albert Beveridge's noted 1900 speech on the Philippines runs the subtext of the quest for youth and immortality, which, he claimed, seizure of those islands would facilitate. In the speech, expansion, the Philippines, the Anglo-Saxon race, America, and heroism and glory are associated with the life and vitality of the nation. This imperial venture, Beveridge claimed, would "renew our youth at the fountain of new and glorious deeds." Death, however, was found in a strict interpretation of the constitution, in the letter of the law, and in the savage and "decaying peoples." He claimed that in taking the Philippines, the United States was taking the path of life and vigor and immortal glory, while relinquishing it would bring about the death of the country. Lodge argued that the policy of expansion, of taking up these new "responsibilities" in the Philippines, was a sign of American vitality, while avoiding empire was a sure sign that "the period of decline is approaching." What was needed, Lodge argued, was action; to win races, he argued, the athlete had to train and race, not sit in an armchair. To abandon this path of action and vitality would mean going "down into nothingness."[27] The subtext of these discussions of the balance of power was an argument about how the "spirit of the nation" was to live on. At stake in the Philippines was the fate of a nation's soul, and the cost of losing would be, as he put it, that troubling notion of nothingness.

For Theodore Roosevelt, it was not so much expansion that was a means for national rejuvenation but the act of war itself. It was the selflessness and sacrifice of the soldiers that epitomized the transcendence of the body. Those who fight "spurn ease and self-indulgence and timidity."[28] In his War College speech of 1897, he declared, "No triumph of peace is quite so great as the supreme triumphs of war. The courage of the soldier, the courage of the statesman who has to meet storms which can only be quelled by soldierly virtue—this stands higher than any qualities called out merely in times of peace." In private, he went so far as to argue in 1915 that Britain and France would "benefit immensely" from the slaughter of trench warfare, as "both of them have shown ugly traits" and "perhaps it was necessary that their manhood should be tried and purged in the ordeal of this dreadful fiery furnace."[29] This could be said of any war, and led Roosevelt to see even such wanton slaughter as occurred in the trenches of World War I as serving a purpose. The act of warring strengthened a nation, according to TR, though the spoils of war could also help increase the chances for survival. There was no peace in life for Roosevelt—life was a war and the choice was whether to fight or die. He would claim that "nature is ruthless, and where her sway is uncontested *there is no peace save the peace of death.*"[30] If, like Jesus on the cross, the soldiers and the élite sending them into battle could show that they were better than simply flesh, their deaths would become a way to life, while peace offered only the prospect of becoming a rotting corpse.

The same language is seen in the writings of John Hay, Douglas Macarthur, and George Kennan. John Hay argued that war often served to purify a people and was necessary to facilitate the "universal tendency" toward republican government.[31] At the ceremony ending the war with Japan, MacArthur spoke of how the war had been a "holy crusade" that had made peace possible and that highlighted the need for a new awakening that "must be of the spirit if we are to save the flesh." The war, he claimed, was a victory of freedom over slavery, and the new threats of atomic warfare only increased the need for a "spiritual recrudescence and improvement of human character."[32] MacArthur saw war as an opportunity for the triumph of the spirit over the flesh, and emphasized the theme of sacrifice for a nation that embodied Christian principles.[33] George Kennan argued that the Cold War should be greeted with "a certain gratitude to a Providence which, by providing the American people with this implacable challenge, has made their entire security dependent on their pulling themselves together and accepting the moral and political leadership that history plainly intended them to bear."[34]

Lyndon Johnson called for physical fitness and self-discipline to overcome the dangers of decadence. When under criticism for the war in Vietnam, LBJ sent a quote of John Stuart Mill to a number of his top advisors:

> War is an ugly thing, but not the ugliest; the decayed and degraded state of moral and patriotic feeling which thinks nothing worth a war is worse. . . . A man who has nothing which he cares about more than his personal safety is a miserable creature who has no chance of being free, unless made and kept so by the exertions of better men than himself.[35]

Within this framework, defeat in war was deeply troubling. Thus, although the international political ramifications of American withdrawal from

Vietnam were not that great (no dominos fell, no nuclear war started, there was no communist triumph but, instead, its eventual collapse), it had a traumatic effect on the American psyche. The nuclear revolution, which for the first time threatened the instantaneous annihilation of a nation, profoundly challenged the notion of national immorality. The 1970s—with the oil shocks, inflation, budget deficits, and Jimmy Carter's pronouncement of a "national malaise"—ushered in a new round of concerns about American decline, and a renewed concern with arguments about imperial decline. In this context, Ronald Reagan's incredible optimism came as a welcome change in the American political context. In his speeches, Reagan repeatedly emphasized that with enough "will" and "resolve" America could remain strong, defeat Communism, and spread its brand of freedom around the globe. Likewise his discomfort with the ontological vulnerability of mutually assured destruction, reflected the widespread discomfort with the tenuousness of life in the nuclear age.

The Gulf War was celebrated as having cured the "Vietnam Syndrome," and the collapse of Communism certainly came as a boost for the morale of those wishing to ensure the continuity of the American way of life. The lack of a clear threat has again raised concerns among foreign policy officials about a new isolationism and American self-absorption—national weaknesses for which, once again, war may be seen as the only cure. The context has changed now, and America is waging wars now in which few (as the in the Gulf) if any (as in Kosovo) Americans are dying (changes explored further in Chapter 6), but war retains its ability to function as a means of symbolically revitalizing the nation.

Élite throughout this period saw war as way of curing the nation of its flabbiness. War provided the opportunity for individuals within the country to transcend their narrow, material existence by asserting their nationalist identity and sacrificing their bodies. The war was proof of that transcendence. By sacrificing their bodies, the soldiers (and the men ordering them into battle) were asserting their victory of the spirit in the war with the body. Thus, the élite could participate in a modern form of the sacrifices that the ancients believed were needed to maintain the social, if not the cosmic, order. This triumph would reinforce several parallel notions of sovereignty—of soul over body, state over nation, and civilization over wilderness. Furthermore, in leading this campaign the élite could achieve some form of immortality by gaining a place in a history in which martial success remains the surest path to fame. Viewing war in this way makes it possible to incorporate some of the seemingly idiosyncratic and richly symbolic elements of élite behavior.

Within the context of this potentially immortal nation, the élite also attempted to firmly establish themselves as immortal individuals. The élite were engaged in this project in a number of ways and had at their disposal a variety of tools that allowed them to associate themselves with the nation. These related to a variety of different artificial "bodies"—bodies of work, of writing, of office, of institutions, and of the nation—with which the élite associated themselves. One of the more common ways the élite sought immortality was through seeking historical fame and forming an identity linked to long-lived institutions. They were self-consciously historical figures, both writing histories and having histories written about them. They had monuments made, commissioned portraits of themselves, and formulated policies and institutions that would live on after them. The office itself took on transcendent importance as a vehicle for immortality. They became famous because they were the president or secretary of state, and so this office and title had to be upheld and honored. They gained a sense of vitality and "life" from the powers of their office. The greater their power, the more alive and happy they were. To leave the places of power, as Acheson would put it, was "to die a little."

THE ÉLITE'S IDENTITY AS OFFICE HOLDERS

In its most basic form, this dualistic identity—mortal body and immortal body politic—is found among the élite in their strong association with the office they occupied. When they assumed office, even though they were not crowned or blessed by the Pope, they assumed a new role, and became the conveyor of a title that had preceded them and would succeed them after leaving that office. Although the corporeal self would die, the office they occupied would not. The office was their link to the nation and a source of great power, both of which could serve as effective antidotes to the powerlessness of the human condition. As well, the office was an entirely artificial identity. As an office holder, one existed completely separate from oneself as a physical being.

This association with the office and public role translated into a sense that the self did not begin until having entered that arena of work. This was particularly true for military men, whose ritual of transformation was so involved and rich in symbolism. Of his time as an adolescent at a Texas military academy, MacArthur would write "that is where I started"; in other words, before he began his training as a soldier, "he"—the person he identified himself as—did not exist.[36] Prior to that time, we must assume, he was merely a physical human being. This sense of transformation and identification with the nation are captured nicely in a passage from Eisenhower's memoirs, in which he would write that when sworn in as a plebe at West Point, "A feeling came over me that the expression 'The United States of America' would now and henceforth mean something different than it ever had before. From here on it would be the nation I would be serving, not myself. Suddenly the flag itself meant something." He would recount as well an episode in which he was identified as a soldier, even when out of uniform. "Unaccountably, and for the first time in my life, a fit of trembling came over me." He explains it by saying "it was such a complete surprise to be *revealed as a soldier*."[37] In the public's eyes, Ike was now seen "as a soldier," that is, as someone holding a position and office with a tradition and set of values associated with it. The identity he had been trying to achieve had then, in the eyes of those around him, been "naturalized," and he had become more than just a body. It was enough to make him tremble.

This transformation was a goal for politicians as well. John Hay noted, half joking but with satisfaction, how several people had mistaken him for the president or some dignitary. "I must be getting to look like some kind of a statesman!" he wrote to his wife. In the last few years of his life, he had both a Sergeant portrait and a Saint-Gaudens bust done. The bust pleased him, for he felt that it "made a statesman" of him. "He is now the statesman pure and complete," Henry Adams would write. "He feels it pathetically but has ceased to struggle. All but the official is dead or paralyzed."[38]

The appeal of these offices and roles lay in the fame one could gain from them and the power one exercised through them. This sense that the élite's life began once they had assumed office or been recognized as occupying a role was reflected as well in their relationship to places of power. The closer they were to the center of power, the more alive they felt; the further away from the White House, the sicker and more depressed they were. The pilgrimage to power involved a move away from the places of primitive nature to the places of civilization and refinement, a move clearly evident in John Hay's career. Hay's biographies outline a strange process, in which his melancholy, "nervous disorders," and concerns about mortality all became more pronounced the further away he got from the centers of civilization. He was happiest in London, slightly less so in New York or Washington, clearly less so in Cleveland, and it did not get much worse than the small-town Illinois of his youth. The cure for his maladies was to go to Europe, still the cultural mecca for the élite. Hay grew depressed and despondent when in the West, writing to an Eastern friend, "I have wondered in the valley of the shadow of death. All the universe, God, earth and heaven, have been to me but vague and gloomy phantasms."[39] He described his time in Warsaw, Illinois, where he returned briefly after leaving Brown, as "this death-in-life of solitude." The prospect of leaving Providence and returning to Illinois was like a dying for Hay. "Fleeting & illusory have been all my dreams. Yet they have died away into silence unheeded & unlamented for they never have possessed the vitality which Hope alone can give."[40]

Hay's friend Henry Adams found political power to be "a diseased appetite, like a passion for drink or perverted tastes," the effect of which was "an aggravation of self, a sort of tumor that ends by killing the victim's sympathies." Public office was to Adams a place of death, and he shunned it as vigorously as Hay pursued it. As Hay noted, "In the workaday world, honors and wealth alike go to the men who seize them, who love and desire them in a practical and aggressive way. If they were less desirable the gentle and good might perhaps have a monopoly of them." About the time Hay wrote this, he became more actively involved in seeking office and actively supported McKinley's campaign for the presidency, delivering speeches and contributing generously to the campaign fund. Whereas Adams associated power with death, Hay associated it with life.[41] Hay was not subtle in his office seeking and was in the habit of giving gifts to incoming presidents (including the two rings that contained strands of Washington's and Lincoln's hair). Despite recurrent health problems and steady complaints about the difficulties posed for him by an obstinate Senate, Hay stayed on as Secretary of State until his death.

Obviously, one of the main reasons politicians seek office is because of their ambition to wield power.[42] What is interesting to note is how the places of power were equated with life, whereas leaving office was equated with dying. One of the reasons why that power was so attractive was that it helped these men address their concerns about mortality. For these politicians, to be out of power was to die. In the politically unsatisfying position of vice president, Theodore Roosevelt described himself as already dead, writing at the time of the "horror of the politician whose day is past . . . and then haunts the fields of his former activity." Life for Roosevelt entailed being at the center of things, having power and influence. Lyndon Johnson, "detested every minute" of his time in the office of the vice presidency, which he said served only as a reminder of his own mortality and was to him a form of "political death."[43]

As gaining power was a means to life, so for the élite losing power or position was often described as a form of destruction or death, and leaving office was almost always referred to as a funeral. Kennedy's *Profiles in Courage* recounts the story of Senator Edmund Ross, who would describe the prospect of leaving office after taking an unpopular stance in the impeachment proceedings for Andrew Johnson as "looking down into my open grave." It was a characterization of the transition from public to private life shared by many élite. At the dinner marking Roosevelt's departure and Taft's arrival in the White House, Taft described the occasion as like a "funeral." The occasion of McNamara's departure from the Department of Defense was likewise described as a "wake." Dean Acheson would write of public life as like a "habit-forming drug," and leaving that realm involved a period of "withdrawal" as a result of his system being overstimulated for too long. "To leave positions of great responsibility and authority," he wrote, "is to die a little." According to Dean Rusk's son Richard, after leaving office Rusk "thought he was dying. He talked about death as if it were imminent; he had all the appearances of a deeply troubled man." After leaving office, Doris Kearns Goodwin writes, Johnson was "drained of all vitality. Retirement became for him a form of little death."[44] As we have seen, for James Forrestal, leaving office literally was his death. Unable to cope with life out of office and suffering from what psychiatrists diagnosed as the civilian equivalent of "battle fatigue," Forrestal had so thoroughly linked his identity to his office that he could not face living without official power.

One component of this power was the élite's ability to create new institutions, socially constructed offspring that might bear the élite's names and embody the principles and values they espoused. Whereas they maintained identities largely separate from their biological families and may have had trouble instilling those values in their biological children, they were more successful with their cultural progeny. While in office, it was the creations and initiatives the élite took that were the locus of their vitality. As Carol Cohn and other feminist writers have pointed out, male politicians often use the language of birth and paternity when referring to their creations, whether they were nuclear bombs or alliance treaties.[45] Cohn found that the subjects in nuclear parlance were the weapons themselves, not the people who might potentially get blown up by them; likewise, in the discourse of the foreign policy élite, what mattered, what lived, and what died were their "baby boys"—Hay's Open Door Notes, Wilson's Fourteen Points, the Marshall Plan, NATO, and Johnson's Great Society. In the élite discourse, the writing of memos, creation of organizations, forwarding of ideas were all framed as matters of life and death. The élite described their creations as living, breathing, embodied beings, about whose fate they were intimately concerned. For instance, George Hoar's "baby," his immortal creation, was the Republican Party. As he put it, "I stood in humble capacity by its cradle. I do not mean, if I can help it, to follow its hearse."[46] To a party stalwart like Hoar, it was the principles of the Republican Party that embodied the essence of America and were his vehicle to immortality.

Dean Acheson's language is a strikingly consistent in this regard. In his memoirs, he describes policies, organizations, and plans as having a parentage and breeding, as being conceived or "fathered," miscarrying, having difficult pregnancies or "gestations," being born or stillborn, growing and aging, thriving, and dying. Thus, Acheson would speak of the "labor pains" of the Truman Doctrine, NSC-68 as having "a difficult pregnancy," and NATO as evidence of "common will made flesh."[47] Whatever concerns he might have had about his existence as a corporeal being were then transferred onto his own disembodied creations. Just as it is easier for nuclear strategists to worry about the survivability of their missiles, Acheson could worry about the survival of his diplomatic initiatives.

That the élite's sense of immortality was wrapped up in the political creations is nowhere more evident than in the life of Lyndon Johnson. After leaving office he cringed at Nixon's gradual weakening of the Great Society programs and described the process as starving his initiatives to death. In language that showed an association between life, female beauty, and his political creations, he said of the Great Society Program,

> She's getting thinner and thinner and uglier and uglier all the time. Now her bones are beginning to stick out and her wrinkles to show. Soon she'll be so ugly that the American people will refuse to look at her; they'll stick her in a closet to hide her and there she'll die. And when she dies, I too will die.[48]

The lack of success of Johnson's program meant that the physical body, as it were, resurfaced. As the mortality of his legislative successes became more apparent, so did its bones and wrinkles.

But while that process was deeply troubling to Johnson he busied himself with overseeing the writing of his memoirs, the construction of the Lyndon B. Johnson Presidential Library, and monitoring how many people visited his birth site and library. For if his programs might have been losing strength, he still could hope to live on in the nation's history books.

MAKING IT INTO THE HISTORY BOOKS

In response to a death of one their own, the élite sought solace in history. In his eulogy for McKinley, the first thing John Hay spoke of was what future historians would say about the dead president, concluding that McKinley was now "among the few whose names may be placed definitely and forever in charge of the historic Muse."[49] Henry Cabot Lodge, in his memorial speech for Teddy Roosevelt, spoke of history as a deity before whom the great go to stand in final judgment. "We must remember that when History, with steady hand and calm eyes, free from the passions of the past, comes to make up the final account, she will call as her principal witnesses the contemporaries of the man or the event awaiting her verdict."[50] Lodge took up this task in his eulogy and went on to tell the story of Roosevelt's public life (his private life being historically irrelevant). After completing the story, Lodge added that his account, "is but a bare, imperfect catalogue into which history when we are gone will breathe a lasting life." History was the means of bringing Roosevelt back to life—breathing a "lasting life" into his new body as it now existed in the body of works written about him. As the nation and political office constituted artificial bodies for the élite, so did the collection of their words embody the transcendent character of the physical and mortal body.

History is the product of a social community and the community itself is partially a product of its history. A large part of community identity is its shared memories and stories. As John Long would argue, material things pass away, while "delicate and invisible" words live on.[51] For those who adopted this quest for fame, part of their self-transformation was to became a word or "make a name for oneself." Élite discourse reflected the sentiments stated at the beginning the Gospel of John, that "In the beginning was the Word, and the Word was with God, and the Word was God." Their identity became thoroughly wrapped up in the symbolization of words, as reflected in the insistence among many of the élite on using proper titles rather than given names. This is seen in extreme form in the behavior of Douglas MacArthur who, after he became a hero in World War I, began to refer to himself in the third person, as if he had already become a disembodied being, a historical figure.[52]

Words themselves are important because they formed the principles and values that are so important to a nation; but the words also are a means whereby politicians' names and specific deeds can become part of the collective memory. For those who were particularly successful in the political game, there would be monuments; their names (or better yet, iconic initials—FDR, JFK, LBJ) would become household words. This search for fame amounted to a form of competition in which the winners gained a place in history. Just a few weeks before he died, Hay wrote in his journal of his reluctance to accept his death, and of the means he had used to attempt to overcome death. These means were of the heroic type, and consisted of the neverending quest for symbolic tokens of power and greatness, such as he had sought in politics and poetry.

> I say to myself that I should not rebel at the thought of my life ending at this time. . . . My name is printed in the journals of the world without descriptive qualifications, which may, I suppose, be called fame. . . . I know death is the common lot, and what is universal ought not to be deemed a misfortune; and yet—instead of confronting it with dignity and philosophy, I cling instinctively to life and the things of life, as eagerly *as if I had not had my chance at happiness and gained nearly all the great prizes.*"[53]

In strikingly similar language, Henry Stimson would note that "the idea of a struggle for prizes, so to speak, has always been one of the fundamental elements of my mind, and I can hardly conceive of what my feelings would be if I ever was put in a position or situation in life where there are no prizes to struggle for."[54]

Related to this quest for prizes was the project of defining what counted as history and the standards of fame. While the élite were engaged in "making history," they also were involved in writing it. As Churchill quipped, he was confident that history would smile on him, since he was going to write it. A fair number of these élite wrote their own histories as well as histories of past statesmen and warriors. At the turn of the century, many of the élite were members of historical societies. John Hay cowrote the first definitive (12 volume) biography of Lincoln. Both Teddy Roosevelt and Henry Cabot Lodge wrote histories of American statesmen and politicians whom they deemed "great" or otherwise worthy of renown. Albert Beveridge, although less prolific, authored works on Lincoln and John Marshall. Woodrow Wilson wrote a history of the United States, and several of the élite wrote biographies or edited memoirs of their predecessors before moving to fill their places. Robert Bacon (TR's boxing partner and briefly secretary of state) edited the works of Elihu Root, and Philip Jessup (later Ambassador to the United Nations) wrote a three-volume biography of Root. McGeorge Bundy worked with Henry Stimson on his memoirs and edited a set of Acheson's speeches.[55] John Kennedy wrote, or at least "authored," the Pulitzer Prize-winning *Profiles in Courage*; when he died, his eulogists made frequent reference to him having "written his own profile in courage."[56] After the establishment of the collection of Franklin D. Roosevelt's official papers, the creation of presidential libraries became a major concern of national executives once they left office.[57]

The standards of historical greatness defined by authors of history mirrored those of their own quest for a transcendent identity. The path to fame lay in transcendence and, ideally, self-sacrifice or martyrdom in battle. The standards for fame held by the élite were tied up intimately with the activities of warring, soldiering, and martyrdom.

DYING LIKE A SOLDIER

As the pilgrimage to empire was accomplished through a series of metaphorical military conquests, so the principal means of achieving historical fame was by doing battle. For the élite, the ideal death was a death in battle. If you were going to have to go (and you were), the way to go was battling (metaphorically or actually) in a crusade. The death of soldiers in battle was glorified, and if the foreign policy leaders failed to make it literally onto the battlefield, they would still describe the deaths of their fellow élite using martial language.

The soldier or military hero was the archetype for the historical figure. The last poem Hay wrote, in 1904, was an ode to the death of the young—Raphael, Shelley, Keats, and "the soldier boys who snatched death's starry prize, . . . Bartering dull age for immortality." This immortality project laid out in his poetry required the heroic death, such as of the young in battle or in some leap of artistic passion. In élite discourse, the soldier is consistently forwarded as a figure who will live on in history. For instance, Hay would describe the Civil War soldiers winning "the joy of ultimate fame" by dying bravely in battle, adding, "It is worth while to die if one could be mourned so gloriously."[58]

In accord with the Christian roots of the élite immortality project, they portrayed the deaths in battle as part of the project of transcending the sinful "body of this death." The act of self-sacrifice itself was inherently compatible with the Christian immortality project; but the soldier also had to be portrayed as pure and selfless. Hay described Ephraim Ellsworth, a soldier killed early in the Civil War, as "stainless and brave," equated him with Sir Lancelot riding off on a crusade to "break the heathen and uphold the Christ." As Hay likened Lincoln to Christ, so the soldiers were akin to saints. "We are charged to fight the good fight of faith; we are to sail through bloody seas to win the prize. The Christian soldier is constantly marshaled to war," he declared in an address to the Boston Peace Conference in 1904. As well, MacArthur saw death in battle as "the highest act of religious teaching" and made sense of the deaths of the men he fought with in World War I as the selfless sacrifice of men who had transcended the flesh. He described the "American soldier" as a "stainless" fighter engaged in "patriotic self-abnegation." Through their willingness to go off to battle, they had become "fit to live." With such a view of death, war was a boon for one's soldiers and citizens—a chance to "become part of that beautiful thing we call the spirit of the Unknown Soldier."[59] Death in battle then became the quintessential "good death," in that it so effectively addressed the project of transcending the mortal body.

The ideal for the élite was to go down in history as a kind of warring saint. George Hoar, for instance, spoke of Charles Sumner, the abolitionist scholar and politician, as a "figure [who] will abide in history like that of St. Michael in art, an emblem of celestial purity, celestial zeal, of celestial courage. It will go down to immortality with its foot upon the dragon of slavery, and with the sword of the spirit in its hand, but with a tender light in its eye and a human love in its smile."[60] In this picture, we see that Sumner has become a disembodied "figure," an "it" (wearing only a smile)

that will live in history and "go down to immortality" because of its martial success. The opponent here is the dragon—the embodiment of all
that is evil, lustful, and destructive, death itself—and Sumner kills it with
complete self-control and a transcendent love. He is a pure figure, "celestial," and, therefore, immortal. This was the ideal—the martyred
saint—toward which the élite, despite all the venality and petty intrigues
of politics, strove.

To the extent that these men sought fame, they attempted to hold
themselves to the standards by which that fame was established, and foremost among those were military success and martyrdom.[61] For élite at the
turn of the century, Abraham Lincoln stood as the preeminent example
of that form of fame. As someone who had successfully guided the country through its bloodiest war and who was martyred by the assassin's bullet, Lincoln had become a high-ranking member of the national political
pantheon. Not surprisingly, Hay wrote that there were two ways to gain
fame "more enduring than any monument." One was through great writing (after all history itself took the form of writing), but more important
were the martial achievements of the statesman—founding states and
conquering lands. The basis on which Hay claimed that McKinley had
gained a place in history was in his role as "Augmenter of the State." Hay
would go so far as to claim that McKinley's assassination was "fortunate,"
because "an event so tragic called the world imperatively to the immediate study of his life and character, and thus anticipated the sure praises
of posterity." As both a war president and a martyr, McKinley had "put on
the august halo of immortality!"[62]

The only *real* death, or good death, then, came in battle. As MacArthur
would quote in his farewell address to Congress, "old soldiers never die,
they just fade away." The pathos of the phrase stemmed from the fact that
old soldiers had failed to die what Hay would call "thanatos athanatos"—
the deathless, and therefore unfading, death. Instead they would simply
fade away. The emotional outpouring from the legislators in response to
the speech stemmed in part from their aversion to that fading away.

For those élite who did not have the good fortune to die on the fields
of glory, those who eulogized them did their best to frame the death of the
élite as sharing something with the war dead. Biographers Hay and Nicolay would say that when Lincoln died, his face showed a "profound happiness and repose, like that so often seen of the features of soldiers shot
dead in battle." Although Hay did not claim that McKinley had died "like
a soldier," he did say that he "was of the stuff of which good soldiers are
made." When Franklin D. Roosevelt died, Forrestal reported that he had
"died like a soldier." Forrestal's choice of a passage from Sophocles' *Ajax*
for his suicide note belied an attempt to model his own death after that

of the Greek warrior hero. Truman said of Forrestal that he "was as truly a casualty of war as if he had died in the firing line," and Bernard Baruch stated that he "died from duty in war and public service." He was buried at Arlington National Cemetery with the band playing "Onward Christian Soldiers."[63]

If the élite tried to die like soldiers, the ideal was to live and die as one. As presidents won fame through martial success, a number of soldiers had become presidents in large part because of their military honors.[64] The surest way to fame was in battle, and so a number of élite strove to win that prize. Henry Stimson felt compelled to enlist, and he took as his role model the "Rough Rider" himself. Teddy Roosevelt spoke of two of the "great prizes of life" that he sought—having a big family, and fighting and dying in battle. Just as Hay described McKinley's assassination as "fortunate," Roosevelt saw death in battle as a cause for celebration. Roosevelt sought battle, and while in battle fought with a bravado that his friends referred to as suicidal drunkenness or madness. On encountering a dying soldier in Cuba, he is reported to have called out to him, "Isn't this splendid!" Dead soldiers need not be pitied but envied, Roosevelt claimed—it was the women who mourned who deserved pity. The soldiers should feel "the most buoyant exaltation," for they had "the supreme good fortune . . . of dying well on the field of battle." "Every man," he wrote in 1892 (before he had been anywhere near a battlefield), "who has in him any real power of joy in battle knows that he feels it when the wolf begins to rise in his heart; he does not shrink from blood and sweat, or deem that they mar the fight, he revels in them, in the toil, the pain and the danger, as but setting off the triumph."[65] Roosevelt thus claimed that war, for those participating in it, was a source of excitement and happiness, not of horror, dread, or chaos.

Roosevelt repeatedly tried to get into battle and expressed the desire to raise an army and fight. He went to great pains to get his horse and his Brooks Brothers uniform to Cuba, bending rules and exploiting his connections and wealth to get the Rough Riders into the fray. In March of 1898 Roosevelt admitted that if he were left behind he would "be eating [his] heart out." As he put it in a letter to his sister Anna, while waiting to see whether he would make into battle, "it will be awful if the game is over before we get into it." While in Cuba, where supplies were often delayed or nonexistent, he wrote that he did not care so much about getting food "as long as we get into the fight." During the war he also kept urging Lodge to push for unconditional surrender and the seizure of Puerto Rico and the Philippines. He obviously loved to fight, sought it out, and reveled in it. "We had a bully fight at Santiago," he wrote to his brother-in-law Douglas Robinson, "the charge itself was great fun." And to Lodge, he wrote that he only wanted to stay in the Army as long as there was "actual fighting on a fairly big scale." After complaining to Lodge about the inefficiencies of the U.S. military, he went on to say, "Don't think I am not having a good time, for I am; this has been, aside from Edith [his wife], *the* time of my life." The period of his life of which he was most proud were the four months when he served in 1898.[66] As well, during the Mexican Civil War and World War I he tried to raise and lead a cavalry force, despite the fact that he was well into his 50s at the time. It is likely that part of his hatred of Woodrow Wilson stemmed from his jealousy of the fact that Wilson, and not Roosevelt, was able to lead the nation during a "real" war. As John Hay had pointed out, TR's war had been splendid, but it also had been little.

He held his sons to the same philosophy of life, and, when World War I came, if Roosevelt would not go, his sons would fight in his stead. After his youngest son Quentin died in France he wrote, "To feel that one has inspired a boy to conduct that has resulted in his death, has a pretty serious side for a father." But he still held fiercely to his convictions that he had done right by his boys. Repeating the credo he held to throughout his adult life, Roosevelt would take consolation that his sons had had their crowded and glorious hour and done their duty. To Edith Wharton, he wrote, "There is no use of my writing about Quentin; for I should break down if I tried. . . . But it would have been far worse if he had lived at the cost of the slightest failure to perform his duty." Even if all four of their sons had been killed in the war and he and Edith had been "crushed by the blow . . . we would rather have it that way than not have had them go." His determination to have his sons fight stemmed in part from his belief in the need for the Allies to defeat Germany, although he had been ambivalent about this at the beginning of the war.[67] More important, for Roosevelt to have behaved otherwise would have undermined his whole philosophy of life and his immortality project, and this to him was worse than the death of his own sons. Like Abraham, Roosevelt was ready to sacrifice his sons as a testament to his faith in that project of transcending the "body of this death."

Although Roosevelt was an extreme case, his life revealed in rarefied form the strategy engaged in by the élite to come to terms with mortality. We see present in the culture of the élite and the activity of war a number of overlapping and mutually reinforcing symbolic or rituals that all contributed to a sense of immortality for the élite. The nation embodied the principles of "freedom," defined as mastery over the material world and over the body and its desires. The nation itself constituted an immortal body. Through their patriotism and as office holders, the élite associated themselves with the nation and its history. They gained a place in history through successfully maintaining the immortality of the nation or increasing its vitality (strength and size).

The nation went to war as a means of overcoming internal weaknesses or signs of the materialism that ran counter to the dominant immortality project; war, in turn, was carried out against an enemy that represented those aspects of the self (such as sin and disease) associated with death. The activity of war involved the acts of martyrdom and sacrifice that were the clearest manifestation of the dominance of spirit over sinful body, and these acts again established those martyrs as historical figures. This was then a symbolic twist of a grand scale—a transformation of that most destructive of activities into an act of transcendence and life. As the process of turning Death into Life involved doing metaphorical battle, so actual battle involved the metaphorical transformation of warfare into a battle with Death itself.

CHAPTER 5

THE BATTLE WITH DEATH

Too often we [the soldiers in Vietnam] made our fantasies real, always to be disappointed, our hunger only greater. . . . in killing I could see the beast, crouched drooling on its haunches, could see it mocking my frailties, knowing I hated myself for them but that I could not get enough, that I would keep coming back again and again.

—William Broyles, Jr.[1]

The rituals examined up to this point allowed American political leaders to symbolically transcend their mortality. In large part, they were attempting to model their own deaths after that of the soldier, but generally they did not die in battle themselves. The same rituals and symbolic transformations used for coming to terms with their own deaths, however, functioned to make sense of the deaths in battle that followed from their decisions.

Perhaps the most common and at least temporarily effective responses to death engaged in by these high-ranking officials were avoidance and denial. This is the dominant response to the problem of mortality in modern Western culture, and the fast pace and high stress of these officials' jobs provided plenty of opportunity for distraction. They immersed themselves in their work, and had little time to dwell on existential dilemmas. Likewise, in their writings and speeches, the statesmen rarely discussed the deaths of soldiers during wartime, and, if they did, would refer to them euphemistically as casualties, losses, attrition, or the "pain" inflicted on a nation.[2] It is telling that in the collected public statements of President Bush, although the word "death" is used in various contexts (such as when referring to drug dealers as "merchants of death"), it is not used at all in speeches on the Gulf War.[3] Foreign policy officials almost never spoke directly about the deaths of Americans overseas, especially in official discourse, and especially while the deaths were occurring (after they were dead, there would be ample opportunity to memorialize them on Veterans Day, the Fourth of July, and Memorial Day).[4]

But as those most centrally responsible for the deaths of these men, the foreign policy leaders could not completely ignore these deaths. On a conscious level, the political leaders reconciled themselves to these deaths as the inevitable and tragic result of life in a hostile, anarchic international system. They could place responsibility for those deaths on the shoulders of some external agent of evil (even if that agent's power was dwarfed by that of the United States). The élite offered a number of explicit, highly formulaic, ways of making sense of death in battle—the nationalistic references to duty to country, defense of the principles of freedom and democracy, and the mantras of national security and interest. Often the élite would refer simply to the effectiveness of the war in achieving specific national political goals. This amounted to the explicit rationale, based on the unquestioned assumption that the goals for which the United States was fighting were noble, that as long as the United States won the war, those who died in it would not have died in vain. In the post–World War II era, these justifications generally amounted to the deterrence or domino theory that a smaller number of deaths now would prevent a larger number later. For instance, Lyndon Johnson, Robert McNamara, and Dean Rusk all offered the rationale for Vietnam that it helped prevent the far worse disaster of a World War III.[5]

But these literal and rational answers, although not without basis or persuasiveness, are not enough. In élite discourse, the vague, abstract notions of duty, principle, success, and security were wrapped up in a highly symbolic language and a set of rituals expressing implicit understandings about life, death, and the immortal soul.[6] The effectiveness of the élite discourse on war in addressing their own, the soldiers', and the general public's concerns about mortality lies in the vast pool of symbols associated with terms such as freedom, security, and honor—symbols in turn associated with life and death. The honor for which America was fighting, Dean Rusk would claim, was not an empty phrase but concerned "the life and death of the nation."[7] The rich symbolism—the Lacanian excess—in which their discussion of war was couched is the subject of this chapter.

To balance out the use of medieval concepts like the king's two bodies, we can draw on but one of the thousands of examples of this symbolism found in American popular culture. The structure and function of the stories and modern mythology produced by Hollywood are certainly dif-

ferent from that of the American foreign policy establishment; but it is far
closer to that symbolic logic of mainstream foreign policy discourse, than,
say, the message of the poetry of Wilfred Owen or the sensibilities embodied in the theater of the absurd. The Hollywood action hero may be
seen as a ridiculous caricature by any given secretary of state, but the
worldview embodied by this Hollywood genre still constitutes a significant
portion of the social context in which foreign policy is made. As Jutta
Weldes puts it, "Popular culture . . . provides a background of meanings
that help to constitute public images of international relations and foreign
policy. As a result, popular culture helps to construct the reality of international politics for officials and non-officials alike and, to the extent that
it reproduces the content and structure of the dominant foreign policy
discourse, it helps to produce consent to foreign policy and state action."[8]
The connection between popular culture and politics was particularly
strong for Ronald Reagan, who slipped back and forth between the two
worlds with amazing grace and drew on the lessons of World War II
movies.[9] Dean Rusk and Douglas MacArthur delighted in old Westerns—
a genre with a particular relevance to American thinking on the utility of
force and proper means to achieve justice.[10] George Bush kept the Terminator close to him as the war in the Persian Gulf approached.

As Richard Slotkin argues in *Gunfighter Nation*, the thinking behind
U.S. foreign policy shared much with the symbolism of Western films, in
which American leaders fancied themselves as "frontier aristocrats" encountering various heathen savages. When transferred directly to the
realm of international politics, perhaps the archetypal Hollywood portrayal
of this frontier aristocrat is the long-lived series of James Bond films. They
are as formulaic as they come, evolving only as the technical sophistication
of the film industry increases, and as the particular manifestation of con-
trived global evil changes. They are focused on the all-powerful, invinci-
ble, refined, sexually irresistible, white, middle-aged male who has a love
affair with technology and has loveless sex with a variety of Barbie looka-
likes. Bond is the epitome of the unemotional, "civilized" man who em-
bodies the illusion of being able to control and overcome all contingency
and opposition in the world. He does not cry; he does not laugh; he drinks
but does not get drunk; he is in complete control. There is, as well, an ongoing "battle with death" in the films that is seen in its most blatant and
obvious form in *Live and Let Die* (1973). The film is a campy example of
how foreign affairs is portrayed in popular culture, but it was not without
its parallels to the élite's construction of death in battle.

In the film's penultimate clash of imperial hero and barbarian anti-
hero, James Bond (Roger Moore) rescues the basically helpless heroine *du
jour,* Solitaire (Jane Seymour), from the pagan voodoo cult worshippers

who are led by a figure known as Baron Samedi (Geoffrey Holder). The Baron is very large, very black, has a stereotypically deep laugh, and is dressed up as a skeleton in a top hat. Given that particular outfit and what he is about to do (kill a helpless victim), it is not too much of a stretch to say that the Baron symbolizes Death, and that Bond's encounter with him is a metaphor for the particular response to mortality outlined in this book. This encounter of Anglo-Saxon technophile with Caribbean mystic illustrates a number of elements of the metaphorical battle with death—not the least of them being its racism and sexism.

This final battle is actually anti-climatic. The Baron rises from the grave as the snake-wielding priests dance wildly to the drums, and the helpless, virgin Solitaire awaits her fate as sacrificial victim. With a few quick shots from his oversize handgun, Bond dispatches the Baron and shatters the simple-minded illusions of the religious fanatics (by literally shattering a life-size puppet of the Baron), who are now shown to be dupes of the evil drug lord (shades of Plan Colombia, the latest campaign in the "war on drugs.") Here in pure form is rational science triumphing over orgiastic primitivism—what Roxanne Lynn Doty writes of as the encounter of "Western peoples" with the "inferior races."[11] It is also a battle with Death. In a symbolic move that could have been taken straight out of Bunyan's *Pilgrim's Progress*,[12] Bond sends this symbol of untamed pagan sinfulness tumbling into a coffin full of venomous snakes. Death is dead, and the audience's concerns about death can be temporarily assuaged, as Bond, as always, gets the girl.

Bunyan's protagonist Christian goes on to heaven, and Bond goes on to find salvation in the sweet embrace of his latest lover. The cigar-smoking Bond has rescued the white woman from the clutches of the black man, disempowered her by taking away her virginity, and turned her into a lovesick fan. Bond thus transforms the "bad" situation (for the white male viewer) of being duped by and completely controlled by the powerful female/black Other, into the "good" situation of the Other being duped, controlled, and dumped into a coffin of venomous snakes.

A central element in most action/adventure films is the protagonist's usually superhuman efforts to avoid death—whether it comes in the form of an evil villain, hordes of demonic aliens, dangerous criminals, a hurtling meteor, or outbreak of the Ebola virus. Certainly this holds true for the Bond films. Each escape is as far-fetched as the next (they are set up so that the viewer "knows" there is no escape), but it is in fact their complete unreality that makes them so appealing. The audience knows on some level no one would really escape these threats, just as we know on some level that no one escapes death. But in these movies, the seemingly inescapable death is always avoided.

As the nineteenth Bond film (and a steady stream of others sharing the same basic logic) rolled off the assembly line in 2000, it seems fair to say that this formula has an enduring appeal to a significant proportion of the American moviegoing public, and that if foreign policy can be construed in somewhat the same way it might appeal to them as well. The goals and practice of U.S. foreign policy, whatever the particular content and morality, are framed in part as an attempt to gain symbolic control over death, to control women and nature, affirm a sense of masculine power, and to defeat the racially different pagans who challenged the Anglo-American sense of how the world ought to be.

THE SOCIAL CONSTRUCTION OF DEATH IN BATTLE

The trick in the action film genre is to escape the inescapable—to symbolically reconstitute the world so that what was otherwise inevitable and unpleasant could be avoided. The symbolic construction of war involves a similar move. The foreign policy élite framed the battles that American soldiers were fighting in terms of the larger project of creating a transcendent identity by doing battle with death. As the Vietnam soldier William Broyles would write of seeing the "beast" of death while fighting in the jungles, and James Bond would dispatch Baron Samedi, so the foreign policy élite in Washington would construct a view of war as an opportunity to face death embodied in the Enemy.

This making sense of death involved a set of paradoxical associations rooted in the tensions of the human condition, which resulted in a symbolic reversal of life and death. The otherwise obvious truths that when you are alive you are alive and when you die you are dead, were transposed—now life was really death-in-life, and death was really life-in-death. This transformation is seen in Lyndon Johnson's April 7, 1965 speech at Johns Hopkins University, in which he laid out his justification for the deaths and other costs that would follow from the war then escalating in Vietnam. In it, we see how war was framed as an answer to the internal and external threats to national immortality and as such constituted a way to "Life" rather than "Death." The speech outlines the familiar list of justifications—America was fighting for freedom, stopping Communism and aggression, protecting national security interests—but Johnson sums up these reasons with an intriguing reference to one of the primary symbolic events in the American political mythos—John Winthrop's 1636 "City upon a Hill" speech. Using fairly apocalyptic language, Johnson stated that, "We may well be living in the time foretold many years ago when it was said [by Winthrop]: 'I call heaven and earth to record this day against you, that I have set before you life and death, blessing and cursing: therefore choose life, that both thou and thy seed may live.' " Johnson continued, "This generation must choose. . . . Well, we choose life. And so doing, we will prevail over the enemies within man, and over the natural enemies of all mankind."[13] His conclusion implied that the various justifications for sending young men to Vietnam to kill and die could be summed up as a matter of life and death; by choosing to fight communism, Johnson implied, America was choosing Life itself (Who would argue with that? Who would be "anti-Life"?) In framing the decision in these terms, Johnson could tap into the concerns about mortality that are elicited during wartime. All the sorrow flowing from the deaths of America's sons and daughters in the distant jungles would be countered by this rhetorical assertion that it was the opposite of those deaths for which they were fighting. What else could compensate for the loss of life but some gain of life? But for this claim to have any resonance it had to be part of a larger rhetorical project of construing death in battle as transcendent.

A number of scholarly works have looked at how the enemy has been demonized, dehumanized, or viewed through a racist lens.[14] This vilification is also part of this process of coming to terms with mortality. Other authors have commented on the symbolic and metaphorical content of foreign policy discourse and discussed the power of that part of the rhetoric.[15] The power of this language can be better understood by placing it in the context of the ritual functions of warfare discussed earlier— to affirm or reify abstract national principles, and to revitalize and remasculinize a nation weakened by decadence. A third ritual function involves reifying death, rendering it solid and manageable, and thereby giving those waging war a sense of control over Death itself. The trick here is to take some abstract fate, something which all humans must undergo and about which none can know directly, and turn that aspect of our fate as mortals into a concrete, identifiable *thing*. This process comes both in religious and secular varieties. The religious aspects of the ritual battle with Death are seen in a set of metaphors centered around the idea of the crusade against a beast representing the body, sin, and death. The secular version uses secular images of the doctor, engineer, or manager engaged in a technical task of combating some force of nature, such as disease or floods. Although both these symbolic constellations were present throughout the period covered here, the religious language declined in prominence, while the technical language became more common. These symbolic vocabularies contained different demarcations between self and other, which formed the basis for that radical differentiation that made killing in the Philippines, Vietnam, and the Persian Gulf seem necessary and justified. This symbolic transformation of war into a symbolic battle with Death involved a number of steps.

The first step was equating the enemy with unbridled physical and sexual desire. As sinfulness was equated with death in Christian ontology, battling a sinful enemy enabled the combatants to gain a sense of control over that projected sinfulness. The war against them then came to stand as the modernist reassertion of rational, virtuous control over the forces of animal nature—the Apollonian triumphing over the Dionysian. As Nature was associated with Death in Modernist ontology, the enemy also was equated with animals and the forces of nature. These themes can be seen in the use of metaphors such as those of the rider and the ridden—to be the rider was to be in control, was to have "bridled" the animal. During the Cold War, Communism also was equated with other large natural forces, and particularly with floods and tides. The Korean and Vietnam wars were described frequently in terms of fluid metaphors—flows, tides, and floods—and so the war also became part of an attempt to control this flood. Not only were communists committing aggression across a boundary sanctified by U.S. and international recognition but, as Paul Chilton points out in *Security Metaphors*, they were engaging in other forms of symbolic border violation.

This transformation of the enemy meant that this battle against Communism was framed as a technical task, akin to a hunt or civil engineering project. The way to battle this animal or stem the tide was through application of America's great technological resources and technical know-how. A prominent form of this technical configuration was that of medical practices. America's enemies were equated with disease, the United States portrayed itself as a doctor, and its foreign policy was described as medical treatment. These symbols were not so clearly linked to death and mortality as those found in *Live and Let Die* but still are part of a constellation of images that gained some of their power from their ability to touch on the deep terror of death. Together these various symbolic configurations helped Teddy Roosevelt, Dean Acheson, and Robert McNamara to persuade themselves and others that the deaths in battle were really a means to a transcendent and eternal life.

FOREIGN POLICY AS CRUSADE

This particular way of viewing the enemy and justifying death in battle fit fairly neatly within the language of crusade, in that it involved viewing oneself as pure and on a mission from God, and viewing the enemy as a force of evil.[16] One source of this sense of self-righteousness and divine mandate on the part of the foreign policy leadership was their belief that they, more than anyone else, had succeeded in controlling or overcoming their "lower" selves. In relation to colonies, Communism, and rogue states, war was framed as a means of asserting the rule of God and virtue over the forces of sin and the body. In Lyndon Johnson's speech at Johns Hopkins, he spoke of the need to conquer both the enemy abroad and the enemy within. One had to overcome some inner weakness or sinfulness in order to triumph in the end. As the diplomatic historian Michael Hunt points out, the United States has always had a somewhat guarded approach to revolutionary or nationalist movements in the Third World and held them to the standards and values that ostensibly had guided the revolution of the United States. John Quincy Adams was particularly adamant that revolutionary movements exercise self-control. These were the standards that élite throughout the twentieth century had held for Latin American and Asian nationalists. "Liberty," Woodrow Wilson would argue, "is the privilege of maturity, of self-control, of self-mastery. . . . Some peoples may have it, therefore, and others may not." This conception of self-rule played itself out in debates over the right of one people to rule over another, and by extension, the definition of a people. In the élite's view of the world, a "people" was defined as a group that could govern itself. In Congressional debates on the Philippines, the issue was thus framed in terms of "self-governance."[17] On the surface, this language reflected a straightforward issue of state capacity, but it tapped into deeper concerns about control of the body and animal passions. Were the Filipinos or Vietnamese capable of setting up their own government or, if left to their own devices, would they run wild, unable to control their lusts and greed? Had Saddam Hussein and Slobodan Milosevic succeeded in conquering their lust for power, or would they need to be disciplined by those who had?

The dominant view among U.S. élite was that Americans could and Filipinos could not. The requisite self-governance was a characteristic of good Christians; the Anglo-Saxons, the élite agreed, had proven themselves particularly capable of it as well. For example, America's Founders succeeded, Senator George Hoar argued, because "they governed themselves, and they believed that a free people should govern itself, by a law higher than their own desire." He would support American involvement in the Spanish-American War as long as it reflected this sense of self-control. As long as America was not "angry, snarling, shouting, screaming, kicking, clawing with her nails" but was, rather, like the Archangel Michael, "inspired by a sentiment even toward her enemies not of hate but of love," then Hoar could go so far as to call the war in Cuba "the most honorable single war in all history."[18] Hoar supported the war because he believed the United States had absolutely no desire for conquest or national gain in Cuba. What allowed this was the grace of God, and what elicited that grace was America's virtue and self-control.

During the 1960s, this language of self-control could still be seen, albeit in muted form. America could avoid decadence and decline, Assistant Secretary of State Roger Hilsman argued, by having "steady nerves," being unafraid, using "cold, deliberate analysis," and possessing that "unemotional self-discipline and self-control that enables one to act effectively." These were the qualities the South Vietnamese lacked, and what legitimized U.S. involvement there. The United States, by contrast, Dean Rusk argued, had made its decision to go to war "with understandable sobriety." Senator Mansfield, in support of the Gulf of Tonkin Resolution argued that the president had acted with a "cool head and a steady hand" and that the aim of the policy in Vietnam was to restrain "the dogs of war." In debates over the necessity for foreign aid, Dean Rusk would frame foreign aid as a manifestation of U.S. selflessness and self-control. If foreign aid were stopped, Rusk warned, "we could easily find ourselves regarded as a voracious, rapacious nation calling upon everyone else to feed our own economy."[19] The foreign policy establishment presented itself as the paragon of selfless and restrained rationality and, thus, the last best hope for mankind to restrain these rogues who were driven by basic instinct. Thus, the foreign policy élite maintained an identity of themselves and the country they led as needing to and generally succeeding in controlling the body.

THE PAGAN OTHER

At the turn of the twentieth century, and in the context of debates over the war in the Philippines, Senator Beveridge argued that the United States did not need to attend to its own problems at home (such as the lynchings, continued disenfranchisement of African-Americans, labor unrest, or fate of the Native American tribes) but should instead create a better government overseas. Through this imperialistic mission, Beveridge claimed, it would be "as if we projected ourselves upon a living screen and beheld ourselves at work."[20] Here, in fairly clear terms, was a manifesto for foreign policy as construction of what the psychologist Jacques Lacan refers to as "fantasy space." If American leaders did not like what they saw in the United States, they could instead create a fantasy, a moving picture of themselves that would somehow be more in accord with their ideals. They would write their own story on the bodies of the Filipinos, a story of the virtuous self and the pagan Other.

If the U.S. élite identified themselves as "self-governing," their authoritarian, uncivilized, and communist opponents were defined by their inability to master themselves. Although the particular opponents (Spain, the Filipinos, the German "Hun," Hitler, Communism, the VC, Iraq, Osama bin Laden) changed over time and across particular crises, they were described using similar language. In accord with the nationalist conception of the body politic, they were referred to as an undifferentiated mass of people, a horde, or single entity.[21] Whereas the United States was seen as having controlled its desires, the Other was not. This in turn led to a characterization of the enemy as uncivilized, un-Christian, and unfit to rule themselves.[22] This Manichean view of the world was clearly expressed in accounts of the Other at the turn of the twentieth century as well as in descriptions of Communism and the Soviet Union.

The beastly Other was a creature of desire and unbridled passion—this is what made it so dangerous. It represented the desires of the body, which were the source and reminder of mortality. In describing the bloody suppression of the Paris Commune, John Hay wrote that, "Death writhed, gorged like a greedy snake," in the streets of Paris. For Hay, Death in this instance had taken the form of the French government troops, which he equated with the creature that had introduced sin into the world. Likewise, during America's early imperial ventures, the élite referred to their Asian and Latin American counterparts as incapable of controlling their desires. Hay would refer to the Colombian officials during the wrangle over Panama as "greedy little anthropoids." As the biographer Clymer put it, "Hay thought of [the] Filipino patriot much as . . . misguided, insincere, [and] venal. . . ."[23]

Theodore Roosevelt likewise reviled any group that did not have what he referred to as "character"—the quality of self-control and subordinating one's own needs to the dictates of principle. This meant that those groups that lacked character would have to be policed by those that had it. Roosevelt, Lodge, and Beveridge—the advocates of the so-called Large Policy of active U.S. involvement abroad—described the Filipinos themselves as children and savages unable to govern themselves. "It is barely possible that 1,000 men in all the archipelago," Beveridge argued, "are capable of self-government in the Anglo-Saxon sense. My own belief is that there are not 100 men among them who comprehend what Anglo-Saxon self-government even means." This meant they did not understand the principles of democratic government, but it also meant that they did not have requisite control over their own desires and impulses. He described the people not as Christians but as Orientals, Malays, lazy, animal-like, and incapable of the august and sacred ability to govern themselves. Beating the body and its lusts into submission had been accomplished in the West, but the Malays had not yet succeeded in that task; therefore, the Anglo-Saxons would have to do it for them. Henry Cabot Lodge would differentiate the Anglo-Saxon from the "Asiatic," arguing that Asians viewed conciliation as weakness. "The Asiatic mind and habit of thought are utterly different from ours," he claimed. They were pagans and Muslims, again unfit for government, because they had never known independence. The Philippine leader, Aguinaldo, despite the fact that he had modeled his manifesto after the U.S. Declaration of Independence, was a akin to a criminal breaking into a house. Lodge would attribute the Japanese success in government to their cleverness and skill in imitation, rather than any intelligence or rationality.[24]

These characteristics added up to a view of these enemies as uncivilized, barbaric, and lawless. Although racism against the people of the Orient was common, Spain also was viewed in derogatory terms. Using language and imagery familiar after America's wars with Japan and Vietnam, politicians described the Spanish as barbarous, impudent, arrogant, and criminal. Some élite made an explicit connection between the enemy and death. Hay described the oppressive King Philip of Spain as a "horrible monster, who is blackened with every crime at which humanity suffers," and who ruled over a "decaying nationality."[25] One clergyman suggested Spanish should be made "the prevailing language of hell." In April 1898, Representative Sulzer from New York claimed the history of Spanish government consisted of "one long, unending, hideous carnival of crime, of public plunder, of rapine, of official robbery, of cruel, torturing death—a frightful big blot on the pages of civilization." In political cartoons of the day, the Spanish General Weyler was depicted as a murderous ape. In December 1896, Senator Cullom claimed that Spanish troops were shooting their victims in the back, whereas the United States was acting completely selflessly toward Cuba. America's only reward would be a free Cuba, and, Cullom argued, the United States would make sure it did "not see that fair island turned again to the mercies of wild beasts and vultures of war whose only stimulus is gain."[26]

This view of the non-Anglo-Saxon world continued during World War II and the Cold War. The historian John Dower has catalogued in great detail how Americans portrayed the Japanese as deranged, primitive, and barbaric (and how the Japanese portrayed Americans in similarly demonic form). During the Cold War, Secretary of State Dean Rusk consistently described the leaders of uncooperative countries—Nasser, Sukarno, Ho Chi Minh, Kim Il Sung, Juan Bosch—in terms of their uncontrolled desires, their inability to "face reality," and their lawlessness. Dean Acheson noted how, after the North Korean invasion, the South Korean ambassador was "weeping"—a sign of the man's inability to control his emotions. Similarly, he described Mossadeq as an emotional and erratic character, "whirling like a dervish," and wrote of the "wild men in Iran who proposed to despoil Britain."[27]

Reflecting the religious underpinnings of foreign policy decision making, when the United States sided with a Third World nation during the Cold War, it showed a preference for Christian nations and leaders. The fact that Chiang Kai Shek and Syngman Rhee were Western-educated Christians helped overcome whatever misgiving the U.S. leaders might have had about their incompetence or authoritarianism. In Latin American politics, the U.S.-backed authoritarian regimes have traditionally been supported by the Catholic churches there as well. In South Vietnam, the United States noted with approval the large Catholic minority there and supported leaders like the Catholic Diem, who was described as a "a relentless Christian" who "did not chase after women the way Sukarno did." The Buddhist majority in South Vietnam, Richard Nixon would argue, was influenced by the Communists, whereas the Catholics were the staunchest anti-Communists. Senator Dodd, in his hawkish speeches on the war in Vietnam, would cite the work of one Father Hoa, the "fighting priest of South Vietnam," whose peasant recruits greeted each other with the Boy Scout salute and put up fierce resistance to Viet Cong advances.[28] Being Christian was not enough, however, if the South Vietnamese were unable to govern themselves, the United States would have to step in and do it for them.

The large U.S. presence in Vietnam and the fact that the Americans were virtually running the country was seen as necessary because of the weakness, backwardness, and generally unrefined nature of the leadership of what LBJ called that "raggedy-ass little fourth-rate country." McNamara, describing the situation in Vietnam in late 1963 as "very disturbing," wrote, "The new government is the greatest source of concern. It is indecisive and drifting," and Lodge would report from Saigon that there is "dry rot and lassitude in the Government of Vietnam."[29]

When hopes of transforming the South Vietnamese into modern-day equivalents of America's Founding Fathers were not realized, Lodge responded, "[W]e have the right and the duty to do certain things with or without the [South Vietnamese] government's consent." Dean Rusk spoke of the need to shake the South Vietnamese leadership "by the scruff of the neck" as if they were unruly schoolchildren. The solution was to clothe them in dignified apparel, get them to stop smoking opium, shower them with Western technology and know-how, and teach them (as NSC staff member Michael Forrestal would put it) some "table manners." In sum, the élite framed foreign policy in Vietnam as an attempt to "pull this undeveloped country into the twentieth century as fast as possible." It was an attitude toward Third World leaders expressed with particular clarity by Johnson during the 1960 national election campaign, when he claimed that the way to deal with Fidel Castro was to wash, shave, and spank him.[30] Since that time, Reagan's characterization of the Sandinistas, Dan Quayle's description of "rogue states," James Baker's characterization of Saddam Hussein, and Madeleine Albright's assessment of current threats all drew on the notion of "lust," "capriciousness," "insatiable appetite," and unrestrained desire.[31]

In world affairs, the élite saw the United States as playing the role of the civilized outsider, controlling the animal lusts and hungers that were running rampant in places such as the Philippines and Vietnam. The Communists were to blame for much of the trouble and much of the world was insufficiently civilized or strong to take care of the problem themselves. Thus, the sober, unemotional, powerful Americans had to intervene.

As the non-Western world was regarded as backward and uncivilized, Communism was viewed in a similar light; and because it was a relatively powerful force in world affairs, it was of proportionally greater concern to the decision-making élite. Painting a Manichean view of the postwar world, Philip Jessup, the first U.S. Ambassador to the United Nations, referred to the "moral strength" of American foreign policy that stemmed from the knowledge that "the Communists are fighting all over the world to capture the mind and the spirit of men so that they can then enslave them by the ruthless totalitarian methods which kill the spirit, darken the mind, and torture the body."[32] Although not without some truth, the stark symbolism of this view fed into élite and public fears about death, as communist philosophy was seen as directly counter to the immortality project dominant among the American élite.

Two of the most troubling aspects of Communism were its materialism and its atheism. As MacArthur would put it, "History teaches us that religion and patriotism have always gone hand in hand, while atheism has invariably been accompanied by radicalism, communism, bolshevism, and other enemies of free government." Marx's philosophy was rooted in the idea, after all, that "life involves before everything else eating and drinking, a habitation, clothing, and many other things." The Russia expert George Kennan, in his seminal characterization of Soviet ideology, would begin by saying that "Communist thought" held that the "central factor of the life of man" is the system by which material goods are produced and exchanged.[33] This reminder and insistence on the primacy of material existence was anathema to the immortality project of the élite, with its emphasis on the transcendence of the material world.

In its materialism and anti-religious stance, Communism became a pagan force against which, in the élite's view, a crusade was necessary. Acheson would write that Russian expansionism was akin to the "invasion by barbarians against classical Greece and Rome" or the attacks on Europe by Islam during the Crusades. In light of the philosophical incompatibility between Communism and Christianity, the primary sponsor of Kennan's "Mr. X" article, James Forrestal, would emphasize the religious or ideological nature of the movement. This sense of the complete "otherness" of the Russians was clearly stated in Forrestal's description of them as actually existing in a completely different "dimension" from the United States—one to which Americans had no access.[34] In Forrestal's account, the Russians did not even occupy three-dimensional space with the "rest of us" but were so foreign as to be beyond our physics and science, an entity that could only be dealt with by force, or perhaps exorcism.

Not surprisingly, Kennan and others would ascribe to the Soviet Union a lack of self-control. Billy Graham preached during the Vietnam War that the underlying cause of war was lust, and, in particular, the lust found in Communism.[35] Although not as explicit in their arguments, the élite made similar symbolic connections between sin and Communism. Their materialist ideology was combined with what Kennan would call the "instinctive desires" of the revolutionary movement. They were "insecure" with a fanaticism "unmodified by any of the Anglo-Saxon traditions of compromise." They were rigid and could not be reasoned with, but "like the white dog before the phonograph, they hear only the 'master's voice.' " In the case of Communism, the "master" was not reason and the soul, but their instinctual desires and aggressiveness. In memoirs and speeches, the élite consistently placed the blame for the start of the Cold War on the Soviets and refused to see any of their own actions as provocative or threatening.[36] It was the Soviet's lack of self-control that necessitated the sober and serious American response of containment and deterrence.

This abstract Communist being was made more tangible by depicting it as an uncivilized beast that gobbled up territory. Johnson pointed out that "aggression is like hunger," and Michael Forrestal described the Communists as "nibbling away" at the periphery. This Communist appetite, however, more commonly was described as voracious. Senator Gale McGee would argue that "an aggressor's appetite is not satisfied by peace offerings of small chunks of territory." China and Communism possessed, Rusk claimed, "appetites and ambitions that grow upon feeding." Johnson would likewise claim that "the appetite of aggression is never satisfied," and assert that this was unnatural and "primitive."[37] Communist aggression was then a manifestation of the unbridled desires of the body, which the élite associated so closely with mortality.

Just as serious were charges of untamed sexual desires, akin to the orgiastic excesses of the "natives" in *Live and Let Die*. After the North Korean invasion of South Korea, MacArthur spoke of the need to counter the "lustful thrusts of those who stand for slavery as against freedom, for atheism against God." Lyndon Johnson, who often resorted to sexual metaphors, also attributed aggressive and uncivilized sexual drives to the Communists. You needed to stand up to aggressors, he argued, just as you needed to stop a rapist before he was in bed with your wife. Communism, he said, was like a robber who had "walked into the house of South Vietnam with the hammer pulled back," and "[I]f you let a bully come in your front yard, he'll be on your porch the next day and the day after he'll rape your wife in your own bed." The way to deal with this was, of course, to dominate sexually or emasculate the Communist beast. After the bombing retaliation following the Gulf of Tonkin incident, Johnson would brag, "I didn't just screw Ho Chi Minh, I cut his pecker off."[38]

In the face of such a mindless and lustful creature, weakness would only unleash the clearly uncontrolled desires of the Soviet Union. Because the Soviets could not control their own bodies or desires, it was incumbent on the United States to do that for them, through the mechanisms of deterrence and containment. Within the framework of this examination of élite culture, the "lesson of Munich" can be reread as a confirmation of the Christian understanding of the need to control physical desires unless they run amok. Acheson wrote that American weakness presented "irresistible invitations" for the Soviets to "fish in troubled waters." Concessions in the international game of the diplomacy of violence would only "whet Communist appetites," and the dangers in the world "flowed" from "Soviet desire." Likewise, Dean Rusk would frequently refer to the problem of weakness, isolationism, or pacifism as "tempting" the Soviets.[39] Since they could not control themselves, they would listen only to force. The battle within the body was mirrored by this global drama in which self-governing élite fought with the political manifestations of the body and desire.

American foreign policy, whether in its manifestations as imperialism, hegemonic rule, or the containment of Communism, has had at its philosophical roots an approach to the various Others that equated them with sin and the body. By controlling or dominating those external entities, the élite were able to participate in that part of their immortality project that sought to control their bodies by doing battle with an Other onto which was projected attributes of mortality. But this aspect of foreign policy as a religious crusade was not the only way in which the élite attempted to create a context in which death was controlled and war seen as a way of choosing life. As the twentieth century progressed, U.S. foreign policy leaders also increasingly engaged in a process of turning war into a scientific experiment in which America's new and immense technological powers could be applied against that which was not simply sinful or evil, but also a force of nature. After projecting all those characteristics associated with death onto the enemy, the enemy was then transformed into something "manageable," an entity with which one did not have to engage in any political dialogue, but simply had to control.

WAR AS A SCIENTIFIC EXPERIMENT

Dean Rusk, quoting Churchill, would refer to the Soviet Union as "a riddle wrapped in a mystery inside an enigma." The Soviets existed behind the opaque "iron curtain." To Acheson, the Chinese were likewise a dark and inscrutable people. The wars against these foes became for the élite a way to master the situations by gaining knowledge about them. This was yet another ritual function of warfare: as a form of scientific experiment, whereby the mysteries of death and the body could be revealed and controlled. If warfare was partially portrayed as a battle with death, and one wanted to gain a sense of power over death, then one needed to think about that battle in ways that gave one a sense of knowledge and control. The aesthetic of this approach is similar to that of the quantitative, formal models of warfare used in political science.

On a certain level, this attempt at understanding the dynamics of a foreign situation is an obvious aspect of any problem in foreign policy. The foreign policy officials were trying to achieve certain goals in these places, and so of course they were trying to gather "intelligence" in order to control events there. But the language used by the élite belied greater concerns—at stake was an overall sense of control over their fate and the forces of nature. The wars gained support in part as they were seen as ways of asserting that the United States had not become what Nixon would call a "helpless giant" but instead was in control of its own fate. This will to knowledge was certainly present during earlier U.S. wars, but became a more and more prominent aspect of élite discourse.

The discourse displayed a tension between a sense of self-assurance and certainty about the need to oppose Communism and, at the same time, a view of Communism as enigmatic, dark, and unknown. Communism's inscrutability was in fact part of what made it so threatening, and this provided further impetus to metaphorically plumb its depths. The difference, the "otherness," was in part what constituted the threat. Thus, the crusade, as with the great scientific project of mapping the globe and shedding light on new realms, attempted to defeat the enemy by knowing them.[40] The symbolic empire that the foreign policy élite strove to set up was one of intelligibility; they strove to create the world in accord with the images found in their mythologies. As noted in Chapter 2, the ritual of war was a way of affirming deeply held beliefs by actualizing them in history. The aircraft carriers and marine corps and napalm bombs were all tools used in part to make the world have meaning within the context of the Anglo-Saxon, Christian worldview of the hegemon.

The ideal of "national security" can then be seen as a goal brought about by gaining this knowledge of the Other. This goal was ultimately unrealizable, however, as complete security could only be achieved by knowing this Other to the extent that it became part of one's "self." This could not be achieved, because the self was in large part constituted in opposition to this Other. Without the Other, this self would disappear, or one's mortality would be reinternalized. To know the Other completely could only be accomplished by knowing death itself, by losing one's self in the cosmos; and this was the exact opposite of the symbolic goals of élite discourse. Just as the human condition of mortality imposes limits on what we can know, and we will never know what death is, so the desire to completely understand the Other can never be completely satisfied. Thus, the élite, while seeking to know and thereby control Communism or the Viet Cong or Saddam Hussein, could never get too close to it, had always to remain somewhat distant and objective in relation to the subject of their "investigation." As long as the Other was associated with death, it had to remain the Other, and could only be known as such—as a dehumanized object.

VISUALIZING WORLD PEACE

This process of gaining knowledge about the enemy was carried out most prominently with the use of visual metaphors. To know the enemy, one first had to see it. As Paul Virilio argues, modern war has more and more become a matter of trying to see an increasingly elusive and distant enemy. War has become a competition in concealment and observation, of long-range missiles and spy satellites. This project of rendering the situation visible and therefore known was reflected in the language of the élite as well. The goal of the élite was to possess the power of the gaze, to be the unseen seer, the census taker.[41] This meant the elimination of the "private" or the interior—rendering everything as surface. This emphasis on the powers of vision, as seen in the title to Dean Rusk's autobiography—*As I Saw It*—meant that special emphasis was placed on the problems of blurred vision. Rusk recounts how the élite felt they were dealing with "kaleidoscopic situations that we saw imperfectly. . . . We were terribly concerned with the limitations of our vision."[42] In international relations, Rusk wrote, the "whole scene is a flux," and therefore it was a priority to try to create an order that allowed a clear view of the problems facing these élite.

If Teddy Roosevelt would refer to death as a "darkness," battle was one way of shedding some illusory light on that shadow. When fighting in

Cuba, Roosevelt expressed the keen—and widely held—desire of wanting to *see* the enemy, and finally getting to shoot one. Through this "sighting," death would be made manifest and then destroyed. Douglas MacArthur, on seeing a dead North Korean soldier, declared it was "a good sight for my old eyes." Eisenhower reported that, in World War II, morale was highest in those units that had direct contact with the enemy; for those that had not, "All they wanted to know was where to find an enemy!"[43] Obviously he reported this as a testament to the general enthusiasm and caliber of the soldiers; but their enthusiasm likely stemmed from the satisfaction of being able to see and engage the enemy as a known quantity rather than some unseen entity about which there was nothing they could do. Thus, despite the fact that such a discovery would dramatically increase the danger to themselves, the soldiers preferred that danger to the uncertainty of a death whose source was unknown. It was a sentiment shared by the statesmen.

In Vietnam—a war in which the enemy was hidden in the dense underbrush of the jungle, moving through tunnels, ignoring political boundaries, not using uniforms, indistinguishable from the peasants farming the fields (because they often were those farmers)—there was a special need to "see" the enemy, and the élite often described the war using visual metaphors. Kennedy and his advisors warned Americans that this was a new and dangerous kind of war—a "subterranean war" that employed "power and deceit" rather than the old-fashioned conventional wars that were fought out in the open. The invisible threat took the form of the "the steady and deadly attack in the night of guerrilla bands that come without warning, that kill people in their sleep." Combining fluid metaphors with imagery of an invisible threat, Johnson described this new kind of aggression as "like poisoning a well, drop by drop, until the water becomes fatal to those who drink it." George Ball expressed his doubts about chances of U.S. success in Vietnam, because "the enemy cannot even be seen." General Westmoreland, equating the enemy with vermin, would recall after the war that trying to estimate the strength of guerrillas was like "trying to estimate roaches in your kitchen."[44]

The solution to this problem was simply to apply the great technological powers at their disposal to make the enemy visible, or, if this failed, to "visualize" the situation in comprehensible terms. So the élite liked to think of the situation not as a jungle but as akin to the American landscape. "We have the sea," Lodge would assert, "Let us visualize meeting the VC [Viet Cong] on our own terms. We don't have to spend all our time in the jungles." General Harkins did visualize meeting the Viet Cong on American terms, equating the situation in Vietnam with the U.S. Revolutionary War and with the long war with those "tough guerrillas," the American Indians. As the historian Larry Berman argues, "Much of the justification for additional [U.S. troop] deployments was based on the reasoning that U.S. troops would *not* be engaged in jungle warfare."[45] Thus, despite the unavoidable reality of the jungle in Vietnam—a jungle which the U.S. troops could not help but enter in order to fight the guerrillas who immersed themselves in it—still the élite tried to visualize the war as carried out in the more comforting environment of the open plains.

In fact, the metaphor of the "jungle" was used by the élite to stand for all that was unknown, dark, and mysterious. On first arriving in the Department of Defense and finding it in need of management and organization, McNamara characterized it as "a jungle." He would likewise describe the situation in Southeast Asia as "a hell of a mess." What he and his associates attempted to do was "clean it up." In public statements, Dean Rusk and McGeorge Bundy would assert that the issues in Vietnam were obvious and uncomplicated. Rusk, in February 1966 testimony before the Senate Foreign Relations committee, claimed that they could cut through "the underbrush of complexity" and find "the simple issues which involve our largest interests and deepest purposes" in Vietnam. As Vietnam veteran-turned-historian Richard Stevens points out, the jungle was also much like a sea, a vast expanse of deep vegetation into which the VC immersed themselves. As part of the process of containment, the technical task of defeating the VC meant "drying up" this sea by battling the environment itself. Metaphorically, the élite had to maintain their distance from the jungle—fly over it, bomb it, or clear it, but not live in it or get sucked into it. As Johnson put it, "This is not a jungle war but a struggle for freedom on every front of human activity."[46]

Opponents of the war in Vietnam, and the earlier war in the Philippines, attempted to dampen support for intervention by characterizing those places as bogs or quagmires—locations in the discursive landscape that were associated with decay, sin, and death. Opponents of annexation of the Philippines would emphasize the diseases that flourished in its tropical climate, while supporters emphasized the benevolence of the Philippine environment. In the case of Vietnam, the two lone dissenters on the Gulf of Tonkin Resolution, Senators Ernest Gruening and Wayne Morse, referred to Vietnam as the "war in the swamps" and called for the rule of reason rather than "jungle law." Clark Clifford, in opposing the war, argued that escalation would lead to a "quagmire." Unlike the die-hard supporters of the war, Clark Clifford did not think there was a "light at the end of the tunnel" and instead referred to the war as a place of unrelieved opacity—a "rathole," "sinkhole," or "bottomless pit," in which American soldiers were getting "chewed up."[47]

In the course of trying to determine whether the United States was pursuing the proper military tactics in Vietnam, Senator A. Willis Robertson asked, "Do they have Johnson Grass in Vietnam that grows higher than a man's head? . . . I read that it is Johnson grass and that it grows higher than a man's head. Senator Stennis and I hunt quail with bird dogs. In a stubblefield we can find quail in a short time, but in India, where one hunts one tiger in the high grass, it takes a hundred men to find the tiger." Switching adroitly to a completely different topic, Robertson continued, "We had a great general from Lexington named Stonewall Jackson. He developed vital tactics, which was interior penetration . . ." and so on.[48] The question of how the war was to be fought was answered with reference to analogies of the hunt, the maneuver of "penetration" used in America's war with the Indians, and with the implication that it would help if Vietnam were turned into a stubblefield. In various, perhaps slightly more sophisticated ways, the metaphors used by the élite reflected this conception of the war.

So, yet another aspect of the task of gathering information was to clear the underbrush and create a clear view of the situation and the enemy. In the case of U.S. involvement in Vietnam, the military first had to establish air superiority over Vietnam and then destroy the foliage and population that hid the enemy. Instead of entering into the jungle, the military goal was to eliminate it as a source of mystery. During the course of the war, "Operation Ranchhand" dropped 100 million pounds of defoliants on Vietnam in an ultimately futile attempt to remove the jungle. In a similar move, McNamara pushed "Operation Duffel Bag," in which the United States used huge bulldozers to try to create a "belt of suitable width completely cleared of all trees and shrub growth, defended by two or more barbed wire barriers and appropriate mine fields, supplied with mutually supporting watch towers and night lighting arrangements existing along Route 9 from the South China Sea to the eastern border of Thailand."[49] Despite McNamara's enthusiastic support, the project failed.

If the enemy could been seen, the next step was to count them; yet another way in which the élite tried control the jungle was through quantification. This involved another sort of ritual move, a kind of transubstantiation through which the blood and mud of the battlefield were turned into tables and graphs. It was a practice honed and refined by the men involved in the U.S. Strategic Bombing Survey after World War II, through which the insane and surreal had been rendered manageable and concrete. A number of the foreign policy élite—including Walt Rostow, Paul Nitze, George Ball, J. Kenneth Galbraith, and Robert McNamara—had been involved in various aspects of waging the "quantitative" air war against Germany and Japan.

This quantitative approach and the search for the clear view and empirical data about the war was epitomized by Robert McNamara. As his biographer Deborah Shapley writes, "The basic logic in mathematics struck a resonant chord in McNamara's mind." When discussing the role of numbers in evaluating success in Vietnam, McNamara would admit that, "Numbers . . . are a language to me." His training and background were in accounting and large-scale manufacturing, and he was part of the group of managers who first applied "statistical control" and "operations research" to problems of manufacturing and government. After the fact, McNamara would admit that not all aspects of the situation were amenable to quantification, but he held to the ideal of attempting to quantify as much as possible: "I am sure that no significant military problem will ever be wholly susceptible to purely quantitative analysis. But every piece of the total problem that can be quantitatively analyzed removes one more piece of uncertainty from our process of making a choice."[50]

His attraction to numbers seemed to stem in part from the certainty, precision, and clarity he associated with them. Where the élite failed to eliminate the literal jungle, they attempted to clear away the linguistic underbrush and provide themselves with the clear vista they needed in order to grasp the dynamics of the war. For McNamara, words were too imprecise, and excessive reliance on words was merely a sign of one's lack of real knowledge. They were in fact, part of the jungle that McNamara was trying so hard to manage and clear. He would refer in public speeches to "the *swampland of semanticism*" and the "semantic jungle." For the man for whom numbers were a kind of language, semantics was like the bog into which the United States had sunk in Vietnam. The tangle of meanings and imprecision rendered words susceptible to misinterpretation and manipulation; numbers, by contrast, were clear and precise.[51] So, again, as part of the process of clearing away the jungle, of controlling the situation, McNamara felt compelled to minimize the use of words in the debate on Vietnam.

With the data in hand, Vietnam could then become not unlike a controlled experiment. The relationships between various aspects of the war often were portrayed in terms of mathematical equations. For instance, Walt Rostow argued that "the likelihood of escalation is inversely proportional to [PRC] judgment of our determination," and Lodge spoke of the need to "introduce something new and significant into the equation." The equation in the experiment looked something like this: increased "pressure" (read bombing) equaled increased levels of morale (even "elation") in the South and decreased level of flow of goods to the VC from the North, leading to a weakening of their will. It was a neat equation with one independent variable (dropping lots of bombs) over which the United States had complete control. The stock of bombs was virtually limitless, and all the United States had to do was gradually increase the pressure until morale in the South reached such high levels, and flow of aid from the North decreased, that the VC would collapse and a friendly regime would remain in power in Saigon. As part of this act of simple mechanics, the U.S. actions would take on the purity of physics, as they "would merge into a single pressure vector" on the North Vietnamese government.[52] In trying to solve this equation, the élite authorized dropping on Vietnam seven times the total tonnage of explosives used during all of World War II.

War as a Technical Task

Whereas earlier campaigns had been framed in moral terms, the war in Vietnam was described primarily as a technical task. By reducing a situation such as that in Vietnam to a set of known, visible elements, that war became not so much a matter of discussion and political negotiation as it did a matter of applying cleanser and scrub brush or hunting an animal. Framed as a technical problem, the "solution" to the Communist advance was not a matter of compromise, of exploring the positions of the enemy, and finding some reasonable and jointly acceptable outcome. As David Halberstam argues, the élite were characterized by a certainty and belief in their cause that left little room for doubt about the morality of their actions. Johnson asserted "[T]here can be no doubt" that the North Vietnamese were aggressors and, therefore, international criminals deserving punishment. This meant that U.S. diplomats saw little need to engage in any sort of political give-and-take with their opponents.

The political élite placed a high value on power and control; part of the allure of this technical view of military problems was that it facilitated the sense that the élite were in fact in control of the situation. Dean Rusk argued that "we have to keep control of events and keep event from getting control of us." Westmoreland emphasized that, in Vietnam, "*Control* is important both as a goal and the measurement of success." This control had both internal and external objectives. In relation to the external world, the ideal was to be in a situation in which the choices of one's opponents were irrelevant or nonexistent and in which one had as wide a range of choices for oneself. Internally, this took the form of the rational control of the emotions and drives that was part of the élite's immortality project. Rational control was the standard by which their work was judged, and the élite attempted to create as rational a picture of their decisions as possible. The two types of control were interrelated—by controlling their (and the people's) emotions and being rational, the élite hoped they would be more likely to be able to control the world around them. As Halberstam writes of the Kennedy and Johnson administrations, "If there was anything that bound the men, their followers and their subordinates together, it was the belief that sheer intelligence and rationality could answer and solve anything."[53]

The project of transcending the emotions in order to make decision making more rational often was framed as part of the project of removing "politics" from decision making in Washington. James Forrestal had a decided dislike of political conflict and felt that successful management involved the ability to "resolve and remove human frictions" so that rational efficiency could be maximized.[54] During World War II, his aim in the Navy Department was to wage a "quantitative war" in which the enemy would be swamped under a "torrent of weapons." Worried about the rapid demobilization and Henry Wallace's attempts at cooperation with the Soviet Union, Forrestal called for "cold and objective thinking" and a "strong and clear mental grasp of events" in regard to U.S. security needs after the war.[55] This view was shared by Forrestal's close friend Robert Lovett, who was "uncomfortable with things that could not be quantified." It was Lovett who got McNamara the job of Secretary of Defense for McNamara—the man whom Johnson would refer to as the "man with the Stacomb in his hair." Behind Robert McNamara's desk in the Pentagon was a portrait of James Forrestal. These associations were fitting, for the three men shared a passion not only for good grooming but management and rational control of the political realm.[56]

The goal in foreign policy deliberations, as so frequently stated in the memos of the foreign policy élite, was to have alternatives and keep one's options open.[57] Those opposed to the war in Vietnam played on this infatuation with control by emphasizing the lack of control over events there. That the war represented a loss of control over the body was reflected in the imagery found in several memos written by George Ball, who would argue that the aim of policy was to prevent "things" from getting in the saddle. In a memo dated June 18, 1965, in which he did his best to persuade Johnson to deescalate, Ball began with the quote from Ralph Waldo Emerson that "[t]hings are in the saddle and ride mankind" and continued, "The most difficult continuing problem in South Vietnam is to prevent 'things' from getting into the saddle—or, in other words, to keep control of policy and prevent the momentum of events from taking command." Ball, in arguing that escalation was a dangerous and uncontrollable process, would warn that, "Once on the tiger's back we cannot be sure of picking the place to dismount,"[58] implying that the United States might be forced to use nuclear weapons if China came in. Ball evoked the troubling image that the United States had not and could not succeed in taming the Communist beast and that, even worse, these Communist "things" were riding us. This was an effective rhetorical ploy by Ball, for it tapped into Johnson's desire to "stay in the saddle"; but, insofar as it disturbed the notion of war as means of staying in control, it was a view that gained few supporters.

Evidence of this conceptualization of war as a technical task against an enemy associated with death is seen as well in the ways the élite spoke of the war either as a civil engineering project or a matter of curing a disease.

Containing the Red Tide.   One manifestation of this technical view of the situation in Vietnam was the élite's description of the war as involving both literal and figurative flood control in Southeast Asia. As Communism was perceived as a steadily spreading red tide, containment involved stemming this flow; this meant that U.S. foreign policy was primarily a technical task to stop a large, dangerous, unthinking force. This formulation was phrased succinctly by Acheson when he argued that trying to talk the Soviets out of expanding was "as futile as talking to a force of nature. One cannot argue with a river; it is going to flow. One can dam it or deflect it, but not argue with it." George Kennan also took up Machiavelli's fluid metaphor of fate, referring to Soviet Communism as a "fluid stream which moves constantly, whenever it is permitted to move, toward a given goal."[59] The élite consistently argued that Communism would flow into areas of weakness and political instability just as water would flow naturally into low-lying areas. Like Machiavelli's image of *Fortuna* as a river that had to be dammed and contained (or as a woman that had to be beaten to keep her obedient), so Communism, as a manifestation of *Fortuna* in the international arena, had to be contained with the military "dikes and levees" built by the Department of Defense.

In fact, one of the initial justifications for U.S. military involvement in Vietnam was to aid in relief from the flooding of the Mekong River in October 1961. General Maxwell Taylor's initial suggestion was taken up by McNamara and others, although it was dropped eventually because the flood waters subsided on their own. In part, the idea's appeal stemmed from the similarity of the troops and supplies needed for the war against the Viet Cong and the battle against the flood. Johnson saw war itself as a great technological challenge that the United States could take on like the Panama Canal or Grand Coulee Dam. Johnson pushed for a huge hydroelectric and flood control project in Vietnam—his "TVA for the Mekong"—as a way of gaining popular support in South Vietnam or even possibly for buying off Ho Chi Minh.[60] Having risen to power in part on the basis of the popularity of such technological government projects, Johnson perhaps hoped for a similar success in Vietnam. The hope was that, by controlling nature, one could eliminate political divisions and conflicts.

This imagery of water, floods, and currents was one of the most common in the élite discussions of the Vietnam War. Communism itself had, since the beginning of the Cold War, been equated with a red tide, and this imagery continued in public debates about the need for U.S. intervention in Southeast Asia. In early 1965, Nixon spoke of the "wave" of communism engulfing the nations of Southeast Asia, and warned of the danger that the Pacific could become a "Red sea." Dean Rusk spoke of the North Vietnamese forces as having a "reservoir" of southern sympathizers. The progress in the war, or momentum of events, was repeatedly referred to in terms of tidal flows. The advances of the North were a tide, which could be turned by the gravitational pull of American technological power. Thus, Senator Gale McGee warned that, without American intervention, "we would find the tides reversed and turning against us," and the élite repeatedly referred to the "tide" of battle turning one way or another. The aim of the policy was to contain the fluids and therefore "stay dry," and the implications of losing were expressed in terms of immersion. Senator John Stennis worried that if we lost, "we might be driven into the sea," and McGeorge Bundy warned that the VC might "engulf" the Khanh regime. Lodge argued that we could not "let Southeast Asia go down the drain," and the cumulative effect of this flow of Communism would be an "erosion of the will to resist."[61]

If the Communist tide could not be contained, U.S. actions were then a matter either of entering the water, mopping it up, or overpowering the flow from the North. The CIA reported that the "pacification effort is like trying to mop the floor before turning off the faucet." Walt Rostow then called for a "shallow invasion" of North Vietnam, that would "mop up" VC at the local level. If the flow could not be stopped, the waters could at least be calmed by implementing what was called "spreading the oil drop"—a form of the rural "pacification" program. Or the tide could be turned by helping the Government of South Vietnam (GVN) succeed. Lodge reported that popular support "swells and floods" when the GVN scored military victories. If all else failed, the tide could be turned by raining down bombs in such volume as to overwhelm any opposing currents. Thus, when things began to look bad in the battle for Khe Sanh, the United States began "Operation Niagara," the most intense bombing campaign of the war. It was a volume of destructive precipitation not matched until George Bush initiated Operation Desert Storm.[62]

One of the requirements for containment was maintaining the integrity of the "container"—the structure that stood as the boundary between in and out, democracy and Communism, freedom and slavery.[63]

The container constituted the border between the orderly flow of water and the flooding waters, and maintaining the integrity of the container entailed clearly drawing the line between self and other. Perhaps the most common cliché in élite discourse was that used by Walt Rostow when he claimed that the United States had to "draw a line in the dust at the borders of South Vietnam." Lodge reported that General Khanh had echoed the sentiment, saying that he saw "some merit in drawing clear lines of battle and thereby engaging men's hearts." Rusk asserted that in Vietnam, "the lines are clearly drawn." Support of these "frontiers," McNamara claimed, "thickens the blood of the free-world family." Senator Thomas Dodd stated that the reasons for being in Vietnam were "crystal clear . . . the security of the entire free world demands that a firm line be drawn against the further advance of Communist imperialism."[64] The clarity with which these lines are drawn, whether in the jungle or in the sand, increases the will of those fighting, for then the battle becomes a matter of keeping out an obviously foreign enemy.

The role of engineer, working out the proper equations necessary to contain the red tide, helped the élite gain a sense of control in the context of chaotic events. Concerns about mortality raised in the context of war could be addressed by constructing the event as a winnable battle against Death. This trope was paralleled by a conceptualization of the war as a problem of disease and America as the good and wise doctor. It was a social construction with particular relevance to the issue of mortality.

Playing Doctor: War as a Medical Procedure.   Another way in which the situation was transformed into a manageable technical task was by employing medical metaphors.[65] In this vision of things, the problem in Asia was one of illness, the United States was the doctor, the Philippines or South Vietnam the patient, and backwardness or Communism the disease. In addition to the commonly known phrases such as "surgical" air strikes and the various "operations," the élite drew on a variety of images and metaphors from the medical world. By placing themselves in the position of the doctor, the élite again gained some sense of control over death. As the doctor had the power of life and death, so the foreign policy decision makers could assuage some of their concerns about the problem of mortality by playing doctor.

The role of doctor has not always conveyed such a sense of power over death. But, over the course of the twentieth century, as doctors became more effective at extending life and curing illnesses, it became a profession that the political élite symbolically utilized. In a striking parallel, as foreign policy came to be seen in terms of medical science, medical practices came to be seen as a kind of war. This conception of death as being caused by a conflict between humans and germs drew on Darwinian theory and used explicitly military imagery.[66]

Politics, the pathologist Rudolph Virchow once said, "is nothing but medicine on a grand scale," and many of the élite embraced this vision of their profession.[67] Medical metaphors elicited deep-rooted fears about mortality and death, thus framing the political issues as ones about which drastic action was absolutely necessary. It likewise placed the élite in the position of the expert doctor, possessing the specialized knowledge needed to cure the disease. And it associated one's political opponents with disease and death, vilifying them in the eyes of the public. By equating persistent social problems with disease, the élite both emphasized the seriousness of the problem and its amenability to technical solutions. If challenges from abroad were akin to microbial or malignant invasions, and the prevalent form of medical treatment was construed as warfare, it is not surprising that the élite would sometimes see the use of force as necessary to save the life of the nation.

Although this conception of foreign affairs was particularly prominent during the Vietnam War, there certainly were signs of it during earlier periods. At the turn of the twentieth century, there was a general sense in the public that the U.S. role overseas amounted primarily to that of a sanitation engineer. To the extent that there might be diseases among the "uncivilized" peoples, American sanitary engineering would take care of the problem. One striking example from popular culture of this theme applied to international politics was found in an advertisement for Pear's soap published in popular magazines following the Spanish-American War. It pictured Admiral Dewey, soap and scrub brush in hand, cleaning up the "dark places" of the globe; the caption read, "The first step towards lightening the White Man's Burden is through teaching the virtues of cleanliness. Pear's Soap is a potent factor in brightening the dark corners of the earth, as civilization advances."[68] In the minds of Americans, the agendas and identities of the missionary, doctor, and the Admiral were converging, and the war on disease and the war on the barbarians were becoming virtually the same.

The discussion of the situation in Cuba and the Philippines drew on the new language about disease and germs. In part, the war with Spain paralleled quite closely the new war on bacteria and microbes. Part of the debate among the statesmen and in Congress was over whether these potential new possessions of America were places of health (and therefore of life) or of disease (and death). The tropics generally were associated with disease, especially the dreaded yellow fever and malaria, and thus supporters of expansion had to overcome the common Anglo-Saxon aversion to the tropics. In the Philippines and Hawaii, opponents of the

U.S. presence there emphasized the diseases of these places. An anti-imperialist editorial referred to the Hawaiians as "leprous descendants of the Sandwich Island cannibals," and Representative Champ Clark of Missouri emphasized that Hawaii had "the largest and most repulsive collection of lepers beneath the sun." Not only were these islands places of disease, but imperialism itself was associated with disease. Clark would speak of the "jingo bacillus," which was more infectious than the plague and he hoped not more fatal.[69] Supporters of expansion, such as Albert Beveridge, objected to the claims that the Philippines was a "sweltering, steaming, miasmatic swamp."[70]

Germ theory also included the idea that diseases were carried by people, thus opening up the possibility that certain groups could be associated with the cause of death.[71] The rise of germ theory saw a resurgence of quarantines and renewed concern among politicians in the 1880s and 1890s about the spread of disease via mobile populations. As well, the Spanish presence was seen as contributing to the foul airs or miasmas on Cuba. Shortly before the outbreak of war in 1898, Senator Fairbanks argued that the "Spanish flag must be withdrawn and cease forever to contaminate the air of this hemisphere."[72] Senator Redfield Proctor's influential speech on the war in Cuba was delivered in the middle of a discussion in the Senate of quarantine legislation, in which concerns about the spread of disease, particularly tropical diseases, were being voiced. In that context, Proctor delivered his report of the conditions he had witnessed on his trip to Cuba. In a letter written from the island, he compared conditions on Cuba to those of St. Bartholomew's massacre and the Inquisition. But in his public speech his support for American intervention on the island was based in part on an association between Spanish policies on the island and the disease and death found there. In the concentration camps, Proctor reported, there was "foul earth, foul air, foul water, and foul food or none," and the Spanish were taking no sanitary measures.[73] The clear implication was that the United States, with its superior skills as sanitary engineer and doctor, had a moral obligation to clean up the mess in Cuba.

In State Department memoranda of the time as well, Spain was portrayed as a source of chaos, disease, and death. The American ambassador to Spain, Stewert Woodford, would recount in his dispatches a series of meetings he had with the representatives of other great powers—Britain, Germany, and Russia. In each instance, he began his explanation of the U.S. position not with a discussion of economics or the balance of power but with the "question of health," that is, with the yellow fever that was widespread in Cuba at the time, due to the "bad sanitary conditions of Cuba."[74] Woodford claimed that Spain was creating the conditions in which this disease was spreading to the United States. The *reconcentrado* camps were described as places of "disease, immorality, and death," and Woodford concluded that "the policy now pursued by the Spanish Government can only restore peace by producing a graveyard that shall be as large as Cuba itself." In another instance, he argued that Spain had turned the formerly fertile Cuba into a desert.[75] Where American business (in the form of sugar plantations) had brought forth life on the island, Spain brought only death. Thus, the American intervention in Cuba was justified in part as being not unlike a battle against death itself.

The social construction of reality is not completely divorced from the obvious perceived realities of a situation. People were dying in Cuba as a result of brutal Spanish rule there, and in that sense the association between Spain and death was literal as much as it was figurative. The "hard, cold facts" worked to lend reality to the portrayal of the war with Spain as a battle against death. Cuba was an active front in the battle against disease, and the Spanish were not cooperating in civilization's struggle against the bacillus. They were, in fact, an ally of disease and their presence in Cuba was leading to the deaths by disease of innocent people. Therefore, the battle against disease necessitated battling the Spanish. The bacteriologist C. Winslow noted in 1903 the successes of Dr. Walter Reed and others in discovering the cause of yellow fever and virtually eliminating it from the island of Cuba within three years of the U.S. military victory there.[76] The military and medical technological prowess of the United States had taken on both Spain and yellow fever, and in both cases they had triumphed; both campaigns were informed by similar philosophies.

Drawing on this tradition, Franklin D. Roosevelt, in a 1937 speech on the situation in Europe, would paint an apocalyptic vision of a "storm" of "invading and violating" that would "rage till every flower of culture is trampled and all human beings are leveled in a vast chaos." War, he said, was "a contagion" and the "epidemic of world lawlessness" was spreading. The necessary response, Roosevelt implied, was a quarantine: "When an epidemic of physical disease starts to spread, the community approves and joins in a quarantine of the patients in order to protect the health of the community against the spread of the disease."

Following World War II, the problems of world politics were similarly construed as diseases. Acheson described Communism like a disease, a corruption of the apple, equated with sin and decay. As he put it in the famous opening line of the Cold War drama, "Like apples in a barrel infected by one rotten one, the corruption of Greece would infect Iran and all to the east. It would also carry infection to Africa through Asia Minor and Egypt, and to Europe through Italy and

France." As with earlier American involvement in Cuba, the United States portrayed countries in the periphery as helpless patients dependent on America for their survival. The spread of Communism, Acheson argued, meant that "Greece was in the position of a semiconscious patient on the critical list whose relatives and physicians had been discussing whether his life could be saved." In arguing for speedy implementation of the European Recovery Program, George Marshall would declare that "[t]he patient is sinking while the doctors deliberate." Eisenhower would likewise refer to the "creeping paralysis of communism." According to John McCloy, the effects of the Red Army in Europe were "locust-like." U.S. Ambassador to the Soviet Union, William Bullitt, argued that the United States had to prevent the "flow of the Red amoeba [*sic*] into Europe." Churchill would worry about France being infected with Communism and that the virus was also beginning to "flow across Germany into Holland and Belgium."[77]

This association between disease and the enemy was made as well when Communism was found within American borders. In several critiques of "Christian pacifism," MacArthur equated pacifism with Communism, sentimentalism, emotionalism, homoeroticism, and disease. In an address at the University of Pittsburgh in 1932, he stated that, "Pacifism and its bedfellow, Communism, are all about us. . . . Day by day this canker eats deeper into the body politic. For the sentimentalism and emotionalism which have infested our country, we should substitute hard common sense."[78] Geoffrey Smith has catalogued how, during the Red Scare of the 1950s, Communism and the suspected Soviet sympathizers often were associated with disease and homosexuality.[79]

The problem in South Vietnam also was seen as one of ill health. The CIA reported that the "political health of South Vietnam was 'precarious,'" and the medical problem in Vietnam was seen either as some sort of decay or infectious disease, a hemorrhaging, or cancer. The metaphor of bleeding meshed nicely with the various liquid metaphors and the calls for "stemming the tide." CIA Director McCone thus proposed to "tighten the tourniquet" on North Vietnam. Élite would describe the Communists as a "rot" or a sort of vermin, which "infest" the Cambodian border. They liked to think of the disease as treatable, or, even better, that they were involved with the process of birth rather than death. George Ball, in opposing escalation, equated Communism in Southeast Asia with cancer, but McGeorge Bundy countered Ball's argument by saying that he "did not believe that Mr. Ball's 'cancer analogy' was a good one. Immaturity and weakness, yes. A non-Communist society is struggling to be born." General Westmoreland also equated progress in South Vietnam with the slow growth of a child.[80]

During the Vietnam War, for both hawk and dove, the role envisioned by the élite was that of the doctor. For the doves, the situation was a lost cause, in which even the application of high-tech radiation therapies would not prevent death. For the supporters of the war, the situation was one of birth, life, and hope, in which the American surgeon or obstetrician would play a crucial and controlling role. Using the familiar equation between the enemy and disease, George Ball cautioned that "we cannot be sure how far the cancer has infected the whole body politic in South Vietnam," but likened U.S. military involvement in South Vietnam to "giving cobalt treatment to a terminal cancer case." Whereas other élite might describe Communism as a disease in order to elicit deep-rooted fears about its possible advances, Ball equated the situation with cancer in terms of its hopelessness, with the disease that modern medicine had had the least success in curing. For Senator Clark, the war was a disease that had infected the American body politic, "a cancer which is devouring our youth, our morals, our national wealth, and the energies of our leadership." For Senator Fulbright, the illness took the form of a "mounting war fever" that "flourished in the current emotionally charged atmosphere."[81]

As foreign policy was seen as a problem of curing diseases, the élite likewise frequently portrayed themselves as doctors. George Kennan argued that Americans would have to adopt the doctor's "attitude of detachment and soberness and readiness to reserve judgment" in foreign affairs. Acheson spoke of the executive branch as being analogous to a doctor, while Congress was like the patient's family needing counsel. In other words, Acheson saw himself as the expert, with the technical knowledge needed to make an unemotional and detached decision concerning life and death. Congressional inquiry only muddied the waters; they could not "plumb the depths," Acheson argued, as the civil servants could. McNamara's principal assistant, John McNaughton, argued in October 1964 that the United States had to emerge from Vietnam looking like a "good doctor"; references to the doctor self-image came up frequently in the memos on Vietnam.[82]

As war was seen as the cure for decadence, and medical treatments were described using military metaphors, so the treatment for the disease of Communism took the form of war. As MacArthur put it in the 1930s, aggression, depravity, greed, and hatred were a "disease which [war] alone could cure." The wars, as with the practices in the modern hospital, were described as involving a heavy reliance on invasive technologies. These included open heart surgery, vaccinations, quarantines, and radiation therapy. During the Vietnam War, whatever the metaphorical treatments espoused by the élite, in practice they all took the form of bombing, which the doctors in Washington claimed would have a "therapeutic effect" on the Vietnamese. McNamara, noting that the situation in late 1966 was bad, wrote that, "[a]ll we can do is massage the heart." General Taylor claimed that bombing the north would "give Pulmotor treatment for a government in extremis."[83] Taylor and Lodge argued that military aid would be "a shot in the arm" for General Khanh. As with the solution proposed for the Cuban missile crisis, the élite often thought of their efforts in South Vietnam as the implementation of a "quarantine." LBJ claimed that "we are quarantining aggressors down there just like the smallpox," and Mc-Namara called for a quarantine of all military aid to North Vietnam.[84]

The medical analogies continued after the war to be used to associate America's opponents with death. Cancer metaphors were used to describe Communism in the Reagan administration's rhetoric on Central America,[85] to refer to international crime and drug trade during the Clinton administration, and in newspaper editorials calling for the ouster of Saddam Hussein. Whenever the nation considers the use of force or wants to heighten audience concern with a problem, these charged metaphors are trotted out, like so many pieces of rhetorical artillery. In selling policies and in justifying losses, the fear of death remains a powerful drive behind and resource to be drawn on by the foreign policy élite. The wars in Asia, the Middle East, and Panama, and the deaths of the soldiers in them, have been justified as part of a metaphorical battle against an enemy equated with disease and death. Death was associated with the natural world, with humanity's animal aspects, with disease, fortune, and all that is beyond our control. By talking about the enemy in terms of those forces, the war became a war against Death itself. The battle against death was then turned into a "manageable" task, a technical problem that America's great wealth and technological resources could be used to solve, and in which the need for discussion or compromise was nonsensical.

The discourse functioned to externalize mortality, to focus attention of the mortality of the Other, thereby drawing attention away from the mortality of the self. During peacetime, there was less of need for this "distraction," but when the body bags started coming home, this need increased. The identity formed through this discourse was of the Self as a rational, controlled problem solver, and of an Other that was a diseased, depraved, and sinful animal. This social construction functioned to dampen anxieties about mortality and death by painting those dreaded facts as completely external qualities of the Other. Within this framework, the deaths of Americans in the jungles were seen as transcendent, as part of that project that asserted and proved that the spirit was separate from and superior to the flesh.

CHAPTER 6

FACING THE WALL

Justice cannot be approximated if the hope of its perfect realization does not generate a sublime madness in the soul.

—Reinhold Neibuhr

I shall die, but that is all that I shall do for Death.

—Edna St. Vincent Millay

As much as we may oppose war, it is still necessary to accept that wars are waged by humans, not monsters, however monstrous or sad the acts of those humans may have been. Having set out to humanize the study of war, it would not make much sense to conclude by reducing these individuals to caricatures, either as callous imperialists or as noble guardians of freedom. This would not get us closer to understanding and being able to think and act more self-consciously about war. Unfortunately, much of the discussion of war and foreign policy seems to be guided by one or the other of these caricatures. Although the field of international relations can be categorized by a fairly healthy diversity, a large number of the investigations of foreign affairs fall roughly into two recognizable camps, each with its own moral cartography and political agenda. The first assumes that the people making foreign policy in powerful countries (particularly the United States) are sensible, rational, and make the right decisions in difficult circumstances. The job of scholars in this camp is to advise the prince on how best to avoid mistakes, the misuse of history, and so on. This view is characterized by a patriotic foundation, precluding any fundamental criticism of the morality or character of America. The country and its leaders may have made some mistakes or miscalculations, but they are in no way evil. This view is most consistently and clearly espoused by the government officials themselves and generally by anyone aspiring to join the ranks of these officials. It likewise characterizes much—although by no means all—of the realist, neoliberal, and rational choice studies of war and foreign policy.

The contrary view holds that these men are essentially evil, imperialist, power-hungry élite. This view characterizes much of the critical, neo-Marxist, and postmodern approaches. I would argue that once you strip away the hyperbole, complex language or formulas, the smoke and mirrors, the often vituperative debate between the left and right boils down to a disagreement over the basic ethical and moral character of these leaders, the issue of responsibility, guilt, and blame. One side accuses, the other defends; both dig in their heals, and are sustained in their work by these deeply felt emotions. The interesting thing about this disciplinary bipolarity is that we all know who is in each camp (although a few quirky free-thinkers continue to defy categorization), even though we might pretend that no such division really exists in the field. It is often quite entertaining to watch the fight as it is played out in journals and conferences and occasionally on the streets; the trouble is, however, that they are both partially right. One of the many challenges facing the field is to acknowledge these underlying value systems, and to learn to live with that complexity. The wars that national leaders wage are in part their own doing, in part the product of the failings and venality of other actors and the vicissitudes of an anarchic world.

To adopt such a perspective leaves us in an indeterminate place; a place without "the answer" to the question about why human beings so often kill each other. We tend to avoid this indeterminate place and to attempt to impose intellectual order on the chaos of world politics; in the end, unfortunately, we must resign ourselves to a pretty heavy dose of chaos; by extension, this means we must resign ourselves to a certain amount of powerlessness, and finally to our own fate as mortals. The two moves are linked, and that is why we need to be wary of clinging too tightly to a neat and tidy view of the world. Accepting ambiguity does not mean that we resign ourselves to helpless passivity or moral indifference, but it means that we seek truth and understanding within the context of a clearheaded acceptance of our limits and of the reality of our impending demise.

There is that traditionally male tendency to want to do something, to be empowered, to understand, which of course is understandable in the face of the tragedy of war. For those who have been through war and survived, it is perfectly healthy and admirable to try to "do something" to prevent it from happening again, or, if that is beyond the grasp of a given individual, to attempt some symbolic reempowerment. In seeking the truth, however, we cannot let those motivations and fears distort what we conclude about the world. The challenge is how to act from that place of uncertainty; although this comes as no great revelation, calls for caution and humility bear repeating, as there is such a great temptation to try to escape the limitations of the human condition. In that spirit of lowered expectations, this book concludes with some observations on the variation, both across individuals and over time, in how these officials thought about death. The hope is that a discussion of changes in the culture of foreign policy at the close of the twentieth century will enable more honest, clearer, and more self-conscious thinking and feeling on these matters.

The metaphors and rituals used by the élite in discussing foreign policy and coming to terms with death in battle are suggestive of an undercurrent of fear and anxiety concerning mortality that shaped the lives and wartime decision making of top foreign policy officials. This study does not establish that fear of death caused particular foreign policy decisions to be made, and it does not explain why wars occur. Human behavior is too complex to reach such a simple answer; we cannot state with certainty, as does Ernest Becker, that the fear of death is "a mainspring of human activity," but it is part of the dynamics of war. This books amounts to a war story, grounded in the historical record, of the meaning attributed to war by certain powerful men, the plausibility of which will depend largely on how it resonates with the reader. It attempts to understand how mass murder-suicide becomes a human possibility at all, and about the sense modern America has made of war. War is more than a matter of economic calculation. It is an activity thoroughly wrapped up in the human condition of mortality, such that war becomes meaningless without consideration of human attempts at coming to terms with that fact of their finitude. Foreign policy is made not by computers but by finite humans who exist within the context of an infinite and ultimately unknowable cosmos; the prevalence of death-related symbols, and the consistent attempt at symbolically overcoming death, point to the need for greater awareness and understanding of how this aspect of élite culture may affect whether and in what manner we decide to use force.

The expansion of foreign policy dialogue can be facilitated by exploring conceptualizations of war that differ from the traditionally masculine response to mortality described in the preceding chapters. Although the dominance of the discourse of denial has left little room for alternatives, we find bits and pieces of a more acceptant stance toward death that amounts, as the title of this chapter implies, to "facing the wall." It in-volves as well a bit of what Neibuhr refers to as the sublime madness that such a facing of death entails. Loved ones die, but we must carry on; fears will continue to drive men to kill, but we must still try to love; wars will continue on, but we must try madly to stop them nonetheless. This stance is reflected in Millay's quote, with its acceptance of mortality and ac-knowledgment of the literal deaths on the battlefield.

This kind of thinking remains far removed from that generally en-countered in the realms of power; still, we can explore some of the vari-ants of the dominant discourse, both as a way of pointing out the contingent nature of élite immortality projects, and to suggest possible al-ternative ways of talking about death in battle. There is, of course, no one "right" way to talk about death, one way that will lead to some perfect for-eign policy; rather, what is being called for here is a certain frame of mind that, at a minimum, is conscious of the ways in which otherwise uncon-scious desires can shape our thinking—a frame of mind that does not try to act out fears about death in a destructive battle against death and re-mains open to the contingency and limits of the *polis*. This is unlikely to be a popular idea, given the modern Western aversion to thinking or talk-ing about death (except in its heavenly variants); but, regardless of whether or not we spend time facing the wall, the wall is always there, fac-ing us. And there are signs that things may be changing. At the turn of the twenty-first century, there appears to be an increased aversion within the body politic to casualties of any kind. From Vietnam on, American de-cision makers have become increasingly unwilling to have any soldiers die in battle, a stance that stands in contrast to the martial enthusiasm of a century earlier.

LIVING WITH DYING

The place to look for alternative discourses is at the boundaries of élite culture—among those officials who found themselves at the periphery of decision-making circles, or out on the battlefield facing death. There were a number of élite who in different ways showed some alternative symbolic or ritual way of coming to terms with death. This group primarily was op-posed to war or imperialism, but not exclusively so; they also partook of many elements of the symbolic battle with death, but by-and-large they found themselves on the outskirts of the places of power. George Hoar was one of a handful of opponents to the campaign in the Philippines; John Long a figure of little consequence in American foreign policy whose career was eclipsed by that of his assistant in the Department of the Navy, Teddy Roosevelt; George Kennan reached the height of his influence with the publication of his hardline "X" article, but his influence in official circles diminished thereafter as his views became decreasingly militaristic. George Ball was the lone dissenter from the prowar members of the National Security Council; and Hubert Humphrey, when he expressed his doubts about the Vietnam War, was in effect banished by Johnson from NSC meetings for over a year. Robert McNamara, although at the center of power up until 1967, was considered to be going soft, and soon left for what he felt was more humane work at the World Bank. These men remained influential, but they were no longer admitted into the inner sanctum in which life-and-death decisions were being made. Some explanation for the relative distance of these élite from the places of power can be found in the incompatibility of some elements of their language with the dominant discourse of the high priests of foreign policy.

As outlined in Chapter 2, the acceptant approach to mortality involves a passive rather than active relationship toward death and entails some emotional expressiveness; among the marginalized members of the élite, there were aspects of this stance. Perhaps the key variation in élite discourse was the extent to which they distanced themselves from mortality by symbolically placing it in a clearly external realm. For some of the élite, death, passion, and sinfulness were portrayed as completely external to the nation and themselves; others distanced themselves from death and sin but did not use national boundaries as the basis for that distinction, metaphorically placing death within the United States. Some of the élite displayed a greater acceptance of mortality than was the norm, and this acceptance seemed to facilitate a less combative stance. As this stance entailed a greater acceptance of the literal deaths on the battlefield, it often was associated with more emotionally painful language. As the dominant discourse involved a control of painful emotions, the alternative was to accept those emotions and express them. Another key divergence from the dominant discourse was the extent to which these "borderline" élite identified with America's new technological and political power. Senator Hoar, in particular, had greater doubts and less faith in the ability of these new technologies to solve America's problems than the bulk of his fellow foreign policy élite. As the twentieth century progressed, and the hold of technology on the American imagination strengthened, it became harder to find such doubters.

There was a certain logic to this acceptant relationship to mortality. If mortality were more accepted and one's own death fully owned, there was less need to exclude death symbolically from one's world. This acceptance was accompanied by and facilitated by the sadness and fear that were expressions of that acceptance. This facilitated the embrace of those characteristics associated with mortality—those faults and sins that the dominant immortality project attempted to locate in an entirely external realm. Such an acceptance of one's own mortality also made it easier to see one's opponents as less than totally evil and meant that compromise and discussion with them was a more acceptable option.

ON THE FRINGE:
HINTS OF AN ALTERNATIVE DISCOURSE

A key element of the élite's immortality project was an embrace of America's new technological power, but there was some variation in the extent to which this was the case. At the turn of the twentieth century, one primary schism in the discourse was between realists and idealists. These two groups practiced different variants of the immortality project—one emphasized material conditions and Darwinian theory, the other the importance of ideals, laws, and the power of words. The realists, with their emphasis on the importance of military strength, not surprisingly tended to identify with America's new economic power, while the idealists emphasized limits and identified with the weak. Those who identified with this material power tended to see it as decisive in international affairs, while those who advocated the positions of weakness emphasized the role of morality, ideas, and divine principles in shaping history. These different stances related to whether the élite adopted an acceptant or resistant stance toward life and death, a split evident in the debate between the imperialists and anti-imperialists at the turn of the century.

The debate over the Philippines was, in large part, a debate between the representatives of an older, less powerful nation, and the representatives of a nascent world power. As Hoar put it in 1900, if taking the Philippines "is being a world power, for my part I would rather be a world weakness." He supported international law, as "the product of Christianity which prevents every weak nation of the earth from becoming the prey of the stronger ones." Rather than embrace the new powers of science, Senator Hoar saw limits to the ability to know or define reality, and instead embraced the mysteries of life. He saw reason and free will as not substitutes but supports "for faith in the divine mysteries which surround all life." This sense of human limitations was reflected in Hoar's notions of national strength. The strength and success of nations was assured by following those laws laid down by the loving Christian God. Reflecting elements of the earlier Puritan sense of man's powerlessness, Hoar held to the argument of his friend Edward Everett Hale: "[W]hen man wields any of the great forces of the Universe, it is God also who is wielding them through him."[1] Thus, for the nation to prosper and survive, first of all it had to be doing God's work.

The different requirements for national vitality were reflected in the relative importance placed on words and principles as opposed to things such as naval power and territorial possessions. To Hoar, war was a matter of words, of the principles embodied in the acts of those involved, and Alfred Mahan's talk of the importance of sea power was of secondary concern.[2] The senior Senator from Massachusetts clearly embraced the Puritan elements of immortality project dominant among the élite, but he did not embrace the activism or technological power of the modern era.

The doves' emphasis on words and faith in the workings of God was compatible with a more passive stance toward the world, and this facet of the acceptant stance can be seen clearly in the writings of John Long, which contain many more passive images than those of the other élite. For example, after his parents died, Long saw the family as drifting "like straws upon the torrent"; during his college days he wrote that he "drifted like a balloon in the air . . . blown about by the winds."[3] In contrast to the identities displayed in the writings of other élite, Long portrayed himself as a passive object, engulfed by his emotions rather than mastering them. Rather than making things happen, things happened to him. This stance was reflected as well in his reaction to international events. Cuban "independence would have come without a drop of blood, as naturally as an apple falls from a tree," he wrote in defense of McKinley's reluctance to go to war. There is no sense of conflict in the imagery Long used but, rather, a view of the world in which natural processes work in a harmonious fashion. The colony of Cuba was now ripe and ready to fall, and all that needed to be done was to let gravity do its work. In discussing the Civil War, Long even went so far as to argue the virtues of a form of passive resistance as more effective than force in international affairs. He delivered a paper before the Massachusetts Historical Society in which he argued that the Confederacy would "have stood a better chance of success by non-resistance than by fighting."[4] The implication was that, for Long, war was not an effective means for accomplishing one's ends in international affairs; when force was used, it was more likely to be the result of passion than self-control.

Following World War II, this idealist and passive stance was not as prevalent or extreme; none of the élite opposed U.S. intervention on principle, as Hoar did, but they did vary in terms of the limits they saw to that intervention. At the turn of the century, the realists had embraced America's new power and pushed for using it to expand; after 1945, it was realists such as George Kennan and Hans Morgenthau, who would call for strictly limiting U.S. involvement overseas to areas of vital interest and avoiding the overextension that often followed from what they termed foreign policy "crusades." Reflecting this sense of limitations and attendant sense of passivity, Kennan argued in regard to Indochina that the United States would have to "permit the turbulent political currents (there) to find their own level." Acheson, in the China White Paper of 1949 made a similar argument regarding American abilities to control events in China, while remaining more optimistic about America's power in Korea and Vietnam. Within the Johnson administration, those opposed to Vietnam would argue against it on the grounds that it was a situation beyond U.S. control. Roger Hilsman, as he was leaving office, wrote that "our ability to control the course of events in Southeast Asia is inherently limited." Likewise, Hubert Humphrey would warn Johnson that "[w]e now risk creating the impression that we are the prisoner of events in Vietnam," and, more simply, that, "[s]ome things are beyond our power to prevent."[5] Much of the growing opposition to the war in Vietnam from McNamara and the "Wise Men" stemmed from their gradual recognition that indeed the United States was overextended. Thus, although most of the élite identified with the vast pool of resources at their disposal and sought to attain as complete a sense of control as possible, a few élite were more willing to face and live with limitations rather than attempt to avoid at all costs the fate of being a "helpless giant."

Another major difference between the élite was the degree to which they engaged in projection as opposed to introspection. For those intent on purging their identity (and the country they identified with) of any hint of mortality, any form of self-criticism or empathy with the enemy was avoided. In such a view, the United States and its leaders were purged of all doubt, sin, or fear (and, by extension, mortality). As with Bunyan's Christian, the self was pure and whatever evil existed in the world was to be found in the "vast external realm." Within the context of the Christian search for immortality through a purification of the self from sin, one imperative was evading any hint of immorality. To the extent that one's own immortality project was wrapped up in the nation, the nation had to be seen as a moral entity, or its fate, and the fate of all those who had died for it in the past, was thrown into question. In general, the élite saw the United States as a special place with a people chosen by God. Not all the élite, however, shared this sense of self-righteousness or lack of self-doubt.

Hoar identified primarily with certain principles rather than with the nation itself, and, therefore, he was able to criticize the nation without endangering his own immortality project. This did not mean that Hoar would object to war in general, but he could stand up in the Senate as one of the few Republicans willing to oppose America's transformation into a global empire. In part, the subordination of his identification with the nation to that with Massachusetts and the Republican Party also enabled Hoar to criticize aspects of both America's past and present. Those who had a more nationalistic identity had a harder time opposing any American acts because they could not do so without also criticizing themselves. Hoar saw the founding of the United States in millennial terms, and clearly saw America as an example to the world. But while those adopting the projective stance would find no fault with the United States, both Long and Hoar did find fault with the country they served. Long, for instance, would give a critical reading of America's past, even noting a number of sordid episodes in the nation's past in a Fourth of July speech. In Senate speeches, Hoar pointed to American ambition and cupidity, the intrigues of the party bosses, and how politicians were concerned more about reelection than sound policy. He went so far as to argue that Spain would have every right, if she were strong enough, to kick the United States out of the Philippines on the same grounds that the United States drove Spain out of Cuba.[6]

Where Hoar differed most from the advocates of imperialism was in his affiliation with the Filipinos. He continually drew parallels between the Filipinos and Americans—particularly those of the Revolutionary era—and argued repeatedly that anyone in America would do the same thing as the Philippine rebels if they were in their place. He did not see them as backward or incapable but, rather, as numerous, proud, and possessing the "right to judge of their fitness for self-government."[7] He repeatedly referred to the purchase of the Philippines as akin to purchasing "people like sheep," when in his eyes these people were not sheep but modern-day equivalents to Hoar's ancestors who had fought at Concord and Lexington.

Although George Kennan would criticize Hoar's idealism, he shared with the Massachusetts Senator a willingness to criticize American policy. Kennan is a complex character, perhaps best known for his hardline stance against Soviet communism; but he often distanced himself from the crusading spirit of the hawks, and his writings provide us with an alternative to the symbolic battle with death. In an August 21, 1950 memo to Acheson (which the Secretary of State did not distribute), Kennan argued for ending U.S. action in Korea as soon as possible and that "sectors of our public opinion and of our official establishment are indulging themselves in emotional, moralistic attitudes toward Korea which, unless corrected, can easily carry us toward real conflict with the Russians." Kennan also showed a greater empathy with the position and needs of the Russians, speaking of them as "human beings like ourselves. . . . [T]hey had been born somewhere [and] had their childhood ambitions as we had." In his writings, far from displaying an unquestioning patriotism, he would often point to the shortcomings and problems with American society and foreign policy.[8]

In Vietnam, opponents of the war would likewise point to the questionable morality of the American position there. Hubert Humphrey, for instance, was one of the few élite actually to call into question the ethics of the war. In a memorandum to Johnson that would lead to his effective exile from the National Security Council, the vice president attempted to bring some moral considerations into the discourse. His one plea to the president to avoid or limit bombing the North is worth quoting at length, as it is so starkly different in tone than the standard foreign policy memo:

> There is obviously no quick or easy solution, and no clear course of right or wrong. . . . The moral dilemmas are inescapable. . . . Our rationale for action has shifted away now even from the notion that we are there as advisers on request of a free government, to the simple and politically barren argument of our "national interest." . . . It is hard to justify dramatic 150 plane U.S. air bombardments across a border as a response to camouflaged, often non-sensational, elusive, small scale terror which has been going on for ten years in what looks largely like a Civil War in the South.[9]

Humphrey still phrased the problem in terms of its "political barrenness," but he also stated that the president faced moral dilemmas that he could not escape, that is, that he could not control. In the post-Vietnam Era, Jimmy Carter's declaration of the "malaise" characterizing American society, and Bill Clinton's confessions of national guilt in for the history of slavery, for American shortcomings in its relations with Africa, and his promotion of the declassification of documents previously considered too politically sensitive, are signs as well of a greater willingness to accept American shortcomings.

If in this acceptant discourse there was less need to purge the self of qualities associated with mortality, and less vilification of the enemy, this discourse likewise held a view of the world as more harmonious than the Darwinian worldview of TR and Lodge or Apocalyptic visions of Reagan. The language of battle is present in the language of all the élite, but with John Long it is found only in his public speeches and generally those delivered to audiences containing veterans. Although he noted the "instinct of self-preservation," he added that when this was tempered by the benevolence of human nature, it would always lead to advancement, not "wreck or chaos"—a sentiment shared by George Hoar.[10] In the post–Cold War Era, the language of conflict, although not gone, is less prevalent, as seen in Clinton's emphasis on progress, the mutual gains from trade, and the need for cooperation.

The dominant response to mortality among the élite involved avoiding, suppressing, or controlling the painful emotions of fear and sadness.

In the lives of John Long, George Kennan, and Robert McNamara, however, we find a few exceptions to this rule. Like the other members of the élite, John Long undertook a form of pilgrimage and underwent the transformation from fearful boy to fearless man.[11] The strategy developed by Long in response to his experience of mortality, however, was clearly one of expressiveness rather than action or projection. Far more than the other élite, Long "was affected" as much as he made effect. Whereas Roosevelt admired the doctrine of works contained in the Epistle of James, Long found comfort in the Biblical passage, "Blessed are they that mourn for they shall be comforted." At another time he would write that "Nothing has such a charm for my mind . . . as a history of the unfolding of the heart, its variableness, its doubts, its fears, hopes, its flutterings, its strugglings." Apparently he was an openly emotional man, recalling crying both when he first arrived at Harvard, and later on seeing his parents at the end of hard term at school.[12]

In his writings, there is much more evidence of any open expression of sorrow than in the writings of any of the other élite. John Long was not one to shunt aside his feelings or mourning for the dead. In fact, he dwelt on the deaths, and returned to them again and again. The year for Long became a series of anniversaries of people's deaths.[13] Where Roosevelt took pleasure and solace in activity and sport—the hard and strenuous— Long was a man of music and words. He wrote that music had a power over him that he "could not resist." His poem "The Old Songs," reflected his appreciation of the expressive power of song,

> Our hearts are full to running o'er
> With raindrops from the skies of yore . . .
> And though they touch the heart with pain
> We sing them o'er and o'er again.[14]

Rather than seek to avoid painful emotion, Long immersed himself in it, returning to his childhood haunts repeatedly in his futile attempt to stop the flow of time, and as this failed, singing the songs over and over, as a source of some comfort in the face of eternity.

John Long's opposition to war was reflected as well in his relatively great concerns about the costs of war. Throughout the discussion of possible war with Spain, Long focused on the possible losses, rather than the glories of battle. The lesson he drew from the *Maine* explosion was that wars now would be even more costly than in the past, as the ships were now loaded with explosives and easily sunk. He noted that the saddest thing about the *Maine* incident "is the constant coming of telegrams from some sailor's humble home or kinspeople, inquiring whether he is saved,

or asking that, if dead, his body may be sent home." Although acknowledging that the United States could defeat Spain easily, he still argued
that "the horrors and costs and miseries of war are incalculable," and later
mentioned the "unutterable evils incident to war—the loss of life, disease,
wounds, debts."[15] War was hard to reconcile with Long's expressive and
emotional response to mortality. It is not surprising then that for Long it
was in what he called "the discordant rage of war" that one lost control.
To someone for whom the harmony of music was central, war was disso-
nant, the product of rage and destructive emotions.[16]

George Kennan was not prone to emotional expression, but Isaacson
and Thomas argue that the arguments he presented to other élite were
often weakened by their emotionalism. Kennan would on occasion com-
mit the sin of crying in public (which did little to improve his standing in
Washington). He was described as "an impressionist, a poet, not an earth-
ling," who found it "hard to divorce his visceral feelings from his knowledge and fact." Reflecting his sense of élitism and alienation from much
of American society, he would describe himself as feeling "like a ghost,"
existing on some other plane of existence and picture himself as having
the "lonely pleasure of one who stands at long last on a chilly and inhos-
pitable mountain top where few have been before, where few can follow,
and where few will believe he has been." Part of this sense of alienation
seemed to stem for Kennan's perception of himself as a particularly sensitive and perceptive soul living in a society in which such sensitivities were
not condoned. As with Long, there was a certain fatalism in Kennan's
views; he argued that history was governed by large forces more than by
the actions of statesmen. And, for Kennan, the use of military force was
associated with a lack of self-control. The American military, he argued,
was "addicted to doing things only in the most massive, ponderous, and
unwieldy manner."[17]

Among the Vietnam Era élite, Hubert Humphrey and later Robert
McNamara, showed an emotionalism that corresponded to their doubts
about the war. Humphrey was someone whom Lyndon Johnson always
pictured "with tears in his eyes," and who was "always able to cry at the
sight of something sad." In his early memos regarding Vietnam,
Humphrey also made the mistake of using emotional language. He
opened his fateful memo to Johnson by writing, "Because these may be
the most fateful decisions of your Administration, I wanted to give you my
personal views. You know that I have nothing but sympathy for you and
complete understanding for the burden and the anguish which surrounds
such decisions." Within the dominant discourse, the decisions concerning
Vietnam were generally not framed as a burden, full of anguish—they
were supposed to be morally clear, simple, and clean. For Dean Rusk, Mc-

George Bundy, and Walt Rostow, there was no need for "sympathy" and "understanding," only a hardheaded analysis of what needed to be done to stop the tide of Communism from sweeping across Asia. Emotions would only get in the way there, confuse analysis, and (using the language of the Joint Chiefs of Staff) perhaps lead to "self-imposed restrictions."[18]

But even Robert McNamara, the paragon of rational self-control, came to express more and more sadness as the war progressed. His break with the Johnson administration was accompanied by an emotional break that frequently left him in tears. He would admit to the biographer Deborah Shapley that "I have always been a very emotional person, ever since I can remember having emotions," and it is perhaps no accident that those strong emotions were accompanied by such heroic efforts to control and master them. Shapley describes a film of McNamara's speech at Millsaps College, in which the frames of the film capture in some detail the efforts McNamara went to control his emotions:

> McNamara came to the line, "If it is not reason that rules man" and then stopped for a second, gulped, and went on: "Then man falls short of his potential." When the film of this moment is run at slow speed, his face can be seen in a terrible convulsion—mouth open, eyes shut, grimacing as though a knife were twisting through him—until the reflex of control stills his features and lets him speak again.[19]

Shapley claims that while he was secretary of defense McNamara was engaged in trying to control both the war and his emotions, and that he succeeded in doing both until some time in 1967. Shapley reports him crying in public on a few previous occasions, but as the reality of the carnage in Vietnam slowly oozed out of the numbers and reports McNamara was receiving from the field, the tears increased. When discussing with one of his assistants how much ammunition would be needed to counter enemy infiltration, he broke down and cried "as though he would never stop." Early in 1968, at a meeting of top advisors, McNamara was described as speaking with "terrible emotion," with tears "in his eyes and in his voice," claiming that all the bombing had accomplished nothing. During this time he often cried and had to turn away from visitors to hide his tears, and at public speaking engagements he was likewise often choked up or even unable to speak.[20]

Although still attempting to overcome death and create a transcendent identity, we see in the language of these élite a greater acceptance of mortality, a recognition of limitations and weaknesses, a corresponding proclivity for emotional expressiveness, and a greater willingness to engage in self-criticism. Use of such a worldview will not inevitably make

war less likely, but it does at least partake of a certain realism and acceptance of the limits of the human condition that was rare among the foreign policy élite, and that should at a minimum make it less likely that
fears of death will drive us to turn foreign policy into a battle against our
own mortality. But this response to death remains at the fringe of political discourse. One way to begin to integrate some acceptance of mortality into our symbolic representation of war is through reformulating our
conception of politics.

THE DECLINE OF POLITICS
AND THE RISE OF THE TECHNICAL

The culture and responses to mortality are not constant, and changes in
the nature of warfare and in American's experiences with death meant
that their responses to mortality and justifications of death in battle were
changing as well. One of those changes has been a decline in a certain
conception of politics. As political analysts as diverse as Robert Putnam
and Carl Boggs argue in regard to contemporary American political culture, we are experiencing a decline in the communitarian and participa-
tory aspects of politics and the continued rise of a fragmented consumer
culture.[21] This survey of historical materials is neither extensive nor rigorous enough to establish that the culture of foreign policy has undergone
a similarly profound change, but there are differences in the discourse
over the course of the twentieth century. The increasing technological,
medical, and economic power in America contributed to a trend away
from a religious view of politics, rooted in a view of humanity's powerlessness and reliance on divine benevolence, to one based more on a secular and technical conceptualization of political problems, in which the
élite increasingly conceived of themselves as playing the role of
demigods.[22] As American technical and economic power increased, the
élite attempted to take advantage of the new array of military and technical tools at their disposal in addressing international problems. As we
saw in the previous chapter, one way to facilitate the use of these tools was
through a conceptualization of situations abroad as technical in nature,
and therefore amenable to the application of engineering and military
know-how.

From the many definitions of the "political," two can be used to illustrate
this change in how we talk about war. One is the concept of politics, formulated by Aristotle and advocated by Hannah Arendt, that sees humans
as inherently social beings who can only exist within the confines of a community of mutually interdependent individuals. The nature of existence
within this community is one in which members share power—citizens in

the *polis*, Aristotle argued, both rule and are ruled. For Arendt, politics is an arena of contested rule and a process of dialogue among equals, through which identities are formed and a meaningful life achieved.[23]

As Arendt argues, this conception of politics has declined in the modern age, replaced by an emphasis on economics, science, and labor in modern society—*Homo faber* has replaced *Homo politicus*. The advent of the "new economy," the triumph of capitalism, and spread of globalization have only further reinforced this shift. With this change has come a view of politics as a matter of technical problem solving rather than an arena in which determinations of identity and right and wrong are made. In this modern view, conflicts between groups are deemphasized, or solutions to them conceived of in technical terms. With enough money and scientific know-how, the thinking goes, any political conflict can be solved. In John Hay's eulogy for William McKinley, he expressed the hope that science would eventually solve the problems of anarchy and social disorder. Hay compared anarchy to the mysterious forces of electricity, implying that political control could come about just as science had begun to understand electricity. As we have seen, this view of the world was clearly evident in the language of Lyndon Johnson as well. Johnson was of course a political operator *par excellence*, a master at bargaining and building coalitions in Congress, but at least some of his success in this regard can be linked to the fact that he frequently framed the political agenda in terms of technical solutions—rural electrification, the space program, flood control, and the war on cancer. Technology, Johnson claimed, was the means to freedom. This celebration of technological power often took on aspects of a hubris that critics such as Loren Baritz argued was one the factors that fueled the tragedy of Vietnam. The United States remained confident, even in the face of contradictory evidence, that its technological superiority could defeat the Viet Cong.[24]

With this new power, the political project of controlling *Fortuna* shifted from one based on dialogue and debate to one of management. The new creed of rational management, represented most clearly by Robert McNamara, now framed politics as a matter of controlling nature and the emotions through the application of cost-benefit analysis and placed more emphasis on the efficient means than on moral ends. As the prospects in Vietnam grew grimmer, the élite increasingly would refer to the "light at the end of the tunnel."[25] This metaphor implied that the problem was solvable, that there was hope, and that America would eventually triumph in this battle against the forces of evil and death. It meant as well that élite faith in the tractability of the universe was upheld. When a reporter commented on how the situation in Vietnam looked like a bottomless pit, McNamara responded, "Every pit has its bottom."[26]

"Bottomlessness" was generally not something countenanced by the men making decisions in Vietnam, and is an idea increasingly anathema to modern American psyche.

This shift in conceptions of the political has been paralleled by changing attitudes toward death. As Arendt argues, the traditional Aristotelian conception of politics involved a conscious recognition of our limited powers and mortality, and provided a means for creating a transcendent identity within the realm of politics. The contemporary political arena provided little such opportunity, with the power of technology used in greater and greater frequency to try to conceal or control death. As sociologists R. Kastenbaum and R. Aisenberg put it, our increased technical capabilities have "led us to expect ourselves to be capable of control or mastery. 'Science' potentially can solve any problem in which we care to invest sufficient time and resources. Money changes the world." This attitude leads then to the "culturally sanctioned expectation that technological answers can be found for all problems, the expectation that man can remove or remake whatever stands in the path of his desires—death not excluded." In extreme form, this technological hubris can reflect a form of denial as well, similar to the narcissistic feeling of omnipotence described by Ernest Becker.[27]

In this way, the discussion of the decline of the "political" brings us back to earlier observations about the attitude toward death prevalent in contemporary Western societies. The French historian Philippe Aries argues that since the Middle Ages there has been a reversal in the way Western cultures have dealt with death. In the Middle Ages and even as late as the nineteenth century, death was an accepted part of life regarding which there were definite rituals and understandings that facilitated that acceptance. As death has become more troubling, it has become distasteful to the point that, in the 1950s, one sociologist noted that talk of death was considered almost pornographic, a distasteful taboo. "Modern death," Octavio Paz writes, is "contrary to all our concepts and to the very meaning of our lives," and so "the philosophy of progress . . . pretends to make it disappear, like a magician palming a coin." Contemporary Western culture has sought to insulate itself from death linguistically, through the use of euphemism and a clean language of death; socially, through the isolation of the dying in hospitals and of the dead in highly manicured cemeteries; and psychologically, through a number of defense mechanisms such as denial and projection.[28]

This decline in the political and increased denial of death share a discomfort with limitations. Rather than face the limits that remain despite our advances in technological abilities, and face mortality despite our ability to isolate ourselves from death, we have attempted to avoid facing the fact that we remain finite, mortal beings. Even William Cohen, whose poetry often dwelt on the topic of mortality, found himself seduced by the allure of technologized power, after a flight in an F-15. As he wrote of the experience,

> on the gleaming wing
> of the death machine
> hung the terrible paradox
> of peace.
>
> For one hour,
> I was fused with beauty, violence and power . . .[29]

The death machine possessed him; he was completely caught up in it; and he saw it as an instrument of peace, while also recognizing the paradox of that view. The allure of that technological power and the temporary sense of transcendence that it can bring, has drawn American élite toward the technical fix. With the post–Cold War triumph of the United States and its elevation to the status of a "hyperpower," these temptations have only become stronger.

The trouble with the technological approach to war is that it can distort our view in harmful ways. One aspect of this distortion was a reduction of the psychological or emotional costs of war that is accomplished in part by hiding the deaths in war from view. As George Lakoff puts it, "The use of a metaphor . . . becomes pernicious when it hides realities in harmful ways."[30] Although removing the dead bodies of the soldiers from the discourse on war may make it emotionally easier to discuss the gruesome and sometimes necessary realities of war, it likewise makes it more likely that we will enter into a war when such a course of action may not be warranted.

In a particularly clear example of this kind of euphemistic view, Paul Nitze, in surveying the damage at Hiroshima, attempted to "measure precisely" the bomb's impact, "to put calipers on it, instead of describing it in emotive terms." The result of this exercise was his determination that the dropping of the atomic bomb was simply equivalent to an incendiary bombing raid by "210 B-29s at Hiroshima and 120 B-29s at Nagasaki."[31] Nitze certainly captured a bit of the truth of those events, and this characterization made the work of surveying such carnage somewhat more bearable; but he was leaving something out. This process of quantification and elimination of death and the horror of war from discussion of even the results of Nagasaki and Hiroshima was a common feature of élite discourse.

During Vietnam, the élite's practice of "visualizing the war in their own terms" meant that they also excluded death from the picture. The most well-known metaphors of the war, the quantified body count, lent itself to a depersonalizing of the human losses in the war.[32] But this hiding of the body was a much more prevalent and pernicious element of the discourse on war. Because the élite could not "see" the enemy in Vietnam, an enemy that embodied death itself, it was possible then to talk about the war as if no Americans would be dying there. For example, Dean Rusk would argue, using rather puzzling language, that "[i]t is difficult to worry about massive casualties when we say we can't find the enemy. I feel strongly that one dead man is a massive casualty, but in the sense that we are talking, I don't see large casualties unless the Chinese come in."[33] Rusk was certainly troubled by American deaths (and perhaps *because* those deaths were so troubling to him), but the picture he created of the war in Vietnam was devoid of death. Any death, he claimed, would be a "massive casualty;" but as there would only be "massive casualties" if the Chinese came in, and it did not look like the Chinese were going to enter the war, it would be as if no Americans were dying. Rusk's words thus created a picture of Vietnam in which he could not "see" any American deaths. Death could only be seen if the large, conventional (highly visible) Chinese forces came in, and as the élite were doing everything they could to keep the Chinese out, it was as if the deaths of American soldiers did not have to enter their field of vision.

As Elaine Scarry points out, during wartime, the "embodying" of the nation is part of a rhetorical move whereby the actual bodies of the soldiers dying in battle are removed from the discourse, while the groups battling are described as having bodies, body parts, anatomies, and so on. In this way, the concern or discomfort with the mutilation of the bodies occurring on the battlefield is appropriated by the strategic discourse, by those who view the "large picture." The injuries and deaths then become "imaginary" injuries to an imaginary creature.[34] This allows those discussing war to address concerns about the body in such a way that the body in question is resilient and potentially immortal. This trope of the artificial body enabled those using that language to relegate the physical, mortal body to the background.

This was another way in which the concerns about mortality were transferred to a realm over which the élite had power. In élite discourse, the physical body disappeared and it was the bureaucratic creations of the élite that lived and died. Woodrow Wilson, in a Fourth of July Speech in 1918 beside Washington's tomb, would refer to the tomb by which he was standing as being not "a place of death, [but] a place of achievement." The gathering that day had many "inspirited associations of that noble death which is only a glorious consummation."[35] In Acheson's memoirs covering the period through World War II and the Korean War, there is no mention of people dying; he briefly mentions a division being "destroyed" and another that "lost half its strength" or had "severe casualties," but of the over 50 million dead in those two wars and countless millions more mutilated bodies and minds, there is no mention. In contrast to this, his discussion of life in Washington within the context of its institutions and official roles reads like a combination of graphic war story and the account from a maternity ward.[36] As we saw in Chapter 4, it was the bureaucratic creations of the élite that lived and died, rather than any actual physical bodies.

In the Vietnam conflict, despite their best efforts to do so, the élite never did escape from the jungle or from the mysteries of death there. As Lyndon Johnson would put it, despite all their best efforts at gaining the clear view, "Everything blurs when you get almost to the gate."[37] In the end, there was no clear choice in Vietnam, and Johnson failed to get to the gate that would release him, give him control, give him the place on Mount Rushmore that he sought. One reason their vision was blurred was that in trying to create too much order where so little existed, the élite, to a certain extent, lost touch with reality. Dean Acheson, who Johnson occasionally sought for counsel on the war, would capture some sense of this in advice he gave to Johnson in early 1968. After getting detailed briefing from people who had gone digging in the "muck" of Vietnam, Acheson had come to oppose the war, and he warned Johnson that the military was "leading you down the garden path." In trying too hard to visualize and turn Vietnam into a "garden," Johnson and his advisors had failed to fully come to terms with what was unavoidably a jungle war.[38] By seeking to completely master the jungle in Vietnam, instead of immersing themselves in it, they doomed themselves to failure. As doctors in their enthusiasm and infatuation with defeating "the disease" often end up neglecting the patient, so the United States—as one army officer put it in Vietnam—often engaged in "destroying the village in order to save it."[39]

In reflecting on the symbolic content of foreign policy discourse we need to be particularly careful about the ways in which death can be hidden from view and enemies vilified. As Americans are a particularly powerful people and their leaders extraordinarily powerful, we need to be aware as well of the ways in which power can contribute to these distortions. This tendency among the élite to shelter themselves from death was related in key ways to the power they possessed. Power breeds both responsibility and corruption. That we should be made responsible because of the great power at our disposal is cause for celebration; that it also has certainly corrupted us should be of some concern.[40] As Dean Acheson observed, exercising power in office was like a "habit-forming drug";

power can have certain addictive qualities. The exercise of power can be used to shelter oneself from harsh realities and inner pain, and in a country and during a time when that drug has been in ample supply, perhaps some attention to potential dangers in its abuse are called for. James Forrestal was referred to as someone "addicted" to power; when that power was taken away, he disintegrated. The habitual and never ending searches for "great prizes" engaged in by Theodore Roosevelt, John Hay, and Henry Stimson have an addictive ring to them as well. As the narcotic effect of each new success wore off, they would feel compelled to search for a new prize, a new high.

For some, however, the power was not sufficient and they resorted to other drugs to help hide the pain, suffering, and mutilation from view; in particularly trying times during the Vietnam War, some of the élite saw the need to resort to other drugs as part of their attempts at dealing with the stresses of war. Dean Rusk claimed he made it through 1968 on a daily diet of "aspirin, scotch, and four packs of Larks." And when asked how he dealt emotionally with the casualties, Robert McNamara replied, "Sleeping pills help. . . . It also helps to believe in what you're doing and to know that the men who are fighting the war also believe clearly in what they're doing." And if even some of Anthony Summer's muckraking on Nixon is true, it appears that the thirty-seventh president dealt with the stresses of office by being "stoned out of his mind on Seconal, single-malt Scotch, Dilantin, and speed," and was kept away from the nuclear button by his secretary of defense.[41] George Ball would claim as well that the massive bombing campaigns in Vietnam were a kind of "pain-killing exercise that saved my colleagues from having to face the hard decision to withdraw."[42] One reason that decision was so painful was that, if the war was a path to Life, admitting defeat in the war was tantamount to acknowledging mortality. This kind of addictive behavior, and the attempt to believe, perhaps a bit too clearly, in what one was doing, is a sign of the unhealthiness of the denial in which these élite engaged. Although not wanting to belittle the pressures and responsibilities resting on these élite, it seems we should be able to come up with better means of coping with death in battle than sleeping pills and Seconal, and that we should be able to think of less destructive means than bombing to assuage the pain elicited by facing our mortality. To keep some sense of perspective and minimize the carnage we seem so good at causing, we would do well to examine ways of socially reconstructing death in battle. And to help in that process, it is helpful to understand the changing social context in which the social construction of death is occurring. As we witness this change toward a depoliticized discourse on war and death, there are other shifts in the cultural context of U.S. foreign policy.

The Dying of Death in Battle

Much of this story about foreign policy leaders and their symbolic land-scapes would seem to apply to a set of premodern (perhaps modern, but not postmodern) notions like heroism, machismo, hand-to-hand combat, and conventional warfare. We are in the era of "post," in which everything from the Cold War to Modernity itself is supposedly coming to an end. Much has changed, especially in regard to how Americans have fought wars since Vietnam, however, many of the atavistic elements of martial culture are still around and unlikely to disappear anytime soon. In looking at events attending the end of the second millennium—in places such as the Persian Gulf, the Balkans, and the Congo—one is struck, not so much by it being a "brave new world," but by the combination of both the old-est and newest of human activities—as indicated by phrases such as "back to the future," "the new Hapsburgs," and the "Lexus and the Olive Tree." We now live in a world in which wars of rape and pillage that are virtually indistinguishable from the fighting in Carthage, Agincourt, or the four-teenth-century Battle of Kosovo, exist alongside the ultra-high tech, long-range wars waged by U.S., UN, and NATO forces. We live in a brave new world in which the importance of religion and myths of autochthony (the idea that a people sprang up from the soil of a particular territory) are not diminished but, rather, has been supplemented by spy satellites, arsenals full of nuclear weapons, the Euro, and the global financial markets.[43]

While knife and gun are still used for most of the killing in wars around the globe today, the technologically advanced nations are waging war over longer and longer distances and at greater speeds, making it possible to minimize the risks for their soldiers. As the standards of living and quality of life have risen for most Americans, peacetime has grown in-creasingly attractive. We are not living in an age in which individual sac-rifice for the good of all is embraced as a widely shared value. Along with this, the increase in the number of women involved in making foreign policy arguably is shifting the cultural and psychological dynamics of in-ternational decision making.[44] Madeleine Albright and the increasing number of high-ranking women in the foreign policy establishment are using many of the traditional elements of foreign policy discourse, but they also are speaking about war and peace in ways that include a greater willingness to openly express and acknowledge the painful emotions stirred up by war.[45] These developments are changing how the American public and leadership are thinking and talking about death in battle. As American society underwent what James Farrell has called the "dying of death" in the late nineteenth century, so at the end of the twentieth, we seem to witnessing at least a temporary end to death in battle.

One ironic result of the increasingly technologized discourse of foreign policy is that it has made it more difficult for the élite to justify war and sell the general public on the idea of death in battle. In a way, the sanitized and technical language of war makes it easier to talk about killing and, thus, makes it easier to go to war. But this language has real limitations, in that it cannot offer a coherent account of the meaning of the deaths occurring during war. In the same way that rational choice theories of war cannot take account of the meaning of death in battle, so the rationalist justifications for war ring hollow. The symbolic and cultural foundation of justifying death in battle has been undermined to the extent now that we have largely lost the political vocabulary for justifying the sacrifice of the young. For TR and MacArthur, what mattered most was the act of martial martyrdom; it did not matter so much *what* the war was being fought for as that soldiers *were willing to die* for that cause. Bill Clinton, by contrast, can only speak of the soldiers who died for America as having died for a particular purpose, say, to maintain the American way of life. But the problem is that it is hard to enjoy the American way of life when you are dead. In America now, what matters is the cause. But it is hard to justify dying for a cause, unless the deaths themselves can be construed as transcendent, and instrumental economic discourse is ill suited for the task. Although the mythoreligious language is not gone, it resonates less in the third millennium than in those that preceded it.

In the American context, in addition to these broad technological and cultural changes, the particular national experience of the Vietnam War seriously undermined the traditional martial logic of foreign policy discourse. The experience of protracted, televised, and morally questionable war shook the faith of a large segment of society. With war framed as a battle against death, the experience of defeat can be a shock to the collective confidence of the American psyche, sufficient in the case of Vietnam to merit the diagnosis of a syndrome that prompted a national effort to repair the shattered national ego and sense of manhood.[46] Up until that time, all the battles with death had finished the same way the James Bond movies had. Thus, it was entirely fitting that the memorial to Vietnam took the form of the black, immovable, grave-deep wall, in which all that remained of the American soldiers was their names, and all that remained of the million dead Vietnamese was their absence.[47] There visitors are forced to stand and face the wall, and see themselves reflected in its depth.

Recent surveys have shown that American citizens still claim to be willing to send troops into battle as long as they think the chances of victory are good.[48] When posed as a hypothetical question this may be the case but, since Vietnam, the minimization of casualties has been a mainstay of the doctrine governing the use of force. History cautions us from leaping to conclusion that this is a real trend, but the signs are that it is harder to find causes for which Americans are willing to die. Nowhere was this more clearly demonstrated than in the Clinton administration and Army's refusal to use the "state of the art" Apache helicopter during the fighting in Kosovo in 1999, for fear that it might get shot down by some soldier with a bazooka hiding behind a tree. The intervention there was guided by the Clinton administration's express desire to "avoid casualties at all cost." Where Teddy Roosevelt stoically thought "only of victory" when his sons were off fighting in World War I, in the war in Kosovo, the commander of the bombing campaign, Lt. Gen. Michael Short choked back tears as he recalled how one night his son's plane was hit by anti-aircraft fire: "And he called me on a secure phone. I picked up the phone and his first words were, 'Don't tell mom,' because he had been hit that night. The litmus test I felt I had to pass every night was if my son were killed in Kosovo, I needed to be able to tell his mother and his wife that he was killed doing something that I thought would help bring the war to a close. . . ."[49] Although General Short, too, was thinking about victory, and like any parent, dreaded losing his child, there was a distinctly un-Pattonesque tone to his statements. America has become very concerned about the fate of particular soldiers, so that the loss of even one individual has become highly charged. As Edward Luttwak argues, we appear to be living now in a postheroic era, in which Americans are increasingly unwilling to accept any casualties.[50] As symbolic of this change, the Defense Department recently announced the opening of its new retirement home, appropriately called the "Home for Heroes." The heroes, it would seem, are mostly all retired.

These heightened political costs associated with the deaths of American soldiers stems from changes both internationally and domestically. War has become potentially so destructive as to completely undermine the old myth of regeneration through violence. New weapons of mass destruction pose threats to the entire global society, thereby rendering total war self-defeating; the symbolic logic of mutually assured destruction does not allow national leaders to construct war as the sacrifice of individual soldiers to insure the survival of the nation.[51] Although the end of the Cold War has pushed this possibility somewhat further into the backs of our minds, the possibility remains. And to the extent it is there, it renders the institution of war itself suspect. If we cannot fight total wars against the Enemy, and defeat them unconditionally (as in World War II), then we are left in the uncomfortable position of having to accept that enemy in some way, and learn to live with them. Limited wars, such as Korea and Vietnam, have never been as psychologically satisfying to Americans as the wholesale destruction of total war, but that is what we are left with in the era of nuclear weapons. Now the technology itself has become the source of death, and the old rituals of war are being reworked.

Changes in military technology have often had profound effects on how wars are waged and, therefore, also how we think about battle.[52] From the visceral experience of hand-to-hand combat to the wanton slaughter of trench warfare to the abstract and sanitized experience of carpet bombing and ICBMs, the experience of those waging wars has been shaped by the technology through which it has been mediated. The technological sophistication and sheer superiority of the U.S. military is now making it easier to avoid American casualties altogether. It is becoming difficult to consider American military engagement abroad as "warfare" at all, in the sense of involving deaths on each side. Perhaps the primary reason why presidents from Carter to Clinton have been so reluctant to risk American lives abroad is because they have had that option of using force with minimal risk of Americans getting shot.

Not that this kind of technological superiority is entirely new—the slaughter of relatively defenseless indigenous peoples has been a mainstay of imperial encounters with the rest of the world. U.S. soldiers in the Philippines during the Spanish-American War would describe their battles with Filipino rebels as like hunting rabbits, and most of the worries and casualties of those wars stemmed from nonhuman dangers such as disease. But as the technology of speed and distance has advanced, it has become possible for the troops of the most technologically advanced armies to obtain that kind of advantage even against relatively powerful and well-armed opponents, and in effect to wage war without being anywhere near the enemy. For the U.S. soldier, combat with Iraq and the Yugoslav Army has amounted to a sophisticated video game of dodging anti-aircraft fire at 40,000 feet and feeding coordinates into the guidance systems of cruise missiles. For the time being, American technological superiority has allowed soldiers to wage war with about as much risk as driving on the average Los Angeles freeway. The old logic of battle is then turned on its head. Instead of military service entailing a significant increase in the chances of dying, it now involves little or no change. In the modern, all-volunteer military, service has become first and foremost a job, and if it is an adventure, it is not generally a life-threatening one.

For a number of soldiers, particularly in élite units such as the Marines, SEALS, and Rangers, there is still a strong sense of the martial spirit, but it appears less and less needed. New recruits still go through the transformative rituals of basic training but recently, when deployed, end up being greeted by the press on the shores of Somalia, or handing out food rations in relief missions, or taking a break from their work-outs in the ship's gym to go fire off another round of cruise missiles at targets hundreds of miles away. As relatively high profile representatives of U.S. hegemony, they are exposed to random terrorist attacks, but so are U.S. embassy workers in Africa and federal employees in Oklahoma City. Whatever inspiration might have been derived from the intensity and *esprit de corps* of wars of the past has significantly diminished, and now soldiers are instead demanding higher pay as compensation for having to deal with the Byzantine workings of the world's largest bureaucracy. The Defense Department continues to struggle with declining recruitment, and is responding not so much with references to the Motherland and Freedom but with higher pay and benefits.[53]

The military leadership is likewise forced now to speak of the soldier not as a hero but as a professional. Secretary of Defense William Cohen and Joint Chiefs of Staff Chairman Shelton concluded in their post-Kosovo report that, "The paramount lesson learned from Operation Allied Force is that the well-being of our people must remain our first priority." In his speeches regarding the troops, Cohen did not say they fought but, instead, that they were creative, they had initiative, they were good engineers, and, therefore, they needed to be adequately compensated. The Secretary of Defense used the language of an employer, saying the workers needed a pay raise, less inconveniences, better benefits—or else the company would lose its workers to some employer who paid better. In a strange turn of events, it seems that the U.S. army has employees, and it is the foreign oil companies in places like Colombia that have the soldiers, hired to protect their operations in the civil war there.

Another characteristic of the era of globalization is that the dangers that remain after the collapse of the Soviet Union are distant and amorphous, not the kind of large-scale, conventional threats that would warrant another D-Day. The U.S. military's emphasis now is on increased global mobility—that is, carrying out policing actions on short notice at great distance from America's borders. The main effort at a strictly territorial defense now involves no troops at all, but the twin efforts of using scrap metal from the Gulf War to build a wall between the United States and Mexico and the to-date failed attempt at developing the technology of ballistic missile defense. In the era of globalization, the nation-state itself—the traditional organizational form of the gravest threats to American national security—appears less relevant. The nation is clearly still the primary locus of military power, but the use of force now occurs across a much more diffuse and shifting set of boundaries. The main actors in the recent American engagements overseas have been the "ethnic Albanians," the Serb army (another ethnic grouping, though linked to a state), and NATO or the United Nations. It is getting harder to determine whether states are using international organizations to pursue their foreign policy agenda or whether international organizations and ethnic groups and multinational corporations are using the state (and its armies) to further their interests instead.

Using familiar language, Madeleine Albright would identify a "viper's nest of perils"—nuclear weapons, regional wars that might spread, terrorism, and "war against narcotics trafficking and the hydra-headed evil of international crime"—but these have not yet proved sufficiently vivid to inspire great sacrifice on the part of the American citizen-soldier.[54] The *New York Times* reported on November 11, 1999, that the United States wanted its European allies to "carry out a 'defense capabilities initiative' within NATO to reshape the alliance's fighting forces, some still designed to defend home territory from *the now nonexistent threat of foreign invasion.*" In the birthplace of sovereignty and power politics, the threat of foreign military invasion appears for the time being to be nonexistent. The main threats to U.S. security now come from a variety of nonstate actors, such as the mythic Osama bin Laden; the cruise missile strikes on Sudan and Afghanistan, dubbed "Operation Infinite Reach" (a bit of a stretch), were supposed to demonstrate U.S. power but, instead, showed U.S. vulnerability and limitations. In the mid-nineteenth century, public health officials used to clear the "foul airs," or miasmas, by firing cannons into the air.[55] Although the scientific basis for this practice was clearly weak, civic leaders still felt compelled to try to destroy the enemy. It seems our current foreign policy is guided in part by a similar symbolic logic. In such a context, the old calls for sacrifice for the nation ring hollow, and the successors to TR and Stimson and Acheson are having a difficult time selling the need for an active foreign policy.

The modern Western reluctance to send teenagers into harms way stems as well from the increased pervasiveness and impact of media coverage of war—first in Vietnam *qua* horror flick, and then war as spectacle *qua* video game in the U.S. bombing of Iraq and Belgrade.[56] The advances in the ability to gather and manipulate these images from war has made it politically hazardous to risk American lives, while at the same time turning the high-tech wars into a kind of national spectator sport. The graphic reality of news footage has made it harder for political leaders to sanitize, glorify, or hide the grim reality of American casualties, on the rare occasions now that there are any. The footage of the U.S. Rangers killed and dragged through the streets of Mogadishu attests to the power of that imagery on foreign policy deliberations. At the same time, the power of television has made it possible to turn the destruction of Iraqis and Serbs into a highly sanitized technological extravaganza. The networks know of no better spectacle to capture the public's attention than images of destruction and death, especially images of American soldiers killed in action. As the media phenomenon of "Survivor" illustrates, the American television-viewing audience has an abiding interest in who lives and who dies in the battles being waged on distant shores. Since Vietnam, the double equation of what's good for the ratings is bad for presidential popularity generally has held. The public eat up scandal, mayhem, death, and disaster with a nearly insatiable appetite, and are then only too happy to blame these troubles on those in charge, or, when "our team wins," to celebrate the victory. The military's ability to limit press access and censor reporting may lessen this effect, but the immediacy and visual impact of televised war make it harder for Americans to accept death in battle.

Beyond these technological changes, the social context on the home front has increased Americans' reluctance to risk their lives. As medicine gradually extends longevity and improves quality of life, the incentive to "do battle with death" in a symbolic realm decreases.[57] Teddy Roosevelt and his generation faced a plethora of mortal threats and incurable diseases that made warfare as much a relief as a danger, since at least in warfare the source of one's death could be known, faced, and, if you were a good enough shot, killed. Many of the people fighting or volunteering for military service do so because their lives are miserable and they want to change, but in the popular imagination of mainstream Americans, as their lives grow ever more comfortable, war is losing the glory previously attributed to it. U.S. interventions abroad are inconvenient for the troops, because they have to be away from their loved ones, and there always is the chance that something might go wrong (as with periodic terrorist attacks); but, generally speaking, the soldiers are not being asked to do anything even approaching the kind of fighting seen at Gettysburg or Verdun or Okinawa.

Although this might make it more likely that force will be used (since the risks are minimal), paradoxically this also weakens the emotional foundations of nationalism. If the nation is built, reified, and reinforced by the deaths of its native sons, when those sons are no longer dying, the need for the nationalistic appeals likewise declines. In such an atmosphere, there also is more room for oppositional voices to be included in foreign policy debates, as those voices cannot be labeled as dishonoring the soldiers killed for "the cause." It is possible that one development of this relatively risk-free warfare is that meaningful political debate will no longer stop so abruptly at the water's edge, but that we will be able to speak somewhat more freely about the merits of our interventions abroad without immediately being charged with dishonoring the noble dead.

It seems then that we will be in a period, for some time, in which the old rituals and understandings of death and nationalism will be shifting. The deaths we will have to make sense of will not be of Americans, but of Serbs, or Iraqis, or Colombian rebels. We have already seen shifts from the Manichean and millennial Cold War rhetoric of the Reagan administration to the language of transition and "new world order" in the Bush administration, to the more optimistic liberalism of the Clinton administration.[58] This, however, could change. Should the technological and geopolitical realities shift sufficiently, and we find ourselves again in another July 1914, our work will be cut out for us. If, by some miracle, we perhaps manage to avoid the maelstrom of our own making the next time, it will require our having plumbed the depths, in a self-aware, courageous, and compassionate way, of our own mortality and fears.

RECONSTRUCTING DEATH IN BATTLE

One of the principal ways in which war has been justified, and could be justified in the future, is by framing it as a way of overcoming death itself. While Hobbes would argue that the "Feare of Death" is one of the "Passions that encline [sic] men to Peace," the fear of death also paradoxically drives people to war.[59] Bismarck once remarked that waging preventive war was "like committing suicide from fear of death." It might seem equally foolish and irrational to justify going to war by drawing on an underlying fear of death; but, to some degree, it appears that this has been a prominent part of American understandings of war. The élite immortality project addressed the underlying fears about mortality raised by the prospect or reality of war by offering some authoritative reassurance that the deaths occurring in battle were in fact a path to life. In and of itself this symbolic construction need not be problematic—there may even be a grain of "truth" in it, to the extent that the nation can serve as basis for a transcendent identity that genuinely meets the needs of those who have faith in it.

What this implies for policy and the study of war is simply that we need to be careful in our use of the rhetorically powerful symbols found within these immortality projects. The language of medicine and disease, beasts and lusts, floods and dams, all tap into powerful emotions that themselves stem from deeply troubling aspects of the human condition.[60] When war is necessary, the prosecution of that war is certainly made easier by the use of such a social construction of death in battle to help those who must face death and those who must mourn their loss.

It should not be *necessary*, however, to glorify death in battle in these ways; for, if as a society we are unable to face the prospect of death without such schemes, it follows that when those schemes are used, it may well appear that the deaths in battle are necessary, no matter what the "real" aims or necessity of fighting. The problem arises when that imagery is used in cases where war may not be called for or justified. The determination of the necessity or justice of a particular war is a complex issue. But whatever justifications or reasoning are given for going to war, we must be certain that they are not based on a social construction of the war as a glorious battle against a foe representing Death. If those charged with selling war to the American public reply that they can only do so through the use of such high-powered rhetoric, then they are selling the wrong wars. If a war is truly justified, we should be able to justify it in plain language, wage it reluctantly, and end with something less than the glee and exuberance expressed at the close of the Gulf War. Such is not our want, but it is what a full facing of mortality warrants.

This separation between "social construction" and "reality" is never completely possible because these metaphors and social constructions are always and necessarily part of how we view the world and make foreign policy decisions. The best we can do is attempt to be as aware and self-conscious as we can be in our use of these metaphors and myths. The best we can hope for is to use our awareness of the contingent and subjective nature of our social constructions as the basis for a healthy skepticism that leads us to a careful analysis of the assumptions, values, and emotional associations that will always form the basis of our understandings of the world.

The lessons to be drawn from this research are similar in many ways to those stemming from the study of the uses and abuses of historical analogies and "lessons" in foreign policy. As Richard Neustadt, Ernest May, Yuen Foong Khong, and others point out, élite frequently used historical analogies in guiding foreign policy decisions in ways that were problematic.[61] These authors call for the more careful and conscious use of these analogies and offer a number of useful guidelines that might help improve the quality of the decision-making process. Likewise, the implications of the new literature on the role of "ideas," ideology, and culture in foreign policy are simply that we need to be aware and careful in our use of the ideas and philosophies that underlie foreign policy decision making.

As with other psychological or sociological explanations, the prescribed remedies are the generally unsatisfying calls for consciousness raising and, to quote Hannah Arendt once again, "thinking what we are doing." But we should not dismiss such prescriptions simply because they are unsatisfying. Rather, it behooves us to examine why we find them unsatisfying. Perhaps one reason this is so is that we want the easy, the technical, and apolitical solution, the solution that does not involve looking within ourselves, or recognizing our fears. If we accept that the human condition is uncomfortable, and that the truth about it therefore unsatisfying, that there may be no easy button to push that will make war go away, then we should seek out the unsatisfying answers, for certainly the human destructive propensities that have been with us for so long are not going to be easily overcome.

That the suggestions offered here are not simple or easy is seen in other ways. We still need rituals and mythologies that make sense of death; at the same time we need to recognize the dangers of the oversimplification that attend this mythmaking. One of the great appeals of these mythologies, and an inherent aspect of them, is their simplification and ordering of the world. But this simplification is often the source of misunderstanding and unnecessary antagonism. What is needed is a self-conscious use of these myths and the development of worldviews that are sufficiently complex to incorporate the paradoxes and contradictions of our existence. But these myths are, of course, only powerful to the extent that they are not seen as myths but as unquestioned truths. To assert their contingency is to destroy them for the faithful. Khong notes as well the difficulty inherent in trying to make the use of analogies more careful and conscious, since they are such an integral part of our thought processes.[62] We need then to devise other forms of faith, other forms of ritual that can incorporate both the need for beliefs and a recognition that it is we ourselves who must devise them. Thus, a call for a conscious structuring of society's unquestioned structures implies existing in that precarious realm in which meaning must be both created, questioned, believed, and used.

As alluded to earlier in this chapter, one of the more promising avenues whereby these metaphors can be used more carefully is through a revival of that form of politics that is so largely absent from the debates over war and peace. In debates in Congress over intervention in the Philippines—as rancorous, emotional, and lengthy as they may have been—the elected officials openly and seriously discussed the basic moral and philosophical issues at stake in the war. To a much larger degree than in the debates in Vietnam or the Gulf War, they directly addressed what the soldiers were dying for. One might think that the arena of war was one devoid of politics and that a call for repoliticizing war talk is misguided. As Arendt points out, politics ends once we stop talking and resort to violence.[63] But there is an element of politics that remains, even in the interaction between armies, and certainly in the decisions leading up to war. One way of reading von Clausewitz's dictum that "war is only a branch of political activity" is to point out that political compromise, dialogue, and bargaining are still integral aspects of war.[64] In another sense, war is the quintessential political act, in that it necessitates defining what one is willing to die for. That such questions are now largely absent from discussions of war is another sign of the depoliticization of foreign policy. Thus, one problem with the rise of technical conception of politics is that it has downplayed the importance of these elements during wartime. There is certainly some merit to the argument for leaving the technical aspects of foreign policy to the experts and technicians in the Executive Branch. But war is a matter of self-definition, a situation in which the very meaning of life and death are brought into question and we are forced to define the core values of our existence. The answers to the questions and the formulation of identity are inherently social and political, and can best be brought about through the process of open discussion, rather than reliance on a set of overworn metaphors and euphemisms trotted out by national security managers and passively absorbed by a media-saturated public.

Whereas it would be both futile and counterproductive to propose some ideal social construction of death in battle, this project suggests some ways of coming to terms with death to which we might want to pay greater attention. One such response to mortality, in broadest terms, combines a greater willingness to accept the tragic nature of death and limitations of the human condition with a sense of the responsibilities and powers that might sometimes need to be used to maintain order or justice. In adopting this stance toward death in battle, we would be better able to face those deaths and accept them as sometimes necessary, even when not framed as part of the battle with death and the search for a transcendence of the body. If we can face death and the pain and sadness that goes with it and yet still recognize the occasional necessity of the use of force, we will have gone a long way toward making the problems of provocation, aggression, and appeasement less likely. Such a response may not be psychologically possible or politically feasible, for it appears that we are generally not willing to accept and mourn deaths in battle as tragic, and repeatedly construct them as part of this ritual overcoming of death that involves vilifying one's opponents.[65] But there are some signs in the élite discourse that some acceptance of death is possible.

As this work has focused on the lives of a few of the foreign policy élite, it is only fitting to conclude by turning to these archetypal "fathers" for some examples of alternative ways of facing mortality and coming to terms with death in battle. There were problematic aspects to the language used by all the élite, and it would not be too much of a stretch to characterize most of them as a power-hungry, vain, racist, sexist, and neurotic group of rich WASP men; there are, however, elements of their lives that provide us with positive alternatives to the dominant discourse on death. Not all the élite hid death from view or sought an escape from the human condition through indulgence in the wonderful powers of science's new technologies. In keeping with the aim of humanizing these men, it is necessary to look at their strengths as well as their weaknesses.

Although this book has painted a fairly critical picture of the discourse used by Teddy Roosevelt, we see in his life a willingness to accept death

as tragic and a willingness to pull his weight and risk his own life when he
felt the cause was just. Although he engaged in ritual battle against death
and glorified war, he did so in part because of his awareness of mortality.
He was, after all, willing to face death in battle, and did not try to gloss
over the material or physical aspects of human existence. As but one example of an alternative discourse, one that recognizes and accepts the
gruesome nature of warfare, we can turn to Roosevelt's own account of
the deaths he witnessed in battle. The graphic nature of his language reflects the tensions in his relationship toward death and is refreshingly devoid of the stale euphemisms of élite discourse. Although glorifying the
death of the soldier, he also worried that, when yellow fever broke out in
their camp, the troops would die like "rotten sheep"; in a letter to his sister Corrinne, Roosevelt went to some length to describe the physical aspects of the deaths in Cuba:

> It was very trying to stand, or advance slowly, while the men fell dead or
> wounded, shot down from we knew not whence; for smokeless powder ren-
> ders it almost impossible to place a hidden foe. The morning after the fight
> we buried our dead in a great big trench, reading the solemn burial service
> over them, and all the regiment joining in singing "Rock of Ages." The vul-
> tures were wheeling overhead by hundreds. They plucked out the eyes and
> tore the faces and the wounds of the dead Spaniards before we got to them,
> and even one of our own men who lay in the open. The wounded lay in the
> path, a ghastly group; . . . a couple died in the night, . . . The woods are full
> of land crabs, some of which are almost as big as rabbits; when things grew
> quiet they slowly gathered in gruesome rings around the fallen."[66]

As in Sledge's account of Okinawa, the image presented by Roosevelt is
both graphic and arresting—war reveals an aspect of the human condition, not as transcendent but instead as food for crustaceans and carrion
fowl. In his fascination with these details, Roosevelt reveals as well something of the horror they held for him. There is something both admirable
and repulsive in this story about land crabs, and in Roosevelt's focus on
the body and its fate in battle. We would do well to question Roosevelt's
motivations for the use of this kind of language in this letter (it smacks of
emotional bullying), but the language has a certain honesty that we
should reintegrate into our policy deliberations and studies of war.

In other élite we see different forms of facing death. There is something
both comic and gruesome in George Hoar's call for America to wage war,
"inspired by a sentiment even toward her enemies not of hate but of
love . . . [with] a dangerous light in her eye, but with a smile on her lips";
if taken seriously, it expresses an admirable sentiment.[67] Although the

image is both hopelessly idealistic and conjures up thoughts of Hitchcock's Norman Bates as much as of Hoar's beloved St. George, it expresses still a profound and difficult challenge—that of loving, even in the midst of battle. If we can imagine for a moment waging war against an enemy who is not portrayed as a cancerous tumor, a "gook," a "Hun," a monkey, or an anti-Christ, but instead who is seen as a human being, not unlike oneself, whom it will always be a tragedy to kill—if we can still convince ourselves with open eyes and hearts that that death needs to happen, and seek it only with the greatest reluctance, then we will have gone a long way toward moving beyond the jingoism to which Hoar so objected, and the destructive crusading mentality of the Cold War and Gulf War.

There was a certain compassion and expression of the tensions of the human condition in Lyndon Johnson as well, who, for all his faults, did appear to genuinely wish to minimize the loss of life, and to be aware of the costs of war. After leaving office, the "very human President" would advise Doris Kearns Goodwin to spend more time with her children, and that he would "have been better off looking for immortality through my wife and children."[68] Johnson's advice should perhaps be more widely heeded by an élite intent on distancing themselves from the family—that site where emotion is more accepted, and that provides perhaps the most basic and profound form of overcoming death, through birth. Part of the project of breaking down the boundaries between life and death, culture and nature, is likewise blurring the already problematic distinction between public and private, male and female.

The "realism" embodied in the honest acceptance of limits and mortality is also found in part in the traditional realism of Reinhold Neibuhr, Hans Morgenthau, and George Kennan, who saw mortality as a central and defining characteristic of human existence and based their foreign policy beliefs on that understanding.[69] In Kennan and Morgenthau's calls for an avoidance of crusades and their recognition that even the United States has limits, there is a welcome antidote to the technological hubris that has dominated our thinking during the last century. And in Niebuhr's arguments that violence is rarely effective and should be avoided whenever possible, but that it still may be necessary, we see how we may be able to live on that tenuous and uncomfortable boundary between war and peace which seems to be our fate. As such, these are aspects of this realism that we would do well to retain, especially in light of the relatively dehumanized and ethereal structural neorealism that has by-and-large replaced it in the field of political science. This, then, is a call for a "realism" grounded in the body's integral role in war and in an emotional realism that is willing to face the pain and sorrow of death without need of engaging in the martial rituals elaborated above.

We get one last example of this of language of acceptance in John Kennedy's 1963 American University speech on world peace. The search for peace, he declared in language uncharacteristic of the élite, must "begin by looking inward." Rather than engage in the projection common in élite discourse, Kennedy argued that the Cold War and dangers of a hot war could not be attributed solely to the Soviet Union or any other external entity. He expressed optimism about the human ability to control their fate, while recognizing that certain aspect of the human condition— including mortality—could not be changed. The basis for cooperation and empathy with those beyond our national boundaries was based, for Kennedy, on some of those shared aspects of the human condition. "For in the final analysis our most basic common link is that we all inhabit this same small planet. We all breathe the same air. We all cherish our children's future. And we are all mortal."[70] That final statement—to which his early death added much poignancy—merits repetition. For all its obviousness, it is a fact that we of late have been too eager to avoid, especially in talking about war, and we are the poorer for it.

If the metaphors we use to come to terms with death may sometimes shape our discussion and thinking about war, perhaps we need to develop, in a more self-conscious manner, new metaphors for war. Instead of seeing death as a hideous beast crouching in the shadows of the jungle, we might want to think of it instead as the shadow cast by our own bodies onto the ground before us. If we are too used to looking at all that is bright and vibrant, we may see the shadow as nothing but blackness. But if we look at it long enough, perhaps our eyes will grow accustomed to the light, and be able to see that in the shadow there is still solid ground on which to stand. Most important, in facing our mortality, as implied by that metaphor, we will fully own that shadow as something that is the inevitable—and perhaps even beautiful—result of being creatures who live in and see the light, and yet have bodies through which that light cannot pass. Perhaps in this image lies one more path along which to struggle if we are to move a little closer to finding less destructive ways of settling our differences and negotiating the complexities of the human condition.

ENDNOTES

ABBREVIATIONS

The following abbreviations are used in citing the most common government sources in the endnotes:

CR   *Congressional Record*
FRUS   *Foreign Relations of the United States*
PP   *Pentagon Papers, Hearings before the House Subcommittee on Government Operations*
PPG   *Pentagon Papers,* Senator Gravel Edition

PREFACE

1. Arthur Bochner, "It's about Time: Narrative and the Divided Self," *Qualitative Inquiry* 3, no. 4 (Dec. 1997), pp. 418–38; James Der Derian's opening passage in *Antidiplomacy: Spies, Terror, Speed, and War* (Cambridge, MA: Blackwell, 1992) with its description of his recurring dream about a dog, bone, and cave is one nice exception to this rule.

2. Benedict Anderson, *Imagined Communities: Reflections on the Origin and Spread of Nationalism,* Revised Edition (New York: Verso, 1991), p. 11.

3. Sigmund Freud, *Thoughts for the Times on War and Death,* in Collected Works of Sigmund Freud, edited by James Strachey and Anna Freud (London: Hogarth Press), p. 289.

4. Slovoj Žižek, *Looking Awry: An Introduction to Jacques Lacan through Popular Culture* (Cambridge, MA: MIT Press, 1993).

5. See Fred C. Ikle, *Every War Must End,* Revised Edition (New York: Columbia University Press, 1991); John Mueller, "Trends in Popular Support for the Wars in Korea and Vietnam," *American Political Science Review* 65, no. 2 (1971), p. 358–72; Scott Sigmund Gartner and Gary M. Segura, "War, Casualties, and Public Opinion," *Journal of Conflict Resolution* 42, no. 3 (June 1998) pp. 278–300; Donald Wittman, "How a War Ends: A Rational Model Approach," *Journal of Conflict Resolution* 23, no. 4 (1979), pp. 743–63.

INTRODUCTION

1. Charles Baudelaire, "On the Essence of Laughter" (1855), in *The Painter of Modern Life, and Other Essays,* translated and edited by Jonathan Mayne (London: Phaidon Press, 1964), pp. 153–54.

2. Sandra Harding, ed., *Feminism and Methodology: Social Science Issues* (Bloomington: Indiana University Press, 1987); Evelyn Fox Keller, *Secrets of Life, Secrets of Death: Essays on Language, Gender and Science* (New York: Routledge, 1992); Norman K. Denzin and Yvonna S. Lincoln, eds. *Handbook of Qualitative Research* (Sage, 1994); Susan Griffin, *A Chorus of Stones* (New York: Anchor Doubleday, 1993).

3. George Lakoff and Mark Johnson, *Philosophy in the Flesh: The Embodied Mind and its Challenge to Western Thought* (New York: Basic Books, 1999), pp. 3–4; also Keller, *Secrets of Life, Secrets of Death.*

4. The early realists noticed and lamented this trend, as in Hans Morgenthau's *Scientific Man Vs. Power Politics,* Midway Reprint (Chicago: University of Chicago Press, 1974); see also K. J. Holsti, *The Dividing Discipline: Hegemony and Diversity in International Theory* (Boston: Allen & Unwin, 1985); Stephen Walt, "Rigor or Rigor Mortis: Rational Choice and Security Studies," *International Security,* 23, no. 4 (Spring 1999); Jonathan Cohn, "Revenge of the Nerds or Irrational Exuberance: When Did Political Science Forget About Politics?" *The New Republic,* online edition, Oct. 25, 1999 (http://www.tnr.com/archive/1099/102599/coverstory102599.html).

5. Gary King, Robert Keohane, and Sidney Verba, *Designing Social Inquiry: Scientific Inference in Qualitative Research* (Princeton, NJ: Princeton University Press, 1994).

6. Thomas Kuhn, *The Structure of Scientific Revolutions,* 2nd ed. (Chicago: University of Chicago Press, 1970); Donna Haraway, *Primate Visions: Gender, Race, and Nature in the World of Modern Science* (New York: Routledge, 1990).

7. Mulford Q. Sibley, "The Limits of Behavioralism," in James C. Charlesworth, ed., *The Limits of Behavioralism in Political Science* (Philadelphia, PA: AAPSS, 1962). The debate on methodology in the Spring 1985 issue of *International Studies Quarterly* is also instructive in this regard.

8. Peter Katzenstein, *The Culture of National Security* (New York: Columbia University Press, 1996), pp. xiii - xiv.

9. Michael Ignatieff, *Virtual War: Kosovo and Beyond* (New York: Henry Holt, 2000); Paul Virilio, *War and Cinema: The Logistics of Perception* (New York: Verso, 1989); James Der Derian, *Antidiplomacy: Spies, Terror, Speed, and War* (Cambridge, MA : Blackwell, 1992); Mary Kaldor, *New and Old Wars* (Stanford, CA: Stanford University Press, 1999).

10. Edward Luttwak, "Toward Post-heroic Warfare," *Foreign Affairs* (May/June 1995), pp. 109–22.

11. For other definitions and studies of this group, see Richard Barnet, "The National Security Managers and the National Interest," *Politics and Society* (Feb. 1971), pp. 257–68; Robert Schulzinger, *The Wise Men of Foreign Affairs: The History of the Council on Foreign Relations* (New York: Columbia University Press, 1984); and David Sylvan and Stephen Majeski, "Rhetorics of Place Characteristics in High-level U.S. Foreign Policy Making," in Francis Beer and Robert Hariman, eds., *Post-Realism: The Rhetorical Turn in International Relations* (East Lansing: Michigan State University Press, 1996), pp. 310–12.

12. John Keegan, *The Face of Battle* (New York: Military Heritage Press, 1986); J. Glenn Gray, *The Warriors: Reflections of Men in Battle* (New York: Harper Touch, 1970); Paul Fussell, *The Great War and Modern Memory* (New York: Oxford University Press, 1975); Studs Terkel, *The Good War: An Oral History of World War Two*, Paperback Reprint edition (New York: New Press, 1997); Stephan Ambrose, *Citizen Soldiers: The U.S. Army from the Normandy Beaches to the Bulge to the Surrender of Germany, June 7, 1944 to May 7, 1945* (New York: Touchstone Books, 1998); Niall Ferguson, *The Pity of War* (New York: Basic Books, 1999); Joanna Bourke *An Intimate History of Killing: Face to Face Killing in 20th Century Warfare* (New York: Basic Books, 1999).

13. The more prominent examples include Robert Jervis, *Perception and Misperception in International Politics* (Princeton, NJ: Princeton University Press, 1976); Irving Janis and Leon Mann, *Decision Making: A Psychological Analysis of Conflict, Choice, and Commitment* (New York: Free Press, 1977); R. Ned Lebow, *Between Peace and War: The Nature of International Crisis* (Baltimore, MD: Johns Hopkins University Press, 1981); Lloyd Etheredge, *A World of Men: The Private Sources of American Foreign Policy* (Cambridge, MA: MIT Press, 1978); Alexander George, "The 'Operational Code': A Neglected Approach to the Study of Political Leaders and Decision-Making," *International Studies Quarterly*, 13, no. 2 (June 1969), pp. 190–222; Margaret Hermann, "Explaining Foreign Policy Behavior Using Personal Characteristics of Political Leaders," *International Studies Quarterly*, 24 (1980), pp. 7–46; Ole Holsti, "Cognitive Dynamics and Images of the Enemy: Dulles and Russia, in D. Finlay, O. Holsti, and R. Fagen, eds., *Enemies in Politics* (Chicago: Rand McNally, 1967), pp. 25–96; David G. Winter, "Power, Affiliation, and War: Three Tests of a Motivational Model," *Journal of Personality and Social Psychology*, 65, 3 (1993), pp. 532–45.

14. Michael Brecher and Wilkenfeld, *Crises in the Twentieth Century* (New York: Pergamon Press, 1988).

15. There were a number of élite whom I would have included or analyzed more thoroughly, had time allowed. Elihu Root, Henry Stimson, Woodrow Wilson, William Jennings Bryan, George Marshall, Harry Truman, John Kennedy, Richard Nixon, Ronald Reagan, and Bill Clinton all deserve much greater attention than they have received in this book.

16. All references are to the World's Classics version of *The Pilgrim's Progress*, edited by N. H. Keeble (New York: Oxford University Press, 1984).

17. Kathleen Swaim, *Pilgrim's Progress, Puritan's Progress* (Urbana: University of Illinois Press, 1993), pp. 1–2.

CHAPTER 1

1. Martin Heidegger, *Being and Time* (New York: Harper, 1962).

2. See Ron Burnett, *Cultures of Vision: Images, Media, and the Imaginary* (Bloomington: Indiana University Press, 1995), p. 127. See also Paul Virilio's discussion of how the cinema functioning to bring the dead to life (*War and Cinema*, Ch. 3).

3. Philippe Aries, *The Hour of Our Death* (New York: Knopf, 1981); Ernest Becker, *The Denial of Death* (New York: Basic Books, 1976); Jacques Choron, *Death and Modern Man* (New York: Collier Books, 1972); James Farrell, *Inventing the American Way of Death* (Philadelphia: Temple University Press, 1980).

4. George Bush, *All the Best, George Bush: My Life in Letters and Other Writings* (New York: Scribner, 1999), p. 503.

5. See David Campbell, *Politics Without Principle: Sovereignty, Ethics, and the Narratives of the Gulf War* (Boulder, CO: Lynne Reinner, 1993); Jean Elshtain, et al. *But Was It Just? Reflections on the Morality of the Persian Gulf War* (New York: Doubleday, 1992).

6. *New York Times*, Jan. 14, 1991, A1.

7. George Bush, *All the Best*, p. 501.

8. Ibid., p. 496.

9. "Remarks at the Simon Wiesenthal Center Dinner in Los Angeles, California" (June 16, 1991), George Bush Digital Library (http://bushlibrary.tamu.edu/papers). In the 32 speeches in which Bush referred to Schwarzenegger, roughly two-thirds of the references to him take the form of jokes.

10. "Remarks at the Great American Workout" (May 1, 1992), Public Papers of the President, George Bush Digital Library (http://bushlibrary.tamu.edu/papers).

11. See Janice Hocker Rushing and Thomas S. Frentz, *Projecting the Shadow: The Cyborg Hero in American Film* (Chicago: University of Chicago Press, 1995).

12. *New York Times*, Jan. 14, 1991, A:14:4.

13. George Bush, *All the Best*, p. 501.

14. Billy Graham, *Just as I Am: The Autobiography of Billy Graham* (San Francisco: HarperCollins, 1997), p. 585.

15. George Modelski and William Thompson, for example, argue that "global war can be viewed, basically, as a macrodecision (that is, as a quasi-electoral process, a phase in which the global system selects a new management group)" and that wars are "likewise part of the political calendar."

"Long Cycles and Global War," in Manus Midlarsky, ed., *The Handbook of War Studies* (Boston: Unwin Hyman, 1989), p. 42.

16. See, for example, Bruce Bueno de Mesquita and David Lalman, *Reason and War: Domestic and International Imperatives* (New Haven, CT: Yale University Press, 1992), pp. 40–44; early works include Lewis F. Richardson, *The Statistics of Deadly Quarrels* (Pittsburgh, PA: Boxwood Press, 1960); Rudolph J. Rummel, *The Dimensions of Nations* (Beverly Hills, CA: Sage Publications, 1972); J. David Singer and Melvin Small, *Resort to Arms: International and Civil Wars, 1816–1980,* 2nd ed. (Beverly Hills, CA: Sage Publications, 1982).

17. See, for example, Bruce Bueno de Mesquita, *The War Trap* (New Haven, CT: Yale University Press, 1981); Robert Gilpin, *War and Change in World Politics* (Cambridge: Cambridge University Press, 1981); Manus Midlarsky, ed., *The Handbook of War Studies* (Boston: Unwin Hyman, 1989); Thomas C. Schelling, *Arms and Influence* (New Haven, CT: Yale University Press, 1966); Kenneth Oye, ed., *Cooperation Under Anarchy* (Princeton, NJ: Princeton University Press, 1986); Donald Wittman, "How a War Ends: A Rational Model Approach," *Journal of Conflict Resolution* 23, no. 4 (1979): pp. 743–63; Michael Howard, *The Causes of War,* 2nd ed. (Cambridge, MA: Harvard University Press, 1983); Geoffrey Blainey, *The Causes of War,* 3rd ed. (New York: The Free Press, 1988).

18. For a discussion of the field, see K. J. Holsti, *The Dividing Discipline: Hegemony and Diversity in International Theory* (Boston: Allen & Unwin, 1985); Stephen Walt, "Rigor or Rigor Mortis: Rational Choice and Security Studies," *International Security,* 23, no. 4 (Spring 1999), p. 5; also Jonathan Cohn, "Irrational Exuberance," *The New Republic,* online edition, October 25, 1999 (http://www.tnr.com/archive/1099/102599/coverstory102599.html).

19. *The War Machine: The Rationalization of Slaughter in the Modern Age* (New Haven, CT: Yale University Press, 1993), p. 32. Pick's understanding of war as resulting from nonrational motivations and dynamics shares much with the approach I use here.

20. Amartya Sen, "Rational Fools: A Critique of the Behavioral Foundations of Economic Theory," *Philosophy and Public Affairs,* 6 (Summer, 1977), pp. 317–44.

21. Alexander Wendt, "Anarchy is What States Make of It: The Social Construction of Power Politics," *International Organization,* 46 (Spring, 1992), pp. 391–425; Jutta Weldes, *Constructing National Interests: The United States and the Cuban Missile Crisis* (Minneapolis: University of Minnesota Press, 1999); Yusef Lapid and Friedrich Kratochwil, eds., *The Return of Culture and Identity in IR Theory* (Boulder, CO: Lynne Reinner, 1996); Michael Shapiro and Hayward Alker, eds., *Challenging Boundaries: Global Flows, Territorial Identities* (Minneapolis: University of Minnesota Press, 1996); Tim Luke, "Discourses of Disintegration, Texts of Transformation: Re-Reading Realism in the New World Order," *Alternatives,* 18 (1993), pp. 229–258.

22. Robert Axelrod, *The Evolution of Cooperation* (New York: Basic Books, 1984), p. 163; Bruce Bueno de Mesquita, *The War Trap* (New Haven: Yale University Press, 1981), p. 58.

23. Bruce Bueno de Mesquita and David Lalman, *Reason and War: Domestic and International Imperatives* (New Haven, CT: Yale University Press, 1992).

24. The account is found in Paul Fussell, *Wartime: Understanding and Behavior in the Second World War* (New York: Oxford University Press, 1989), pp. 293–94.

25. See Paul Fussell, *Wartime*; J. Glenn Grey, *The Warriors: Reflections of Men in Battle* (New York: Harper Torch, 1970); John Keegan, *The Face of Battle* (New York: Military Heritage Press, 1986); Joanna Bourke, *An Intimate History of Killing: Face to Face Killing in 20th Century Warfare* (New York: Basic Books, 1999); Niall Ferguson, *The Pity of War: Explaining World War I* (New York: Basic Books, 1999).

26. Quoted in Joanne Martin, "Deconstructing Organizational Taboos: The Suppression of Gender Conflict in Organizations," *Organizational Science*, 1, no. 4 (Nov. 1990), p. 340.

27. My use of the terms "absence," "surplus," and "excess" takes some inspiration from the work of Slavoj Zizek, *Looking Awry*, pp. 8–16, and Georges Bataille; for a quick summary of Bataille's work, see John Lechte, *Fifty Key Contemporary Thinkers: From Structuralism to Postmodernity* (New York: Routledge, 1994), pp. 98–99.

28. This work shares some of the spirit of Theda Skocpol's *Bringing the State Back In* (New York: Cambridge University Press, 1985), and of the agenda proposed by Hayward Alker in "The Humanistic Moment in International Studies: Reflections on Machiavelli and las Casas," *International Studies Quarterly*, 36, no. 4 (Dec. 1992), pp. 347–71. For other work attempting to "embody" studies of politics and war, see Anthony Giddens, *The Constitution of Society* (Berkeley: University of California Press, 1984), pp. 34–37; Francis Beer and Barry Balleck, "Body, Mind, and Soul in the Gulf War Debate," Paper prepared for the International Studies Association Meeting, March 1993, Acapulco, Mexico. For a discussion of the body as a symbol of death and its association with the state of liminality (of existing on the threshold or border), see Peter Metcalf and Richard Huntington, *Celebrations of Death: The Anthropology of Mortuary Ritual*, 2nd ed. (New York: Cambridge University Press, 1991), p. 50; and for a particularly vivid example of this reintroduction of the body, see Michel Foucault, *Discipline and Punish: The Birth of the Prison* (New York: Vintage, 1979), pp. 3–6.

29. Jack Valenti, *A Very Human President* (New York: Norton, 1975).

30. James March and Johan Olson, *Rediscovering Institutions: The Organizational Basis of Politics* (New York: Free Press, 1989), p. 50; idem, "The New Institutionalism: Organizational Factors in Political Life," *American Political Science Review*, 78, no. 3 (Sept. 1984), p. 741. This view is found as early as Aristotle's *Politics*, and is stressed by Hannah Arendt, in *The Human Condition* (Chicago: University of Chicago Press, 1958); the use of

concepts such as "operational code" and "cult of the offensive" are likewise premised on the understanding that humans construct a view of their world that enables them to pursue goals and understand their place in the world. See Stephan Van Evera, "The Cult of the Offensive and the Origins of the First World War," *International Security*, 9, no. 1 (1984), pp. 58–107. The symbolic function of information is noted in Martha Feldman and James March, "Information in Organizations as Signal and Symbol," *Administrative Science Quarterly*, 26 (1981), pp. 171–186; Murray Edelman, *Politics as Symbolic Action: Mass Arousal and Quiescence* (Chicago: Markham Pub. Co., 1971); idem, *The Symbolic Uses of Politics* (Urbana: University of Illinois Press, 1964), p. 12.

31. John Long, "Address at the Dedication of the Wallace and Converse Memorial Library Buildings, at Fitchburg and Malden [Mass.], July 1 and October 1, 1885," in *After Dinner and Other Speeches* (Cambridge, MA: The Riverside Press 1895), p. 179.

32. Quoted in David Campbell, *Writing Security: United States Foreign Policy and the Politics of Identity* (Minneapolis: University of Minnesota Press, 1992), p. 3. Campbell also points out the highly symbolic content of the official, top secret National Security Council memoranda in *Writing Security*, Chapter 2. This conception of the nation is found in G. W. F. Hegel's *Introduction to Lectures on the Philosophy of World History*, translated by H. B. Nisbet (New York: Cambridge University Press, 1975), pp. 93–107; and Carl Schmitt, *The Concept of the Political*, translated by George Schwab (New Brunswick, NJ: Rutgers University Press, 1976), pp. 25–27; Martha Finnemore, *National Interests in International Society* (Ithaca, NY: Cornell University Press, 1996).

33. Quoted in Margaret Leech, *In the Days of McKinley* (New York: Harper, 1959), pp. 344–45; *Congressional Record*, [CR] 55th Cong., 1st sess., 1138; 55th Cong., 3rd sess., pp. 288, 294; 56th Cong., 1st sess., pp. 711–12, 2617–20, 2630, 4301–06, 5798.

34. John Hay, *Addresses of John Hay* (New York: The Century Co., 1906), p. 173. The account of these rings is found in Nathan Miller, *Theodore Roosevelt: A Life* (New York: Morrow, 1992); and Tyler Dennett, *John Hay: From Poetry to Politics* (Port Washington, NY: Kennikat Press, 1963). One can only wonder how he procured these reliquaries. Theodore Roosevelt, "The Rough Riders," in *The Works of Theodore Roosevelt*, Memorial Edition, vol. XIII (New York: Charles Scribner's Sons 1924); Walter Isaacson and Evan Thomas, *The Wise Men: Six Friends and the World They Made* (New York: Touchstone, 1986), p. 191.

35. Townsend Hoopes and Douglas Brinkley, *Driven Patriot: The Life and Times of James Forrestal* (New York: Knopf, 1992); Arnold A. Rogow, *James Forrestal: A Study of Personality, Politics, and Policy* (New York: Macmillan, 1963); quoted in Larry Berman, *Planning a Tragedy: The Americanization of the War in Vietnam* (New York: W. W. Norton, 1982), p. 73; Doris Kearns Goodwin, *Lyndon Johnson and the American Dream* (New York: St. Martin's Press, 1991), pp. 286–87, 342–44.

36. For an interesting argument on the virtues of life on the borders, see Spike Peterson, "Transgressing Boundaries: Theories of Knowledge, Gender, and International Relations," *Millennium*, 21, no. 2 (1992), pp. 183–206.

37. Roosevelt, "The Rough Riders."

38. We should note that in the account Roosevelt indirectly constructs a similar picture of himself, by first describing and praising certain traits in his associates and then later briefly mentioning that he displayed these same characteristics. Thus, Roosevelt's account of O'Neil can be read in part as a construction of Roosevelt's identity as well.

39. Roosevelt, "The Rough Riders," p. 94.

40. This is not to say that it is an illusion of no consequence; as Berger and Luckmann and Clifford Geertz argue, it is a creation of the utmost significance to an understanding of society. See Geertz's *The Interpretation of Cultures* (New York: Basic Books, 1973) and Peter Berger and Thomas Luckmann, *The Social Construction of Reality: A Treatise in the Sociology of Knowledge* (New York: Doubleday, 1966).

41. See C. Wright Mills, "Situated Actions and Vocabularies of Motive," in *Language and Politics*, edited by Michael Shapiro (New York: New York University Press, 1984), p. 17.

42. Berger and Luckmann, p. 51.

43. This attempt at looking at both experience and interpretations draws its inspiration in part from Weber's sociology and the work of Anthony Giddens; see also the essay by Peter Hall, "Ideas and the Social Sciences," in Robert Keohane and Judith Goldstein, eds., *Ideas and Foreign Policy* (Ithaca, NY: Cornell University Press, 1992); and George Lakoff's discussion of "basic realism" in *Women, Fire, and Dangerous Things: What Categories Reveal about the Mind* (Chicago: University of Chicago Press, 1987), p. 158.

44. Anthony Giddens, *The Constitution of Society* (Berkeley: University of California Press, 1984), pp. 1–37.

45. This distance or separation between observer and observed is a central feature of the phenomenological social theory of, among others, Alfred Schutz, *Reflections on the Problem of Relevance* (New Haven, CT: Yale University Press, 1970); see James Aho, *This Thing of Darkness: A Sociology of the Enemy* (Seattle: University of Washington Press, 1994), p. 107–08.

CHAPTER 2

1. "Death in the Nuclear Age," in Nathan Scott, ed., *The Modern Vision of Death* (Richmond, VA: John Knox Press, 1969), pp. 73–74.

2. John Hay, *The Complete Poetical Works of John Hay* (Boston: Houghton Mifflin Company, 1916), pp. 98, 111–14, 146, 234. The "stirrup cup" is a farewell drink taken before leaving on a journey.

3. John Hay, *A College Friendship: A Series of Letters from John Hay to Hannah Angell* (Boston: Priv. print., 1938), p. 34; Patricia O'Toole, *The Five of Hearts: An Intimate Portrait of Henry Adams and his Friends, 1880–1918*

(New York: C. N. Potter, 1990), pp. 41, 59, 112, 228; Tyler Dennett, *John Hay, from Poetry to Politics* (New York: Dodd, Mead & Company, 1934), pp. 21, 150, 152, 344; William Roscoe Thayer, *The Life and Letters of John Hay* (New York: Houghton Mifflin Company, 1915), vol. I, p. 69; Howard Kushner and Anne Sherrill, *John Milton Hay: The Union of Poetry and Politics* (Boston: Twayne Publishers, 1977), p. 164.

4. John Long, *Journal*, edited by Margaret Long (Rindge, NH: R. R. Smith, 1956), pp. 31, 34, 132, 251, 271, 286, 342. The themes of reminiscence and domestic images run throughout his speeches and poetry. See Long, *After Dinner*, pp. 32, 48, 65, 69–70, 124, 132, 177; idem, *At the Fireside* (Boston: Albert Harrison Hall, 1914), 23; idem, *Journal*, pp. 120, 129–30, 155, 158, 299; idem, *America of Yesterday*, pp. 136, 150, 229. See also the poetry of William S. Cohen, *A Baker's Nickel* (New York: William Morrow, 1986) and *Of Sons and Seasons* (New York: Hamilton Press, 1987), in which the themes of mortality, death, transience, and the passage of time figure prominently.

5. For numerous examples of Johnson's concern with mortality, see Goodwin, *Lyndon Johnson and the American Dream*, pp. i - iv, 29, 32, 40, 121, 125, 143, 164, 167, 172, 253, 287, 342, 344, 354; William Martin, *A Prophet with Honor: The Billy Graham Story* (New York: William Morrow, 1991), pp. 348–49; Halberstam, p. 640; Robert Caro, *The Years of Lyndon Johnson, Vol. 1: The Path to Power* (New York: Knopf, 1982), p. 544.

6. Edmund Morris, *Dutch: A Memoir of Ronald Reagan* (New York: Random House, 1999), pp. 11–12, 249–66, 431–32.

7. Roosevelt's *Diaries of Boyhood and Youth* (New York: Charles Scribner's Sons, 1928) are full of references to death, the passage of time, and nightmares; see pp. 18, 20, 21, 22, 25, 30, 31, 35, 36, 59, 64–65, 74, 78, 91, 95, 103, 128, 129, 148–49, 164, 205, 287, 304–05, 308, 309; see also Nathan Miller, *Theodore Roosevelt: A Life* (New York: Morrow, 1992), pp. 31, 45, 80–82, 101, 156; Theodore Roosevelt, *Theodore Roosevelt, an Autobiography* (New York: Charles Scribner's Sons, 1946), p. 13; David McCullough, *Mornings on Horseback* (New York: Simon and Schuster, 1981), p. 107. For descriptions of asthma attacks and their effect on Roosevelt, see Chapter 4 of McCullough's work.

8. Edward Wagenknecht, *The Seven Worlds of Theodore Roosevelt* (New York: Longmans, Green, 1958), pp. 193–95; Theodore Roosevelt, *Letters* (Cambridge, MA: Harvard University Press, 1951–54), vol. 2, p. 992; for example, "As our eyes close, and we go out into the darkness," from Roosevelt's *Biological Analogies in History* (New York: Oxford University Press, 1910), p. 43.

9. Murray Edelman (*The Symbolic Uses of Politics*, pp. 2, 13) refers only to certain needs and fears as driving the creation of symbols. James March and Johan Olsen (*Rediscovering Institutions: The Organizational Basis of Politics*) refer to a widely held norm of freedom and choice as underlying the "broader social visions" they speak of but do not attempt to give an account of in what ways these are important.

10. This is the argument of phenomenologically informed sociologists such as Berger and Luckman, Garfinkle, Schutz, and Giddens. See also Paul Chilton, *Security Metaphors;* and George Lakoff and Mark Johnson, *Philosophy in the Flesh: The Embodied Mind and its Challenge to Western Thought* (New York: Basic Books, 1999).

11. See, for instance, Michael Rogin, *Ronald Reagan, the Movie,* Ch. 9; also discussions of the emotional dimensions to rhetoric and metaphor as in Francis Beer and Robert Hariman, eds., *Post-Realism: The Rhetorical Turn in International Relations* (East Lansing: Michigan State University Press, 1996).

12. See Joseph Underhill-Cady, "Nine Walls to Keep out Nothing," *Dimensions* IX (1995).

13. See Richard Cottam, *Foreign Policy Motivation: A General Theory and a Case Study* (Pittsburgh, PA: University of Pittsburgh Press, 1977), Ch. 3; David Winter, *The Power Motive* (New York: Free Press, 1973).

14. Berger and Luckmann, pp. 92–104.

15. Ibid., p. 101.

16. Anderson, *Imagined Communities,* p. 10.

17. See the discussion of drives and limits in Harold Lasswell, *Psychopathology and Politics* (Chicago: University of Chicago Press, 1977). Various versions of these notions of human nature are found in other students of Freud, including Jacques Lacan. My account is informed as well by Ernest Becker's *The Denial of Death.*

18. U.S. Congress, *Congressional Record [CR] 56th Congress 1st session* (Washington, DC: GPO, 1900), p. 2630.

19. Irving Janis and Leon Mann, *Decision Making: A Psychological Analysis of Conflict, Choice, and Commitment* (New York: Free Press, 1977); Robert Jervis, *Perception and Misperception in International Relations;* Berger and Luckmann, *The Social Construction of Reality,* pp. 47–52.

20. CR, *55th Congress 1st session,* p. 1139.

21. Clifford Geertz, "Religion as a Cultural System," in *The Interpretation of Cultures,* pp. 100–08; William Connolly, *Identity/Difference: Democratic Negotiations of Political Paradox* (Ithaca, NY: Cornell University Press, 1991); Anderson, *Imagined Communities,* pp. 10–11.

22. In Ernest Becker's *The Denial of Death* (p. 3), humans are characterized by a "cherished narcissism" and seek a sense of meaning and self-esteem in their lives. See also Žižek, *Looking Awry,* Ch. 1.

23. This, at least, is the argument of Ernest Becker and Martin Heidegger in *Being and Time.*

24. I have not seen this specific term used elsewhere, but it is consonant with Heidegger's notion of *zein sum Tode,* or "being toward death," and with the main thrust of Becker's argument in *The Denial of Death.*

25. The phrase is the subtitle to John Bunyan's *Pilgrim's Progress.*

26. John Davis Long, *America of Yesterday, as Reflected in the Journal of John Davis Long,* edited by Lawrence Mayo (Boston: The Atlantic Monthly Press, 1923), p. 113.

27. Long, *After Dinner*, p. 30.

28. See the works by Becker, Aries, and Farrell cited in Chapter 1, and also Octavio Paz, "The Day of the Dead," in David Fulton, ed., *Death and Identity* (New York: Wiley & Sons, 1965), pp. 382–95; Jacques Choron, *Death and Modern Man* (New York: Collier Books, 1972).

29. Ann Tickner, *Gender and International Relations* (New York: Columbia University Press, 1992); Cynthia Enloe, *Bananas, Beaches, Bases: Making Feminist Sense of International Politics* (Berkeley: University of California Press, 1990).

30. For examples of women's varied involvement with war, see the feminist trio of *Women on War*, edited by Daniella Gioseffi (New York: Touchstone, 1988); Shelley Saywell's *Women in War* (New York: Penguin, 1985); and Jean Bethke Elshtain's *Women and War* (New York: Basic Books, 1987).

31. Morgenthau, "Death in the Nuclear Age," p. 69.

32. Arguing along similar lines, Hannah Arendt (*The Human Condition*, p. 8) posits that the various forms of human activity—labor, work, and action—as "intimately connected with the most general condition of human existence: birth and death, natality and mortality."

33. Quoted in Robert Fulton, ed., *Death and Identity* (New York: Wiley & Sons, 1965), p. 67. The example of Socrates calmly drinking the hemlock and asking that a debt of his be paid off comes to mind as well.

34. This is recounted in Phillipe Aries, "The Reversal of Death" in David Stannard, ed., *Death in America* (Philadelphia: University of Pennsylvania Press, 1975), p. 142. Sartre's short story, "The Wall," nicely illustrates both the terror and the liberating, transformative effects of facing the wall, the symbol of one's mortality.

35. Paul Rosenblatt, R. Patricia Walsh, and Douglas Jackson, *Grief and Mourning in Cross-cultural Perspective* (Washington, DC: Human Rights Area Files Press, 1976), pp. 1–9, 105; Thomas J. Scheff, *Catharsis in Healing, Ritual, and Drama* (Berkeley: University of California Press, 1979); Elizabeth Kubler-Ross, *On Death and Dying* (London: Macmillan, 1969); Peter Metcalf and Richard Huntington, *Celebrations of Death: The Anthropology of Mortuary Ritual*, 2nd ed. (New York: Cambridge University Press, 1991), pp. 23–24.

36. David Halberstam, *The Best and the Brightest*, 20th anniversary ed. (New York: Random House, 1992), p. 312.

37. Goodwin, p. i; Alexander George and Juliette George, *Woodrow Wilson and Colonel House: A Personality Study* (New York: Dover, 1964); Kushner and Sherrill, p. 164.

38. Dwight G. Anderson, *Abraham Lincoln: The Quest for Immortality* (New York: Knopf, 1982), pp. 77–99.

39. Paul De Man, "The Epistemology of Metaphor," in Michael Shapiro, ed., *Language and Politics* (New York: New York University Press, 1984); see also George Lakoff and Mark Johnson, *Metaphors We Live By* (Chicago: University of Chicago Press, 1980); J. Sapir and J. Crocker, eds., *The Social Uses of Metaphor: Essays on the Anthropology of Rhetoric* (Philadelphia:

University of Pennsylvania Press, 1977), pp. 35–44; Kenneth Burke, *Language as Symbolic Action* (Berkeley: University of California Press, 1966).

40. Geertz (*The Interpretation of Cultures*, p. 90) defines religion as "a system of symbols which acts to establish powerful, pervasive, and long-lasting moods and motivations in men [*sic*] by formulating conceptions of a general order of existence and clothing these conceptions with such an aura of factuality that the moods and motivations seem uniquely realistic."

41. Long, *After Dinner and Other Speeches*, pp. 179–85.

42. For a discussion of the importance of metaphors in the creation of identity, see James Fernandez, *Persuasions and Performances: The Play of Tropes in Culture* (Bloomington: Indiana University Press, 1986), p. 31, and David Campbell, *Writing Security*, pp. 68–79.

43. Quoted in Barbara Ehrenreich, *Blood Rites: Origins and History of the Passions of War* (New York: Henry Holt & Co., 1997), p. 212.

44. Berger and Luckmann, p. 183.

45. Long, *After Dinner and Other Speeches*, pp. 186–87, italics added.

46. Ibid., p. 181.

47. Richard G. Hutcheson, *God in the White House: How Religion Has Changed the Modern Presidency* (New York: Macmillan, 1988).

48. See Edwin Gaustad, *A Religious History of America* (New York: Harper & Row, 1966); Martin Marty, *Righteous Empire: The Protestant Experience in America* (New York: Dial Press, 1970); Roger Fink and Rodney Stark, *The Churching of America, 1776–1990: Winners and Losers in our Religious Economy* (New Brunswick, NJ: Rutgers University Press, 1992); Furio Colombo, *God in America: Religion and Politics in the United States*, translated by Kristin Jarratt (New York: Columbia University Press, 1984). For a discussion of the role of morality in U.S. foreign policy, see Samuel P. Huntington, "American Ideals versus American Institutions," in G. John Ikenberry, ed., *American Foreign Policy: Theoretical Essays* (Glenview, IL: Scott, Foresman, 1989), pp. 223–58; and Kenneth W. Thompson, *Traditions and Values in Politics and Diplomacy: Theory and Practice* (Baton Rouge: Louisiana State University Press, 1992).

49. Ron Hirschbein, *Newest Weapons/Oldest Psychology: The Dialectics of American Nuclear Strategy* (New York: Peter Lang, 1989); Stephen W. Twing, *Myths, Models & U.S. Foreign Policy: The Cultural Shaping of Three Cold Warriors* (Boulder, CO: Lynne Reinner, 1998); Michael Hunt, *Ideology and U.S. Foreign Policy* (New Haven, CT: Yale University Press, 1987).

50. Edwin S. Gaustad, "America's Institutions of Faith: A Statistical Postscript," in W. C. McLoughlin and R. C. Bellah, eds., *Religion in America* (New York: Houghton Mifflin, 1968); National Opinion Research Center, 1986, cited in Robert and Beatrice Kastenbaum, eds., *Encyclopedia of Death* (New York: Avon, 1989), p. 170; Garry Wills, *Under God: Religion and American Politics* (New York: Simon and Schuster, 1990).

51. Finke and Stark, pp. 15–16.

52. Anderson, *Imagined Communities*, p. 12; George Mosse, *Fallen Soldiers: Reshaping the Memory of the World War* (New York: Oxford University Press, 1990), Ch. 2.

53. Bronislaw Malinowski, *Magic, Science, and Religion, and Other Essays* (Garden City, NY: Doubleday, 1954), p. 29.

54. Robert Bellah, "Civil Religion in America," *Daedelus*, 96, no. 1 (1967), pp. 3–4.

55. Edmund Morris, *Dutch: A Memoir of Ronald Reagan*, p. 351.

56. For a more detailed analysis of the role of religion in U.S. foreign policy, see Underhill-Cady, "Doing Battle with Death," Ch. 4, and "Faith and Foreign Policy: Death and Religion in the American Discourse on War," in *Religion, War and Peace*, Conference Proceedings of the Wisconsin Institute (Ripon, WI, Jan. 1997).

57. I have seen this rhyme on road signs near fundamentalist churches and cemeteries.

58. For an interesting discussion of these aspects of Christian theology and their political implications, see Thomas Hobbes, *Leviathan*, Part III, Ch. 38; for a telling dissent on this issue, see George Kennan, *Around the Cragged Hill: A Personal and Political Philosophy* (New York: W. W. Norton, 1993), p. 38.

59. On the conceptions of gender in early Western thought, see, among others, Susan Griffin, *Woman and Nature: The Roaring Inside Her* (San Francisco: Sierra Club Books, 2000).

60. Vera Brittain, *Testament of Youth: An Autobiographical Study of the Years 1900–1925* (New York: Wideview Books, 1980), p. 446.

61. For a useful discussion of how this is accomplished, see Aho, *This Thing of Darkness*, pp. 27–32; Geertz, *Interpretation of Cultures*, pp. 109–18.

62. For discussions of death and ritual, see Arnold van Gennep, *The Rites of Passage* (Chicago: University of Chicago Press, 1960); Robert Hertz, *Death and The Right Hand* (Glencoe, IL: Free Press, 1960); Robert G. Hamerton-Kelly, ed., *Violent Origins: Walter Burkert, Rene Girard, and Jonathan Smith on Ritual Killing and Cultural Formation* (Stanford, CA: Stanford University Press, 1987).

63. Isaacson and Thomas, p. 570.

64. Dwight D. Eisenhower, *At Ease: Stories I Tell to Friends* (Garden City, NY: Doubleday, 1967), p. 52.

65. CR, *55th Congress 3rd session*, p. 297.

66. Jean Bethke Elshtain, "Sovereignty, Identity, Sacrifice," in Marjorie Ringrose and Adam Lerner, eds., *Reimagining the Nation* (Philadelphia: Open University Press, 1993), pp. 159–75; James Aho, *Religious Mythology and the Art of War: Comparative Religious Symbolisms of Military Violence* (Westport, CT: Greenwood Press, 1981); Bruce Lincoln, *Death, War, and Sacrifice: Studies in Ideology and Practice* (Chicago: University of Chicago Press, 1991); Ehrenreich, *Blood Rites*.

67. Lawrence Wittner, *MacArthur* (Englewood Cliffs, NJ: Prentice Hall, 1971), p. 30. Appropriately enough, MacArthur's account of the "final

reckoning" was actually a quote from Theodore Roosevelt, a man who had likewise held self-sacrifice as the highest act, and who was now portrayed as speaking from heaven.

68. Goodwin, p. 310.

69. Elaine Scarry, *The Body in Pain: The Making and Unmaking of the World* (New York: Oxford University Press, 1985), p. 125.

70. Kushner and Sherrill, p. 144.

71. James Garfield, "Strewing Flowers on the Graves of Soldiers," Oration delivered at Arlington, VA, May 30, 1868, in *The Works of James Abram Garfield* (Boston: J. R. Osgood and Company, 1882–83), vol. 1, p. 322, italics added.

72. Quoted in Michael Rogin, *Ronald Reagan, the Movie*, p. 88; italics added.

73. Quoted in J. Glenn Grey, *The Warriors*, p. 223; italics added.

74. Michael Blain, "The Role of Death in Political Conflict," *The Psychoanalytic Review* 63, no. 2 (1976), pp. 249–65.

75. Aho, *This Thing of Darkness*, p. 17; this is similar to the transference dynamics described by Becker, *The Denial of Death*, pp. 139–50.

76. Theodore Roosevelt, *Selections from the Correspondence of Theodore Roosevelt and Henry Cabot Lodge, 1884–1918* (New York: Da Capo Press, 1971), vol. 2, p. 333; John Long, *American of Yesterday*, p. 180.

77. See William Broyles, Jr., "Why Men Love War," *Esquire*, November 1984, pp. 55–65. This enthusiasm is by no means universal and it does seem to be more common among men than women.

78. For discussions of America's martial enthusiasm, see Ernest May, *Imperial Democracy: The Emergence of America as a Great Power* (New York, Harcourt, Brace & World, 1961), p. 268; John L. Offner, *An Unwanted War: The Diplomacy of the United States and Spain over Cuba, 1895–1898* (Chapel Hill: University of North Carolina Press, 1992), p. 190; Ehrenreich, pp. 216–23.

79. For further discussion and use of the "representative character," see Stephen W. Twing, *Myths, Models & U.S. Foreign Policy*.

CHAPTER 3

1. The account is found in an appendix to Theodore Roosevelt's *African Game Trails: An Account of the African Wanderings of an American Hunter-naturalist* (New York: Charles Scribner's Sons, 1910); see also Nathan Miller, *Theodore Roosevelt: A Life* (New York: Morrow, 1992) pp. 497–98.

2. See Theodore Roosevelt, "A Book-lover's Holiday," in *Works of Theodore Roosevelt*, Vol. IV (New York: Charles Scribner's Sons, 1923–26), p. 187.

3. Kermit Roosevelt, Jr., *A Sentimental Safari* (New York: Knopf, 1963); Kermit Roosevelt, Sr., *The Happy Hunting Grounds* (New York: Charles Scribner's Sons, 1920).

4. Kermit Roosevelt, Jr., *Countercoup: The Struggle for the Control of Iran* (New York: McGraw-Hill, 1979).

5. Doris Kearns Goodwin, *Lyndon Johnson and the American Dream* (New York: St. Martin's Press, 1991), p. 38.

6. *Public Papers of the Presidents, 1965*, Vol. I, pp. 358–60, 398–401; Vol. II, p. 1172; Lyndon Johnson, *The Quotable Lyndon B. Johnson* (Anderson, SC: Droke House, 1968), pp. 3, 119.

7. William Martin, *Prophet with Honor: The Billy Graham Story* (New York: Morrow, 1991), pp. 348–49; Michael Beschloss, ed., *Taking Charge: The Johnson White House Tapes, 1963–64* (New York: Simon & Schuster, 1997). This was a regular practice for Johnson, who took Kennedy out to shoot deer as well.

8. George Bush, "Getting it Right," *Forbes*, 160, no. 6 (Sept. 22, 1997), pp. 114–20.

9. See Underhill-Cady, "Doing Battle with Death," Ch. 4.

10. In a similar manner, Richard Drinnon, in *Facing West: The Metaphysics of Indian-hating and Empire Building* (Minneapolis: University of Minnesota Press, 1980), emphasizes the motifs of escapism and westward movement informing American political culture.

11. Victor Turner and Edith Turner, *Image and Pilgrimage in Christian Culture* (New York: Columbia University Press, 1978); Victor Turner, "Death and the Dead in the Pilgrimage Process," in *Religion and Social Change in Southern Africa* (Cape Town: David Philip, 1975), pp. 107–27.

12. George Kennan, *Around the Cragged Hill: A Personal and Political Philosophy* (New York: W. W. Norton, 1993), p. 42.

13. Johnson, *Quotable LBJ*, pp. 3, 116.

14. George F. Hoar, *Autobiography of Seventy Years* (New York: Charles Scribner's Sons, 1903), vol. II, pp. 437, 446. This was a common motif in Hoar's speeches in the Senate; see CR—*Senate*, 55th Cong., 1st sess. (May 18, 1897), p. 1137.

15. John Long, *After Dinner and Other Speeches* (Cambridge, MA: The Riverside Press, 1895), pp. 44, 47, 81, 85, 87, 93, 128, 167, 179, 207.

16. John Bunyan, *The Pilgrim's Progress* (New York: Oxford University Press, 1984), pp. 23, 31.

17. In addition to Forrestal's portrayal of himself in these terms, Billy Graham would equate Johnson with Christ, and Johnson would refer to himself as being crucified (Goodwin, p. 251); assassinated presidents were particularly susceptible to this characterization. See, for instance, Robert Niemi, "JFK as Jesus: The Politics of Myth in Phil Ochs's 'Crucifixion,'" *Journal of American Culture*, 16, no. 4 (Winter 1993), pp. 35–40; also Michael Rogin, *Ronald Reagan, The Movie and Other Episodes in Political Demonology* (Berkeley: University of California Press, 1987), pp. 81–114.

18. John Hay, *The Complete Poetical Works of John Hay* (Boston: Houghton Mifflin, 1916), pp. 5, 47–51, 74, 162–63.

19. Nelson W. Aldrich, *Old Money: The Mythology of America's Upper Class* (New York: A. A. Knopf, 1988), pp. 141–90.

20. Bunyan, p. 10.

21. Theodore Roosevelt, *Theodore Roosevelt, an Autobiography* (New York: Charles Scribner's Sons, 1946), p. 27.

22. See Richard Collins, *Theodore Roosevelt, Culture, Diplomacy, and Expansion* (Baton Rouge: Louisiana State University Press, 1985), introduction; Edward Wagenknecht, *The Seven Worlds of Theodore Roosevelt* (New York: Longmans, Green, 1958), pp. 2–3; Dean Acheson, *Present at the Creation: My Years in the State Department* (New York: Norton, 1969), pp. 595–96; Deborah Larson, *Origins of Containment: A Psychological Explanation* (Princeton, NJ: Princeton University Press, 1985), p. 128.

23. A number of the élite were avid riders—Teddy Roosevelt, Elihu Root, William McKinley, William H. Taft, Woodrow Wilson, Warren Harding, Averell Harriman, Lyndon Johnson, and Ronald Reagan were all horsemen. Henry Stimson while secretary of war actually lobbied for maintaining a horse cavalry during World War II. For other uses of the metaphors of rider and the ridden, see Chapter 5.

24. Theodore Roosevelt, *Letters*, vol. VII (Cambridge, MA: Harvard University Press, 1910), p. 343 fn; Wagenknecht, p. 38; Theodore Roosevelt, *Biological Analogies in History: The 1910 Romanes Lecture* (London: Oxford University Press, 1910), p. 7. This view is evidenced in his arguments on how to control violence in cities. He argued that setting up boxing clubs in cities would decrease violent crime in tough neighborhoods, by allowing for the healthy release of man's inherent aggressiveness (Roosevelt, *Autobiography*, p. 42). See also David H. Burton, "Theodore Roosevelt's Social Darwinism and Views on Imperialism," *Journal of the History of Ideas*, 26 (Jan. 1965), pp. 103–18.

25. His asthma and diarrhea attacks tended to come before going to church, which may have reinforced or stemmed from his connection between sin and physical weakness. See N. Miller, p. 30; also Roosevelt, *Letters*, vol. I, p. 33.

26. Roosevelt, *Autobiography*, pp. 50, 524; N. Miller, pp. 543–44; Roosevelt, *Autobiography*, pp. 232, 534; idem, *Letters*, Vol. VI, pp. 942–44 and Vol. VIII, p. 1022.

27. Quoted in N. Miller, p. 47.

28. Roosevelt, *Autobiography*, p. 28. He kept up boxing while president and entertained a few prizefighters in the White House. Robert Lansing, who would later serve as secretary of state, was one of his boxing partners.

29. See Tyler Dennett, *John Hay: From Poetry to Politics* (Port Washington, NY: Kennikat Press, 1963), pp. 144–45, 196, 326, 432, 443. This same motif of self-transformation characterizes A. Robert Smith's biography of Senator Wayne Morse, in which he is described as a "fighter" who made a "Legend" of himself to support him in the "darkest moments of defeat and rejection"; *The Tiger in the Senate: The Biography of Wayne Morse* (New York: Doubleday, 1962), Chs. 1 and 22.

30. William Roscoe Thayer, *The Life and Letters of John Hay* (Boston: Houghton Mifflin, 1915), Vol. I, p. 40 fn.

31. See Robert Caro, *The Years of Lyndon Johnson: The Path to Power* (New York: Knopf, 1982), pp. 46–53; and idem, *The Years of Lyndon Johnson: The Means of Ascent* (New York: Vintage, 1990), pp. 196–206; Goodwin, pp. xv, 62, 65.

32. Dean Rusk, *As I Saw It* (New York: W. W. Norton, 1990), pp. 30, 513, 197, 198, 293, 630.

33. Henry L. Trewhitt, *McNamara* (New York: Harper and Row, 1971), p. 209.

34. Robert S. McNamara, *The Essence of Security: Reflections in Office* (New York: Harper & Row, 1968), pp. 109, 116, italics added.

35. Townsend Hoopes and Douglas Brinkley, *Driven Patriot: The Life and Times of James Forrestal* (New York: Knopf, 1992), pp. 14, 28, 54, 88, 144, 353, 411, 414, 478.

36. As secretary of the navy, Forrestal had gone ashore on Iwo Jima and was apparently deeply moved by the carnage there.

37. Hoopes and Brinkley, p. 432.

38. James Forrestal, *The Forrestal Diaries* (New York: Viking Press, 1951), p. 448.

39. Roosevelt, *Letters*, Vol. II, p. 1100; Roosevelt, *Autobiography*, pp. 128, 304.

40. Roosevelt, *Diaries*, pp. 205, 277; N. Miller, p. 354; Roosevelt, *Letters*, Vol. VII, pp. 35–37; James E. Amos, *Theodore Roosevelt: Hero to his Valet* (New York: John Day Co., 1927), pp. 160–61.

41. Acheson, *Present at the Creation*, p. 405; Dwight D. Eisenhower, *Letters to Mamie* (New York: Doubleday, 1978), pp. 61, 175; Plato, *The Republic*, translated by George M. Grube (Indianapolis, IN: Hackett Pub. Co., 1974), pp. 56–57.

42. Thomas Hobbes, *Leviathan* (New York: Penguin Classics, 1987), Part I, Ch. 6.

43. Acheson, *Present at the Creation*, pp. 22, 28, 359, 519, 589; Brian VanDeMark, *Into the Quagmire: Lyndon Johnson and the Escalation of the Vietnam War* (New York: Oxford University Press, 1991), p. 205; Clark Clifford, with Richard Holbrooke, *Counsel to the President: A Memoir* (New York: Random House, 1991), p. 419.

44. Goodwin, pp. 55, 172, 269.

45. Acheson, *Present at the Creation*, pp. 141, 213, 216; also Walter Isaacson and Evan Thomas, *The Wise Men: Six Friends and the World They Made* (New York: Touchstone, 1986), pp. 237, 390–91; Rusk, pp. 130–32.

46. Long, *America of Yesterday as Reflected in the Journal of John Davis Long* (Boston: The Atlantic Monthly Press, 1923), p. 71; William Manchester, *American Caesar: Douglas MacArthur, 1880–1964* (Boston: Little, Brown, 1978) p. 41; Deborah Shapley, *Promise and Power: The Life and Times of Robert McNamara* (Boston: Little, Brown, 1993), p. 10.

47. Eisenhower, *At Ease: Stories I Tell to Friends* (Garden City, NY: Doubleday, 1967), p. 52; idem, *The Eisenhower Diaries* (New York: Norton, 1981), p. 52.

48. See Acheson, *Present at the Creation*, pp. 47, 169, 256, 303, 307, 387–88, 648, 694; Forrestal, pp. 57, 128, 133, 321, 346, 361, 363, 495.

49. Larry Berman, *Lyndon Johnson's War: The Road to Stalemate in Vietnam* (New York: Norton, 1989), p. 48. On McNamara's emotional control see Shapley, pp. 10, 99, 103, 168, 190, 586; Trewhitt, pp. 49–50, 96, 119; on Johnson, see Goodwin, pp. 34, 55, 269.

50. John Hay, *A College Friendship: A Series of Letters from John Hay to Hannah Angell* (Boston: Priv. print., 1938), p. 50.

51. Hay, *Complete Poetical Works,* pp. 82–83.

52. Howard Kushner and Anne Sherrill, *John Milton Hay: The Union of Poetry and Politics* (Boston: Twayne Publishers, 1977), p. 139.

53. Ibid., 22; Thayer, Vol. I, p. 69; Hay, *A College Friendship,* p. 48; Dennett, p. 154 fn; Hay, *Complete Poetical Works,* pp. 57, 169–70, 242.

54. John F. Kennedy, *Profiles in Courage* (New York: Harpers, 1956), p. 1.

55. Trewhitt, p. 50.

56. N. Miller, pp. 38–39, 562; Roosevelt, *Autobiography,* pp. 27, 347; see also Donna Haraway, "Teddy Bear Patriarchy," in Pease and Kaplan, eds., *Cultures of United States Imperialism* (Durham, NC: Duke University Press, 1993), p. 239.

57. Soren Kierkegaard, *Fear and Trembling and The Sickness unto Death,* translated by Walter Lowrie (Princeton, NJ: Princeton University Press, 1954), p. 145.

58. For a useful account of the large role played by Roosevelt's father in his life, see David McCullough, *Mornings on Horseback* (New York: Simon & Shuster, 1981). The fact that Roosevelt's father avoided fighting in the Civil War and the shame Roosevelt felt from not having a veteran father may have had the effect of spurring TR to avoid a similar fate for his own children. He wanted to be sure to have a good answer when his children asked what he did in the war.

59. N. Miller, p. 32; Roosevelt, *Autobiography,* p. 8.

60. Roosevelt, *Autobiography,* pp. 32, 52, 93.

61. These four recalled in their memoirs seminal events in their youths when they were attacked by some threatening animal or local bullies. The lessons in "power politics" they drew from these events were that one needed to strong in order to fight back. See Paul H. Nitze, et al., *From Hiroshima to Glasnost: At the Center of Decision: A Memoir* (New York: Grove Weidenfeld, 1989), p. xi; Isaacson and Thomas, p. 54; Eisenhower, *At Ease,* p. 30.

62. Godfrey Hodgson, *The Colonel: The Life and Wars on Henry Stimson, 1867–1950* (New York: Knopf, 1990), p. 85, italics added.

63. The phrase is John Eisenhower's, describing his father's lack of clout among European military leaders because of his lack of actual battle experience (Eisenhower, *Letters to Mamie,* p. 30).

64. Dennett, p. 337; Patricia O'Toole, *The Five Hearts: An Intimate Portrait of Henry Adams and his Friends, 1880–1918* (New York: C. N. Potter, 1990), p. 352.

65. Townsend Hoopes, *The Devil and John Foster Dulles* (Boston: Little, Brown, 1973), p. 41.

66. From Roosevelt's "The Deer Family," quoted in Wagenknecht, pp. 17–18. I leave it to the reader to judge whether his choice of imagery here had anything to do with his repeated problems with "cholera morbus."

67. Theodore Roosevelt, *Letters* (Cambridge, MA: Harvard University Press, 1951–54), vol. IV, pp. 1059–60.

68. Ibid., *Selections from the Correspondence of Theodore Roosevelt and Henry Cabot Lodge, 1884–1918* (New York: Da Capo Press, 1971), vol. I, p. 41. Similarly, Eisenhower would write that his greatest loves were a shotgun and an obedient dog, and of the great pleasure he derived from training a horse (Eisenhower, *At Ease,* pp. 106, 193). Other hunters and shooters among the élite included Henry Cabot Lodge, Elihu Root, Henry Stimson, John Hay, William Howard Taft, Calvin Coolidge, Charles Bohlen, John McCloy, James Baker III, and Bill Clinton.

69. Roosevelt, *Diary,* pp. 240–70.

70. A visit to the house reveals the macabre collection relatively intact. Along with his guns and books, the house is full of reminders of Roosevelt's power over these dangerous animals. The feel of the place is not unlike that of a shrine to the death, and, at the same time, the preservation of the animal.

71. Haraway, "Teddy Bear Patriarchy."

72. Quoted in Gerald Linderman, *The Mirror of War: American Society and the Spanish-American War* (Ann Arbor: The University of Michigan Press, 1974), p. 93. The same was said of those who followed Roosevelt's example. Amos Pinchot would comment about Henry Stimson that he must "continually be killing some damned animal or other;" quoted in Elting E. Morison, *Turmoil and Tradition: A Study of the Life and Times of Henry L. Stimson* (Boston: Houghton Mifflin, 1960), p. 89.

73. Kushner and Sherrill, p. 15; Kenton J. Clymer, *John Hay: The Gentleman as Diplomat* (Ann Arbor: University of Michigan Press, 1975), pp. 35, 45, 57; Drinnon, *Facing West,* pp. 261–78. "Feculance" is derived from the Latin *faeces,* meaning dregs, and is defined as "muddiness; foulness; excrement." The word reflects an association between the rural poor and the dirt and foulness of the body, which in Christian thought was in turn associated with sinfulness and death.

74. Clymer, p. 41.

75. Acheson, *Present at the Creation,* pp. 360–69, 400, 460–61, 513, 528.

76. Ibid., p. 461.

77. Charles G. Dawes, *A Journal of the McKinley Years* (Chicago: Lakeside Press, 1950), p. 449.

78. The themes of battle are frequently found in Acheson's *Present at the Creation.* See also John Long, *After Dinner,* pp. 48, 91, 135, 159; Hay, *Complete Poetical Works,* pp. 88–204, 255; Shapley, pp. xv, 234.

79. Roosevelt, *Autobiography*, pp. 91, 131, 158, 199, 259, 288, 292, 465; and idem, *Letters*, vol. I, pp. 55, 131 and vol. V, p. 307; N. Miller, pp. 324, 336, 440, 522, 528.

80. Anthony Giddens, *The Constitution of Society* (Berkeley: University of California Press, 1984), p. 35.

CHAPTER 4

1. Quoted in Ernst Kantorowicz, *The King's Two Bodies* (Princeton, NJ: Princeton University Press, 1957), p. 13.

2. "Remarks to Officers and Troops at Hickam Air Force Base in Pearl Harbor, Hawaii" (October 28, 1990), *Public Papers of the President*, Bush Presidential Library, online (http://bushlibrary.tamu.edu/papers/1990/90102800.html).

3. The initial reports of Iraqi atrocities have now been determined to be the product of a concerted Kuwaiti advertising campaign, carried out with the assistance of the public relations firm of Hill and Knowlton, and worthy of the fictional producers in *Wag the Dog*. Although the Iraqi troops carried on the long-standing military tradition of plunder, the Bush administration's assertions of these hideous killings appears to have been themselves premature; see David Campbell, *Politics Without Principle: Sovereignty, Ethics, and the Narratives of the Gulf War* (Boulder, CO: Lynne Reinner, 1993), pp. 65–66.

4. For another use of Kantorowicz's work for analyzing contemporary American politics, see Michael Rogin, "The President's Two Bodies," in *Ronald Reagan, the Movie and other Episodes in Political Demonology* (Berkeley: University of California Press, 1987).

5. Benedict Anderson, *Imagined Communities*.

6. This parallelism between religion and nationalism was particularly strong in George Hoar. See, for instance, Hoar, *Autobiography*, vol. 2, pp. 435, 437, 448; Welch, *George Hoar*, p. 317.

7. Hay, *Addresses*, pp. 138, 199; Manchester, p. 313; Hoar, *Autobiography*, vol. 1, p. 5 and vol. 2, p. 434.

8. Roosevelt, *Letters*, vol. 2, p. 1217.

9. Acheson, *Present at the Creation*, p. 489.

10. Theodore Roosevelt, *Biological Analogies*, pp. 22–23, 34.

11. Acheson, *Present at the Creation*, p. 375.

12. Ibid., pp. 257, 293, 297, 331; Rusk, p. 423.

13. M. Miller, *Great Debates*, p. 243.

14. CR, 56th Cong., 1st sess., (Washington, DC: GPO, Mar. 1900), p. 2630.

15. Roosevelt, *Biological Analogies*. He made the same argument in abridged form in a letter to Arthur Balfour in 1907. See *Letters*, vol. 6, pp. 960–63; see also Arthur J. Balfour, *Decadence* (Cambridge: Cambridge University Press, 1908).

16. Roosevelt, *Autobiography*, p. 223; idem, *Letters*, vol. 6, pp. 1138–39 and vol. 2, pp. 1113, 1217.

17. The Union League Club was a bastion of respectable Eastern New York Republicans, and its members included Theodore Roosevelt and his father, many of their wealthy Long Island associates, William Howard Taft, Elihu Root (club president for a time), and John Hay. Ernest May describes the members as feeling that "America had degenerated morally to become soft and materialistic" since the Civil War (*Imperial Democracy*, p. 141).

18. Wittner, p. 27; Eisenhower, *At Ease*, p. 317; Isaacson and Thomas, p. 708.

19. Isaacson and Thomas, p. 19; Halberstam, pp. 41, 273, 621; Rusk, pp. 262, 406, 504.

20. Roosevelt, *Autobiography*, p. 253; *Letters*, vol. 1., pp. 504, 620; Roosevelt, *Fear God and Take Your Own Part* (New York: George H. Doran Co., 1916), p. 74.

21. Bruce Lincoln, *Death, War, and Sacrifice: Studies in Ideology and Practice* (Chicago: University of Chicago Press, 1991); see also Jean Bethke Elshtain, "Sovereignty, Identity, Sacrifice;" Barbara Ehrenreich, *Blood Rites*.

22. James Aho, *Religious Mythology and the Art of War: Comparative Religious Symbolisms of Military Violence* (Westport, CT: Greenwood Press, 1981), pp. 9–10.

23. Hunt, *Ideology and U.S. Foreign Policy*, p. 95.

24. George Bancroft, in *Memorial Addresses Delivered before the Two Houses of Congress on the Life and Character of Abraham Lincoln, James A. Garfield, William McKinley* (Washington, DC: GPO, 1903), p. 55.

25. Long, *After Dinner*, p. 77.

26. Quoted in Frederick H. Gillett, *George Frisbie Hoar* (New York: Houghton Mifflin, 1934), p. 203; CR, 56th Cong., 1st sess., p. 4279; 56th Cong., 1st sess, p. 4302; also 57th Cong., 1st sess., p. 5792.

27. CR, 56th Cong., 1st sess., p. 2629.

28. Roosevelt, *Autobiography*, p. 220; *Letters*, vol. 6, p. 1285.

29. N. Miller, p. 255; Roosevelt, *Letters*, vol. 7, p. 890.

30. Roosevelt, *Letters*, vol. 6, p. 943; Wagenknecht, p. 259; Theodore Roosevelt, *Fear God and Take Your Own Part*.

31. Kushner and Sherrill, pp. 48, 148; Hay, "Colonel Baker," p. 106.

32. Manchester, pp. 453–54.

33. Wittner, p. 26; Dean Rusk would speak of how, following World War II, "Our minds and hearts had been purged in the fires of a great war . . ." (Rusk, pp. 136, 401).

34. George Kennan ("X"), "The Sources of Soviet Conduct," *Foreign Affairs*, 25 (1947), p. 582.

35. Quoted in Berman, *Johnson's War*, p. 139.

36. Manchester, p. 44.

37. Eisenhower, *At Ease*, pp. 4, 22.

38. Dennett, pp. 298, 362; O'Toole, p. 376. Henry Adams also claimed that, "Politics poisoned [Hay]. The Senate and the diplomats killed him. He would have had to resign at McKinley's death, if he were to save his own life" (Dennett, p. 436). Mark Twain, another more distant friend of Hay's, would write of Hay, "It is interesting, wonderfully interesting the miracles

which party-politics can do with a man's mental and moral make-up" (quoted in Clymer, p. 15).

39. Kushner and Sherrill, p. 24; also Thayer, vol. 1, p. 62. The biblical description of the Valley of the Shadow of Death as a "wilderness," and Hay's association of the place with miasmatic fogs, probably heightened his aversion to the Mississippi Valley.

40. Hay, *A College Friendship*, pp. 16, 21–26, 40–42; Kushner and Sherrill, pp. 143, 145.

41. O'Toole, p. 5; Kushner and Sherrill, p. 79; Dennett, p. 325.

42. Long, *America of Yesterday*, pp. 117–18.

43. N. Miller, p. 346; Goodwin, pp. 164–65, 194; Ball, *The Past has Another Pattern*, p. 395; Robert McNamara would display a similar penchant for control and power (Shapley, pp. 21, 62, 85, 90, 480, 517).

44. Kennedy, *Profiles in Courage*, p. 118; Hoopes and Brinkley, p. 457; Rusk, p. 595; Acheson, pp. 238–39, 633, 708; Shapley, p. x; Goodwin, p. xviii.

45. Carol Cohn, "Sex and Death in the World of Defense Intellectuals," *Signs: Journal of Women in Culture and Society*, 12, no. 4 (1987), pp. 687–718; Eva F. Kittay, "Womb Envy: An Explanatory Concept, " in Joyce Trebilcot, ed., *Mothering: Essays in Feminist Theory* (Totowa, NJ: Rowman & Allanheld, 1984), pp. 94–128; Elaine Tyler May, *Homeward Bound: American Families in the Cold War Era* (New York: Basic Books, 1988).

46. Quoted in Gillett, p. 248; Hoar, *Autobiography*, vol. 1, p. 130 and vol. 2, p. 324; Lodge, "Tribute to Senator Hoar," *Massachusetts Historical Society* (Oct. 1904), p. 388.

47. For these and numerous other examples, see Acheson, *Present at the Creation*, pp. 27–8, 41, 81–83, 127, 223–24, 373, 383, 396, 400, 440, 487, 495, 556, 564, 571, 586, 625, 633, 644, 701. This same trope, particularly the emphasis on the "death" of issues, runs with somewhat less frequency through Rusk's reminiscences as well; see Rusk, pp. 222, 243, 255, 265, 266, 275.

48. Goodwin, pp. 286–87.

49. Hay, *Addresses*, pp. 160.

50. Lodge, "Memorial to Theodore Roosevelt," p. 90.

51. Long, *After Dinner*, p. 164.

52. Manchester, p. 110. Both Henry Adams, in *The Education of Henry Adams*, and George Kennan (*Around the Cragged Hill*, p. 23) refer to themselves in the third person.

53. Kushner and Sherrill, p. 164.

54. Hodgson, *The Colonel*, p. 37.

55. This tradition has been carried on to the present: Richard Holbrooke, the special ambassador in Bosnia and United Nations representative, assisted Clark Clifford in writing his memoirs.

56. United States, Congress, *Memorial Addresses in the Congress of the United States and Tributes in Eulogy of John F. Kennedy* (Washington, DC: GPO 1964), pp. 1, 3. The phrase was used by Everett Dirksen and the Rev. Frederick Brown Harris.

57. Welch, *George Hoar,* p. 317. Eisenhower in his diary would compile a list of those he thought would make good presidents (*Diary,* p. 238); James Forrestal, as his political fortunes improved, would speculate on the qualities necessary to become president (*Diary,* pp. 32–33).

58. Hay, *Complete Poetical Works,* p. 237; see also McKinley, *Speeches and Addresses,* pp. 83–84; Hay, *Addresses,* pp. 212–13; idem, *Compete Poetical Works,* pp. 82–83; idem, "Colonel Baker," p. 107.

59. Hay, "Ellsworth," p. 125; idem, *Addresses,* pp. 113, 147–51, 160, 172, 174, 312; Wittner, pp. 29–30

60. Hoar, *Autobiography,* vol. 1, p. 215

61. See Russell Alger, *Eulogy on the late General Philip H. Sheridan* (Detroit: J. F. Eby & Co., 1888), p. 14.

62. Hay, *Addresses,* pp. 54–59, 93–94.

63. Hay, *Addresses,* p. 151; Hay and Nicolay, *Lincoln,* vol. 10, p. 350; Forrestal, *Diaries,* p. 42; Hoopes and Brinkley, p. 466 and Ch. 31; Arnold A. Rogow, *James Forrestal, a Study of Personality, Politics, and Policy* (New York: Macmillan, 1963), pp. 10–20.

64. Presidents Washington, Jackson, Taylor, Grant, Garfield, Roosevelt, and Eisenhower all came to office in large part because of their military accomplishments. George Bush's record approval ratings following the Gulf War, and the strong appeal of General Colin Powell in the 1996 electoral season, are continued testament to the appeal of military figures in the American psyche.

65. Roosevelt, *Roosevelt-Lodge Correspondence,* vol. 2, pp. 325–27; Wagenknecht, pp. 249–50; Roosevelt, "The Cuban Dead," p. 625. MacArthur also took a certain pleasure in facing death, and like Roosevelt, while in battle exhibited a kind of death wish (Manchester, p. 704).

66. Roosevelt, *Letters,* vol. 2, pp. 802, 829–31, 833, 838, 842, 860, 863; vol. 6, pp. 1441–42; vol. 8, pp. 1094–95, 1153; idem, *Roosevelt-Lodge Correspondence,* vol. 1, p. 334, italics in original; idem, *Autobiography,* p. 253. After leaving the presidency, he liked to be referred to as Colonel Roosevelt.

67. Roosevelt, *Letters,* vol. 8, pp. 1355, 1363, 1382, italics added. He supported Germany's desire to expand, and "would not go into the abstract rights or wrongs of it," but simply argued that if Germany tried to expand into the Americas, they "would have to whip us first." He had visited the Kaiser during his postpresidential tour of Europe, and the two had apparently found that they had a few things in common, including their love of the cavalry.

CHAPTER 5

1. William Broyles, Jr., "Why Men Love War," *Esquire* (November 1984), p. 65.

2. David Halberstam, *The Best and the Brightest* (New York: Random House, 1992), p. 513.

3. See United States, President, *Public Papers of the President*, George Bush Digital Library (http://bushlibrary.tamu.edu/papers).

4. See G. R. Boynton and Francis A. Beer, "Speaking about Dying," in Sally Jackson, ed., *Argumentation and Values, Proceedings of the Ninth SCA/AFA Conference on Argumentation* (Annandale, VA: Speech Communication Association, 1995), pp. 550–56.

5. For a sample of these more explicit justifications, see Dean Rusk, *As I Saw It* (New York: W. W. Norton, 1990), pp. 435–36, 494; Neil Sheehan, *A Bright Shining Lie: John Paul Vann and the American War in Vietnam* (New York: Random House, 1988), p. 554 ; Berman, *Planning a Tragedy: The Americanization of the War in Vietnam* (New York: W. W. Norton, 1982), pp. 140, 184; Roosevelt, *Autobiography*, 206–07; United States Congress, House, *The Pentagon Papers*, Hearings before the Committee, Vol. VII, V.A.C and V.A.D (1971–72); Yuen Foong Khong, *Analogies at War: Korea, Munich, Dien Bien Phu, and the Vietnam Decisions of 1965* (Princeton, NJ: Princeton University Press, 1992), p. 132; Doris Kearns Goodwin, *Lyndon Johnson and the American Dream* (New York: Random House, 1992), p. 311.

6. Mosse, *Fallen Soldiers*; Debra Umberson and Kristen Henderson, "The Social Construction of Death in the Gulf War," *Omega* 25, no. 1 (1992), pp. 1–15.

7. Rusk, p. 494.

8. Jutta Weldes, "Going Cultural: Star Trek, State Action, and Popular Culture," *Millennium: Journal of International Studies*, 28, no. 1 (Spring 1999), pp. 67–91. See also Emily Rosenberg, "'Foreign Affairs' after World War II: Connecting Sexual and International Politics," *Diplomatic History*, 18, no. 1 (Winter 1994), pp. 59–70.

9. Frances Fritzgerald, *Way Out There in the Blue: Reagan and Star Wars and the End of the Cold War* (New York: Simon & Schuster, 2000); Michael Rogin, *Ronald Reagan: The Movie and Other Episodes in Political Demonology* (Berkeley: University of California Press, 1987).

10. Richard Slotkin, *Gunfighter Nation: The Myth of the Frontier in Twentieth-Century America* (Tulsa: University of Oklahoma Press, 1998).

11. Roxanne Lynn Doty, "The Logic of Difference in the International Relations: U.S. Colonization of the Philippines," in Francis Beer and Robert Harriman, eds., *Post-Realism: The Rhetorical Turn in International Relations* (East Lansing: Michigan State University Press, 1996).

12. When the protagonist of that novel, Christian, spies the cross, his heavy burden rolls from his back down into a coffin.

13. *Public Papers of the President*, 1965, Vol. I, pp. 398–99. Winthrop's quote is from Deuteronomy 19:30. As evidence that hawk and dove alike drew on this imagery, we see Andrew Bard Schmookler using the same language in arguing for a movement away from possible nuclear holocaust; in *The Parable of the Tribes: The Problem of Power in Social Evolution* (Boston: Houghton Mifflin, 1984), pp. 323–36.

14. See John Dower, *War Without Mercy: Race and Power in the Pacific War* (New York: Pantheon, 1986); Michael Hunt, *Ideology and U.S. Foreign*

Policy (New Haven, CT: Yale University Press, 1987); Edward Said, *Orientalism* (New York: Vintage, 1979); J. Glenn Gray, *The Warriors: Reflections of Men in Battle* (New York: Harper Torch, 1970); Paul Fussell, *The Great War and Modern Memory* (New York: Oxford University Press, 1975).

15. See works by Christ'l De Landtsheer and Ofer Feldman, *Politically Speaking: A Worldwide Examination of Language Use in the Public Sphere* (Westport, CT: Praeger, 1998); Paul Chilton, *Security Metaphors: Cold War Discourse from Containment to Common House* (New York: Peter Lang, 1995); George Lakoff, "Metaphor and War: The Metaphor System used to Justify War in the Gulf," *Peace Research*, 23 (1991), pp. 25–32; Beer and Harriman, *Post-Realism.*

16. For examples of this self-righteous, crusading language, see John Hay, *Addresses of John Hay* (New York: The Century Co., 1906), pp. 184, 253; idem, *Complete Poetical Works of John Hay* (Boston: Houghton Mifflin, 1916), pp. 30–34; Dwight D. Eisenhower, *The Eisenhower Diaries* (New York: Norton, 1981), p. 200; Harry Truman, "Public Opinion and American Foreign Policy," in Department of State, *DOS Bulletin* (Aug. 1, 1949), p. 147; Isaacson and Thomas, *The Wise Men: Six Friends and the World They Made* (New York: Touchstone, 1986), p. 369; Acheson, *Present at the Creation,* p. 729; *FRUS*, 1950, Vol. VII—Korea, p. 460–1; CR, 56th Cong., 1st sess., p. 704.

17. Hunt, Ch. 4; quoted in Rogin, p. 91; CR, 56th Cong., 1st sess, p. 4304; George Hoar, *Autobiography of Seventy Years,* Vol. II (New York: Charles Scribner's Sons, 1903), pp. 305–06; Vincente L. Raphael, "White Love: Surveillance and Nationalist Resistance in the U.S. Colonization of the Philippines," in Amy Kaplan and Donald Pease, eds., *Cultures of United States Imperialism* (Durham, NC: Duke University Press, 1993), p. 186.

18. Welch, *George Frisbee Hoar and the Half-breed Republicans* (Cambridge, MA: Harvard University Press, 1971), p. 315; Hay, *Addresses,* p. 148; Frederick Gillett, *George Frisbee Hoar* (New York: Houghton Mifflin, 1934), p. 203.

19. *Pentagon Papers,* V.A.C.34; and V.A.D.83; CR, 88th Cong., 2nd sess. (1964): p. 18399; Rusk, p. 406.

20. CR, 56th Cong., 1st sess., p. 710.

21. Dwight D. Eisenhower, *Letters to Mamie* (New York: Doubleday, 1978), p. 209; Rusk, p. 173.

22. This attitude shared much with the particular form of ethnocentrism described in Edward Said's *Orientalism,* although it was applied not only to the Arabic and Asian world but to any force or opponent that did not co-operate or agree with the international political agenda of the United States.

23. Howard Kushner and Anne Sherrill, *John Milton Hay: The Union of Poetry and Politics* (Boston: Twayne Publishers, 1977), p. 149; Tyler Dennett, *John Hay: From Poetery to Politics* (Port Washington, NY: Kennikat Press, 1963), pp. 81, 376; Hay, *Complete Poetical Works,* p. 64; Kenton Clymer, *John Hay: The Gentleman as Diplomat* (Ann Arbor: University of Michigan Press,

1975), p. 131; John Hay, *A College Friendship: A Series of Letters from John Hay to Hannah Angell* (Boston: Priv. print., 1938), p. 43.

24. CR, 56 Cong. 1st sess. (Jan. 9, 1900), p. 705, and (Mar. 7, 1900), pp. 2617–25.

25. John Hay, "Ellsworth," *Atlantic Monthly* (July 1861), p. 121.

26. Ernest May, *Imperial Democracy: The Emergence of America as a Great Power* (New York: Harcourt, Brace and World, 1961), p. 69, 141; John L. Offner, *An Unwanted War: The Diplomacy of the United States and Spain over Cuba, 1895–1898* (Chapel Hill: University of North Carolina Press, 1992), pp. 19, 169; Marion Miller, *Great Debates in American History* (New York: Current Literature Publishing, 1913), pp. 100, 108–09.

27. Dower, pp. 94–146; Rusk, pp. 295, 369, 379, 394, 398, 425; Acheson, pp. 407, 500–05, 679.

28. Halberstam, p. 147; CR, 88th Cong., 2nd sess. (1964), pp. 9619–22.

29. *Pentagon Papers,* [PP] Gravel ed., vol. 3, p. 494; *FRUS, 1964—Vietnam,* 1.

30. *FRUS, 1964—Vietnam,* pp. 54, 345, 413; Halberstam, pp. 20, 512; Khong, p. 125.

31. See U.S. *Department of State Dispatches,* 9 no. 1 (Jan - Feb 1998), pp. 1–4; 5, no. 10 (Nov. 15, 1994), p. 21; 3, no. 26 (June 29, 1992), pp. 522–5; 3, no. 7 (Feb. 17, 1992), pp. 103–4; 1, no. 15 (Dec. 10, 1990), pp. 307–9; 1, no. 14 (Dec. 3, 1990), pp. 295–6; 88, no. 2140 (Nov. 1988), pp. 1–8; 85, no. 4 (Nov 1985), pp. 14–15.

32. Philip Jessup, "The Foreign Policy of a Free Democracy," *Department of State Bulletin* (Sept. 5, 1949), p. 346.

33. Lawrence Wittner, *Macarthur* (Englewood Cliffs, NJ: Prentice Hall, 1971), p. 26; Karl Marx, "The German Ideology," in *The Marx-Engels Reader,* 2nd ed., edited by Robert C. Tucker (New York: W. W. Norton, 1978), p. 156; Kennan, "Sources of Soviet Conduct," p. 566.

34. Acheson, pp. 197, 376; Forrestal, p. 264.

35. Martin, *Prophet with Honor,* p. 346.

36. Kennan, "Sources of Soviet Conduct," p. 566; Acheson, p. 194; Rusk, p. 364.

37. PP V.A.D.88; V.A.C.1; V.A.D.20, 30, 81; V.A.D.32; *Congressional Digest,* 44, no. 4 (Apr. 1965), p. 124; Rusk, p. 227.

38. William Manchester, *American Caesar: Douglas MacArthur, 1880–1964* (Boston: Little, Brown, 1978), p. 568; Goodwin, pp. 95, 328; Isaacson and Thomas, p. 642; Halberstam, p. 414. This view of the Soviet Union as a criminal or an armed robber was common; see, for example, Acheson, p. 263; Rusk, pp. 82–83.

39. Acheson, pp. 379, 418, 421; Rusk, pp. 82–83, 156, 224, 363.

40. Gearoid O Tuathail, *Critical Geopolitics: The Politics of Writing Global Space* (Minneapolis: University of Minnesota Press, 1996).

41. Paul Virilio, *War and Cinema: The Logistics of Perception,* translated by Patrick Camiller, (New York: Verso, 1989). For discussions of the gaze, see Slavoj Zizek, *Looking Awry,* pp. 125–28; Michel Foucault, *Discipline and*

Punish: The Birth of the Prison (New York: Vintage, 1979), pp. 170–77, 195–228; Raphael, "White Love," pp. 187–88.

42. Rusk, pp. 513, 533.

43. T. Roosevelt, *Roosevelt-Lodge Correspondence*, Vol. II, p. 306; Manchester, p. 580; Eisenhower, *Letters to Mamie*, pp. 135, 150.

44. PP V.A.C.7, 17; V.A.D.42; Johnson, *The Quotable LBJ* (Anderson, SC: Droke House, 1968), p. 156; Khong, p. 126; Larry Berman, *Lyndon Johnson's War* (New York: Norton, 1989), p. 113; and FRUS, 1964—Vietnam, p. 197. Westmoreland's imagery, as well, is illuminating for its portrayal of the Vietnamese as a kind of vermin typically exterminated by the use of poison. For a discussion of the portrayal of Japanese in these terms, see Dower, pp. 71–92, 184–85.

45. Khong, p. 129; Berman, *Johnson's War,* p. 172; Berman, *Planning a Tragedy,* p. 80 (italics in original); Halberstam, p. 406.

46. Henry Trewhitt, *McNamara* (New York: Harper & Row, 1971), p. 15; Deborah Shapley, *Promise and Power: The Life and Times of Robert McNamara* (Boston: Little, Brown, 1993), p. 113; *Congressional Digest*, 44, no. 4 (1965), pp. 118–19, and 45, no. 4 (1966), p. 113; Richard L. Stevens, *The Trail: A History of the Ho Chi Minh Trail and the Role of Nature in the War in Viet Nam* (New York: Garland, 1993); CR, 88th Cong., 2nd sess. (1964), pp. 18132–33; David Barrett, "The Mythology Surrounding Lyndon Johnson, his Advisors, and the 1965 Decision to Escalate the Vietnam War," *Political Science Quarterly* 103, no. 4 (1988), p. 656.

47. Berman, *Johnson's War,* pp. 174, 178, 180, 184, 192, 194; Barrett, p. 657.

48. Trewhitt, pp. 223–24.

49. Stevens, p. 166; Shapley, pp. 323, 362–3.

50. Shapley, 13, 359; Robert McNamara, *In Retrospect: The Tragedy and Lessons of Vietnam* (New York: Times Books, 1995), p. 6; Trewhitt, p. 17; Halberstam, p. 405; Sheehan, p. 290; and McNamara's memos of June 26, and July 30, 1965, in Berman, *Planning a Tragedy,* pp. 140, 179 ff.

51. Robert McNamara, *The Essence of Security: Reflections in Office* (New York: Harper & Row, 1968), p. 117, 150, italics added.

52. FRUS 1964—Vietnam, pp. 81, 334, 413; PPG, pp. 590–91, 620 (italics in original).

53. FRUS, 1964—Vietnam, p. 410 and 416 (italics in original); Halberstam, p. 44.

54. Townsend Hoopes and Douglas Brinkley, *Driven Patriot: The Life and Times of James Forrestal* (New York: Knopf, 1992), pp. 168, 408.

55. Forrestal, *Diaries*, pp. 57, 61, 128, 280, 281, 321, 346, 359, 361, 495.

56. Isaacson and Thomas, pp. 183–84, 208; Trewhitt, p. 257; Halberstam, p. 214; McNamara, *The Essence of Security*, p. 109; Berman, *Johnson's War,* p. 11; Barrett, p. 661.

57. PPG, Vol. III, pp. 558, 562, 600, 616; PP, V.A.D.25–30, p. 69.

58. Quoted in Berman, *Planning a Tragedy,* pp. 73–4; George Ball, "Top Secret: The Prophecy the President Rejected," *The Atlantic*, 230, no. 1 (July 1992), pp. 41, 49.

59. Acheson, p. 379; he would also refer to communism as a "clap of thunder," ibid., p. 629; Kennan, "The Sources of Soviet Conduct," p. 575. Douglas MacArthur used similar metaphors in describing warfare (Manchester, p. 622).

60. FRUS 1961—Vietnam, pp. 335, 347, 424, 489; FRUS 1964—Vietnam, p. 901; PP 2.IV.B.1, p. 122; Goodwin, pp. 94, 266.

61. Khong, p. 123; *Congressional Digest*, 44, no. 4 (Apr. 1965), pp. 110, 122; and 45, no. 4 (Apr. 1966), p. 115; for a sample of the use of the phrase "turning the tide," see PPG p. 619; FRUS, 1964—Vietnam, pp. 66, 84, 171, 330, 336; Berman, *Planning a Tragedy*, p. 184. The phrase was used four times in the July 22, 1965 meeting the president had with his military advisors (Khong, 130–31). See also Senator Thomas Dodd's Feb. 23, 1965 Speech in the *Congressional Digest*, 44, no. 4 (Apr. 1965), p. 122.

62. *Congressional Digest*, 45, no. 4 (Apr. 66), p. 127; FRUS, 1964—Vietnam, pp. 375, 460, 429, 87, 66; Berman, *Johnson's War*, pp. 8, 140, 170.

63. For discussions of foreign and military policy as boundary maintaining activities, see David Campbell, *Writing Security;* and Klaus Theweleit, *Male Fantasies* (Minneapolis: University of Minnesota Press, 1987).

64. FRUS, 1964—Vietnam, pp. 74, 317; PP V.A.D.3, 10; *Congressional Digest*, 44, no. 4 (Apr. 1965), p. 118.

65. On other uses of medical metaphors, see Geoffrey Smith, "National Security and Personal Isolation: Sex, Gender, and Disease in the Cold-War United States," *The International History Review*, XIV, no. 2 (May 1992), pp. 307–35; Rogin, pp. 236–71; Susan Sontag, *Illness as Metaphor* and *AIDS and its Metaphors* (New York: Anchor Doubleday, 1990).

66. For a fuller discussion, see Underhill-Cady, *Doing Battle with Death* (Ph.D. Dissertation, University of Michigan, 1995), pp. 172–84.

67. Quoted in David Arnold, ed., *Imperial Medicine and Indigenous Societies* (New York: St. Martin's, 1988), p. 18.

68. Richard E. Welch, *Response to Imperialism: The United States and the Philippine-American War, 1899–1902* (Chapel Hill: University of North Carolina Press, 1979), p. 103.

69. May, *Imperial Democracy*, p. 16; M. Miller, pp. 196, 199–200.

70. CR, 56th Cong., 1st sess., p. 705. It turned out that in the Philippines, for every one American soldier killed in battle, nearly ten would die from disease.

71. For a discussion of the association made in American culture between immigrants and disease, see Alan M. Kraut, *Silent Travelers: Germs, Genes, and the "Immigrant Menace"* (New York: Basic Books, 1994).

72. M. Miller, p. 158.

73. Gerald Linderman argues persuasively that Proctor's speech was crucial to swinging the consensus in the Senate toward intervention in Cuba. See *The Mirror of War*, pp. 43 ff; CR, 55th Cong., 2nd sess., (Mar. 1898), p. 2915; quoted in Offner, p. 131.

74. FRUS, 1898, p. 562.

75. See also Lewis L. Gould, *The Spanish-American War and President McKinley* (Lawrence: University Press of Kansas, 1982), p. 28.

76. C. E. A. Winslow, "The War Against Disease," *Atlantic Monthly*, 91 (Jan. 1903), p. 49.

77. Franklin D. Roosevelt, *Public Papers and Addresses of Franklin D. Roosevelt, 1937* (New York: Macmillan, 1941), pp. 406–411. The staying power of this metaphor was evidenced by President Clinton's recent reference to it in his speech commemorating the fiftieth anniversary of the founding of the United Nations; the only change was that now the disease was terrorism rather than fascism. Acheson, pp. 219, 221, 228; Eisenhower, *At Ease*, p. 368; Hoopes and Brinkley, pp. 251, 261, 273, 305–06; Isaacson and Thomas, pp. 262 fn., 380.

78. Wittner, p. 27.

79. G. Smith, pp. 311–13.

80. Berman, *Johnson's War*, pp. 27, 40; see also Halberstam, p. 176; Berman *Planning a Tragedy*, p. 59; PPG, p. 627; FRUS, 1964—Vietnam, p. 302; Khong, p. 128.

81. Khong, pp. 126–7; Berman, *Planning a Tragedy*, p. 74; Joseph S. Clark, *Stalemate in Vietnam: Report to the Committee of Foreign Relations, United States Senate* (Washington, DC: GPO, 1968), p. 22; *Congressional Digest*, 45, no. 4 (Apr. 1966), p. 119.

82. Sherwin Nuland, *How We Die: Reflections on Life's Final Chapter* (New York: Knopf, 1994), p. 229; George Kennan, *American Diplomacy*, expanded ed. (Chicago: The University of Chicago Press, 1984), pp. 102–03; Acheson was quoting Woodrow Wilson (*Present at the Creation*, p. 100); see also Isaacson and Thomas, pp. 302, 553; PPG, pp. 559, 547, 549, 582, 600; CR, 88th Cong., 2nd sess. (1964), pp. A648, 6255.

83. In the mid-1960s, CPR had not yet been developed and the best-known method of trying to revive heart attack victims surgically was to open the abdominal cavity, reach in, and massage the heart in an attempt to start it beating again.

84. Wittner, p. 24; Berman, *Johnson's War*, pp. 44, 14; Halberstam, p. 488; FRUS, 1964—Vietnam, pp. 374, 413, 423; Goodwin, p. 329; Berman, *Planning a Tragedy*, p. 181.

85. Rogin, p. xv fn.

CHAPTER 6

1. CR, 56th Cong., 1st sess., pp. 4304, 4283; Welch, *George Hoar*, pp. 313–14; Hoar, *Autobiography*, Vol. I, p. 4; Vol. II, pp. 436, 445.

2. Hoar, "Remarks on the Role of Individuals in History," p. 237; Hoar, "Charles Allen of Worcester," *Proceedings of the American Antiquarian Society* (Oct. 1901): 371; CR, 56th Cong., 1st sess., pp. 4282, 4284.

3. Long, "Reminiscences of my Seventy Years' Education," p. 354; Long, *Journal*, pp. 29, 106.

4. Long, *America of Yesterday*, p. 179; John D. Long, "The Civil War," *Massachusetts Historical Society Proceedings* (Oct. 1912), pp. 175–77.

5. Hans Morgenthau, "Globalism: Johnson's Moral Crusade," *The New Republic* (July 3, 1965), pp. 19–22; see also Townsend Hoopes, *The Limits of Intervention* (New York: W. W. Norton, 1987); Kennan, *Around the Cragged Hill* and *American Diplomacy*; FRUS, 1950—Korea, p. 625; Acheson, p. 303; Hubert H. Humphrey, *The Education of a Public Man: My Life and Politics*, edited by Norman Sherman (Garden City, NY: Doubleday, 1976), p. 322; see discussion of George Ball's dissent, Chapter 5, above.

6. Long, *After Dinner*, pp. 199, 204, 208, 223; CR, 57th Cong., 1st sess., p. 5797.

7. CR, 56th Cong., 1st sess., pp. 714, 4299, 4301; 57th Cong., 1st sess., p. 5789; Hoar, *Autobiography*, Vol. II, p. 305.

8. FRUS, 1950—Korea, p. 624; Isaacson and Thomas, p. 158; Kennan, *American Diplomacy*, expanded ed. (Chicago: University of Chicago Press, 1984), pp. 90, 93.

9. Humphrey, p. 321–3.

10. Long, *America of Yesterday*, pp. 111, 114; idem, *After Dinner*, pp. 31, 39, 55–56, 62, 91, 136, 143, 162, 165, 214; Gillett, p. 277; Hoar, *Autobiography*, Vol. I, p. 69; quoted in Welch, *George Hoar*, p. 320.

11. Leech, *In the Days of McKinley*, p. 155; Long, *After Dinner*, p. 71.

12. Long, *Journal*, pp. 77, 302; idem, *America of Yesterday*, pp. 86, 109; idem, *After Dinner*, p. 61.

13. Long, *Journal*, pp. 58, 114, 259, 265. His emotionalism extended as well to the death of pets. When their dog "Brownie" died, Long gave an extensive, emotional account of the dog's life and how it was part of the family (*Journal*, p. 328).

14. Ibid., pp. 46, 241; for an example of the theme of music in his public speeches, see *After Dinner*, pp. 134–36; *At the Fireside*, pp. 24–25.

15. Long, *America of Yesterday*, pp. 6, 163–80; John D. Long, "General Robert E. Lee," *Massachusetts Historical Society Proceedings* (Apr. 1911), p. 595; idem, *Journal*, p. 215.

16. Long, *Journal*, pp. 25, 97.

17. Isaacson and Thomas, pp. 154, 164–67, 228, 238, 240, 243, 286, 405, 436–37, 477, 487–88.

18. Goodwin, p. 133; Humphrey, p. 321.

19. Shapley, pp. 473–4.

20. Ibid., pp. 39, 215–6, 263, 408, 415, 444, 458, 499, 586.

21. Robert Putnam, *Bowling Alone: The Collapse and Revival of American Community* (New York: Simon & Schuster, 2000); Carl Boggs, *The End of Politics: Corporate Power and the Decline of the Public Sphere* (New York: Guilford, 2000).

22. J. Glenn Gray, *The Warriors*, pp. 235–37.

23. Hannah Arendt, *The Human Condition* (Chicago: University of Chicago Press, 1958); Aristotle, *Politics*, translated and edited by Ernest Barker (New York: Oxford University Press, 1958), pp. 5–6.

24. Hay, *Addresses*, p. 141; Goodwin, p. 331; Loren Baritz, *Backfire: A History of How American Culture Led Us into Vietnam and Made Us Fight the Way We Did* (New York: W. Morrow, 1985), pp. 29–40; Neil Sheehan, *A Bright Shining Lie*, pp. 285, 374); Halberstam, *The Best and the Brightest*, pp. 44, 134–35; J. William Fulbright, *The Arrogance of Power* (New York, Random House, 1967); CR, 89th Cong., 1st sess., (1965), p. 9221.

25. Berman, *Johnson's War*, pp. 19, 93, 99, 118, 120.

26. Halberstam, p. 616. During the Persian Gulf War, Carol Cohn argues that there was a "supplanting of political and moral discourse by a military-techno-bureaucratic one." In "The Language of the Gulf War," *Center Review*, 5, no. 2 (Fall 1991).

27. R. Kastenbaum and R. B. Aisenberg, *The Psychology of Death* (New York: Springer 1972), pp. 207–8; Becker, pp. 2–3.

28. Aries, *The Hour of Our Death*, p. 560; Robert Fulton, *Death and Identity* (New York: Wiley & Sons, 1965), p. 82; this characterization of America's relationship to death is found in Geoffrey Gorer, *Death, Grief, and Mourning in Contemporary Britain* (Garden City, NJ: Doubleday 1965), p. 111; and idem, "The Pornography of Death," *Modern Writing* (1956), pp. 56–62; see also Robert Fulton, *Death and Identity*, p. 82; Octavio Paz, "The Day of the Dead," pp. 382–95. For a study of these mechanisms at work in media and government portrayals of the Gulf War, see Umberson and Henderson, "The Social Construction of Death in the Gulf War," *Omega*, 25, no. 1 (1992), pp. 1–15.

29. Cohen, *A Baker's Nickel*, p. 56.

30. George Lakoff, "Metaphor and War: the Metaphor System used to Justify War in the Gulf," *Peace Research*, 23 (1991), pp. 25–32; see also George Orwell, "Politics and the English Language," in *Shooting an Elephant and Other Essays* (New York: Harcourt, Brace, 1950), pp. 162–78.

31. Nitze, *From Hiroshima to Glasnost*, pp. 42–43.

32. See Sheehan, pp. 287–88.

33. Khong, p. 128.

34. Scarry, p. 71.

35. FRUS, 1918, Supplement, Part I, p. 268.

36. As noted in Chapter 4, the language runs throughout Acheson's, *Present at the Creation*, pp. 27–8, 41, 81–83, 127, 223–24, 373, 383, 396, 400, 440, 487, 495, 556, 564, 571, 586, 625, 633, 644, 701. This same trope, particularly the emphasis on the "death" of issues, runs with somewhat less frequency through Rusk's reminiscences as well (*As I Saw It*, pp. 222, 243, 255, 265, 266, 275).

37. Quoted in Barrett, p. 658.

38. *Congressional Digest*, 45, no. 4 (Apr. 66), p. 113; PP V.A.D.42, 55, 12–13; Isaacson and Thomas, p. 694.

39. For a discussion of the focus on the disease rather than the patient, see Nuland, *How We Die*, p. 249.

40. For discussions of the corrupting effects of power, see David Kipnis, *The Powerholders* (Chicago: University of Chicago Press, 1976); Pitirim Sorokin,

Power and Morality: Who shall Guard the Guardians? (Boston: P. Sargent, 1959); Neibuhr, *Moral Man and Immoral Society*, pp. 10–13.

41. Anthony Summers, *The Arrogance of Power: The Secret World of Richard Nixon* (New York: Viking Press, 2000).

42. Rusk, p. 417; Shapley, p. 447; Berman, *Planning a Tragedy*, p. 45.

43. Thomas Friedman, *The Lexus and the Olive Tree: Understanding Globalization*, rev. ed. (New York: Anchor Books, 2000).

44. Nancy McGlen and Meredith Sarkees, *The Status of Women in Foreign Policy* (New York: Foreign Policy Association, 1996); Rhodri Jeffreys-Jones, *Changing Differences: Women and the Shaping of American Foreign Policy, 1917–1994* (New Brunswick, NJ: Rutgers University Press, 1995).

45. Joseph Underhill-Cady and Andrea Cobery, "The Throat of War: Evolving American Justifications of Death in Battle at the end of the Cold War," paper presented at the International Studies Association Conference, Los Angeles, CA (March 2000).

46. Susan Jeffords, *The Remasculinization of America: Gender and the Vietnam War* (Indianapolis: Indiana University Press, 1989).

47. Kristin Ann Hass, *Carried to the Wall: American Memory and the Vietnam Veterans Memorial* (Berkeley: University of California Press, 1998).

48. Peter D. Feaver and Christopher Gelpe, "How many Deaths are Acceptable? A Surprising Answer," *Washington Post* (Nov. 7, 1999), p. B3.

49. *New York Times* (May 1, 1999).

50. Edward N. Luttwak, "A Post-heroic Military Policy: Post–Cold War U.S. Military Policy," *Foreign Affairs*, 75, no. 4 (July-August 1996), pp. 33–44.

51. On the effects of nuclear weapons on American culture, see Paul S. Boyer, *By the Bomb's Early Light: American Thought and Culture at the Dawn of the Atomic Age* (Chapel Hill: University of North Carolina Press, 1994).

52. See John Keegan, *The Face of Battle*.

53. Steven Lee Myers, "Drop in Recruits Pushes Pentagon to Return New Strategy," *The New York Times Online*, September 27, 1999.

54. Madeleine Albright, "U.S. Efforts to Preserve America's Security," *U.S. Department of State Dispatch*, 9, no. 5 (June 1998), pp. 11–15.

55. Sylvia Tesh, *Hidden Arguments: Political Ideology and Disease Prevention Policy* (New Brunswick, NJ: Rutgers University Press, 1988).

56. Michael Ignatieff, *Virtual War*; Paul Virilio, *War and Cinema*; Jean Baudrillard, *The Gulf War Did Not Take Place*, translated and with an introduction by Paul Patton (Bloomington: Indiana University Press, 1995).

57. Abdel R. Omran, "Epidemiological Transition in the United States: The Health Factor in Population Change," *Population Bulletin*, 32, no. 2 (1977).

58. Underhill-Cady and Cobery, "The Throat of War."

59. Hobbes, *Leviathan*, p. 188.

60. Lakoff and Johnson, *Metaphors We Live By* and *Philosophy in the Flesh*.

61. Ernest May, *"Lessons" of the Past: The Use and Misuse of History in American Foreign Policy* (New York: Oxford University Press, 1973); Richard

Neustadt and Ernest May, *Thinking in Time: The Uses of History for Decision-makers* (New York: Free Press, 1986); Yuen Foong Khong, *Analogies at War: Korea, Munich, Dien Bien Phu and the Vietnam Decisions of 1965* (Princeton, NJ: Princeton University Press, 1992).

62. Khong, pp. 254–58.

63. Hannah Arendt, *On Violence* (New York: Harcourt, Brace & World, 1970).

64. This bargaining in warfare is a central feature of Schelling's discussion of *The Strategy of Conflict* (New York: Oxford University Press, 1963).

65. This is Freud's prescription at the end of "Thoughts for the Times on War and Death," pp. 299–300.

66. Roosevelt, *Letters*, Vol. II, pp. 845, 862, 864.

67. Gillett, *George Frisbie Hoar*, p. 203.

68. Goodwin, pp. i - iii.

69. Kennan, *Around the Cragged Hill*, Ch. 1, pp. 35–6, 59, 98; Hans Morgenthau, *Politics Among Nations*, 5th ed. (New York: Knopf, 1985), pp. 550–58; idem, "Globalism: Johnson's Moral Crusade;" Reinhold Neibuhr, *Moral Man and Immoral Society*.

70. Bill Adler, ed., *The Kennedy Reader* (Indianapolis, IN: Bobbs-Merrill Co., 1967), pp. 123–26.

BIBLIOGRAPHY

I. THEORY AND METHOD

Aho, James. *Religious Mythology and the Art of War: Comparative Religious Symbolisms of Military Violence*. Westport, CT: Greenwood Press, 1981.

———. *This Thing of Darkness: A Sociology of the Enemy*. Seattle: University of Washington Press, 1994.

Alker, Hayward. "The Humanistic Moment in International Studies: Reflections on Machiavelli and las Casas." *International Studies Quarterly*, 36, no. 4 (Dec. 1992), pp. 347–71.

Anderson, Benedict. *Imagined Communities: Reflections on the Origin and Spread of Nationalism*, rev. ed. New York: Verso, 1991.

Anderson, Dwight G. *Abraham Lincoln: The Quest for Immortality*. New York: Knopf, 1982.

Arendt, Hannah. *On Violence*. New York: Harcourt, Brace & World, 1970.

———. *The Human Condition*. Chicago: University of Chicago Press, 1958.

Aries, Philippe. *The Hour of Our Death*. New York: Knopf, 1981.

———. "The Reversal of Death." In David Stannard, ed., *Death in America*. Philadelphia: University of Pennsylvania Press, 1975.

Axelrod, Robert. *The Evolution of Cooperation*. New York: Basic Books, 1984.

Baudelaire, Charles. "On the Essence of Laughter." In *The Painter of Modern Life, and Other Essays*, pp. 153–54. London: Phaidon Press, 1964.

Baudrillard, Jean. *The Gulf War Did Not Take Place*, translated and with an introduction by Paul Patton. Bloomington: Indiana University Press, 1995.

Becker, Ernest. *The Denial of Death*. New York: Basic Books, 1976.

Beer, Francis, and Barry Balleck. "Body, Mind, and Soul in the Gulf War Debate." Paper prepared for the International Studies Association Meeting, March 1993, Acapulco, Mexico.

Beer, Francis, and Robert Hariman, eds. *Post-Realism: The Rhetorical Turn in International Relations*. East Lansing: Michigan State University Press, 1996.

Bellah, Robert. "Civil Religion in America," *Daedalus*, 117, no. 3 (1988), pp. 97–118.

Berger, Peter, and Thomas Luckmann. *The Social Construction of Reality: A Treatise in the Sociology of Knowledge*. Garden City, NY: Doubleday, 1966.

Blain, Michael. "The Role of Death in Political Conflict." *The Psychoanalytic Review*, 63, no. 2, (1976), pp. 249–65.

Blainey, Geoffrey. *The Causes of War,* 3rd ed. New York: The Free Press, 1988.

Boggs, Carl. *The End of Politics: Corporate Power and the Decline of the Public Sphere.* New York: Guilford, 2000.

Boynton, G. R., and Francis A. Beer. "Speaking about Dying." In Sally Jackson, ed. *Argumentation and Values, Proceedings of the Ninth SCA/AFA Conference on Argumentation,* pp. 550–56. Annandale, VA: Speech Communication Association, 1995.

Bueno de Mesquita, Bruce. *The War Trap.* New Haven, CT: Yale University Press, 1981.

Bueno de Mesquita, Bruce, and David Lalman. *Reason and War: Domestic and International Imperatives.* New Haven, CT: Yale University Press, 1992.

Burke, K. *Language as Symbolic Action.* Berkeley: University of California Press, 1966.

Burnett, Ron. *Cultures of Vision: Images, Media, and the Imaginary.* Bloomington and Indianapolis: Indiana University Press, 1995.

Campbell, David. *Politics Without Principle: Sovereignty, Ethics, and the Narratives of the Gulf War.* Boulder, CO: Lynne Rienner, 1993.

———. *Writing Security: United States Foreign Policy and the Politics of Identity.* Minneapolis: University of Minnesota Press, 1992.

Chilton, Paul. *Security Metaphors: Cold War Discourse from Containment to Common House.* New York: Peter Lang, 1995.

Choron, Jacques. *Death and Modern Man.* New York: Collier Books, 1972.

Cohn, Carol. "Sex and Death in the Rational World of Defense Intellectuals." *Signs: Journal of Women in Culture and Society,* 12, no. 4 (1987), pp. 687–718.

Cohn, Jonathan. "Revenge of the Nerds or Irrational Exuberance: When did political science forget about politics?" *The New Republic,* online edition, October 25, 1999; available at http://www.tnr.com/archive/ 1099/102599/coverstory 102599.html.

Connolly, William E. *Identity/Difference: Democratic Negotiations of Political Paradox.* Ithaca, NY: Cornell University Press, 1991.

Cottam, Richard W. *Foreign Policy Motivation: A General Theory and a Case Study.* Pittsburgh, PA: University of Pittsburgh Press, 1977.

De Landtsheer, Christ'l, and Ofer Feldman. *Politically Speaking: A Worldwide Examination of Language Use in the Public Sphere.* Westport, CT: Praeger, 1998.

De Man, Paul. "The Epistemology of Metaphor." In Michael Shapiro, ed., *Language and Politics.* New York: New York University Press, 1984.

Denzin, Norman K., and Yvonna S. Lincoln, eds., *Handbook of Qualitative Research.* Thousand Oaks, CA: Sage, 1994.

Der Derian, James. *Antidiplomacy: Spies, Terror, Speed, and War.* Cambridge, MA: Blackwell, 1992.

Doty, Roxanne Lynn. "Foreign Policy as Social Construction: A Post-positivist Analysis of U.S. Counterinsurgency Policy in the Philippines." *International Studies Quarterly,* 37 (1993), pp. 297–320.

Ehrenreich, Barbara. *Blood Rites: Origins and History of the Passions of War.* New York: Henry Holt & Co., 1997.

Edelman, Murray. *Politics as Symbolic Action: Mass Arousal and Quiescence.* Chicago: Markham Pub. Co., 1971.

———. *The Symbolic Uses of Politics.* Urbana: University of Illinois Press, 1964.

Elshtain, Jean Bethke. "Sovereignty, Identity, Sacrifice." In Marjorie Ringrose and Adam Lerner, eds., *Reimagining the Nation.* Philadelphia: Open University Press, 1993.

———. *Women and War.* New York: Basic Books, 1987.

Elshtain, Jean Bethke, et al. *But Was it Just? Reflections on the Morality of the Persian Gulf War.* New York: Doubleday, 1992.

Enloe, Cynthia. *Bananas, Beaches, and Bases: Making Feminist Sense of International Politics.* Berkeley: University of California, 1990.

Etheredge, Lloyd. *A World of Men: The Private Sources of American Foreign Policy.* Cambridge, MA: MIT Press, 1978.

Feaver, Peter D., and Christopher Gelpe. "How many Deaths are Acceptable? A Surprising Answer." *Washington Post* (Nov. 7, 1999), p. B3.

Feldman, Martha, and James March. "Information in Organizations as Signal and Symbol," *Administrative Science Quarterly*, 26 (1981), pp. 171–86.

Fernandez, James. *Persuasions and Performances: The Play of Tropes in Culture.* Bloomington: Indiana University Press, 1986.

Finnemore, Martha. *National Interests in International Society.* Ithaca, NY: Cornell University Press, 1996.

Foucault, Michel. *Discipline and Punish: The Birth of the Prison.* New York: Vintage, 1979.

Freud, Sigmund. "Thoughts for the Times on War and Death." In James Strachey and Anna Freud, eds., *Collected Works of Sigmund Freud*, pp. 275–300. London: Hogarth Press.

Friedman, Thomas L. *The Lexus and the Olive Tree: Understanding Globalization*, rev. ed. New York: Anchor Books, 2000.

Fritzgerald, Frances. *Way Out There in the Blue: Reagan and Star Wars and the End of the Cold War.* New York: Simon & Schuster, 2000.

Fulton, Robert, ed. *Death and Identity.* New York: Wiley & Sons, 1965.

Fussell, Paul. *The Great War and Modern Memory.* New York: Oxford University Press, 1975.

Gartner, Scott Sigmund, and Gary M. Segura. "War, Casualties, and Public Opinion." *Journal of Conflict Resolution*, 42, no. 3 (June 1998), pp. 278–300.

Geertz, Clifford. *The Interpretation of Cultures.* New York: Basic Books, 1973.

George, Alexander. "The 'Operational Code': A Neglected Approach to the Study of Political Leaders and Decision-Making." *International Studies Quarterly*, 13, no. 2 (June 1969), pp. 190–222.

Giddens, Anthony. *The Constitution of Society.* Berkeley: University of California Press, 1984.

Gilpin, Robert. *War and Change in World Politics.* Cambridge: Cambridge University Press, 1981.

Gioseffi, Daniella, ed. *Women on War: Essential Voices for the Nuclear Age from a Brilliant International Assembly.* New York: Touchstone, 1988.

Gorer, Geoffrey. *Death, Grief, and Mourning.* New York: Arno Press, 1977.

———. "The Pornography of Death." *Modern Writing* (1956), pp. 56–62.

Gray, J. Glenn. *The Warriors: Reflections of Men in Battle.* New York: Harper Torch, 1970.

Griffin, Susan. *A Chorus of Stones.* New York: Anchor Doubleday, 1993.

———. *Woman and Nature: The Roaring Inside Her.* San Francisco: Sierra Club Books, 2000.

Hall, Peter. "Ideas and the Social Sciences." In Robert Keohane and Judith Goldstein, eds., *Ideas and Foreign Policy.* Ithaca, NY: Cornell University Press, 1992.

Hamerton-Kelly, Robert G. *Violent Origins: Walter Burkert, Rene Girard, and Jonathan Smith on Rithual Killing and Cultural Formation.* Stanford, CA: Stanford University Press, 1987.

Harding, Sandra, ed. *Feminism and Methodology: Social Science Issues.* Bloomington: Indiana University Press, 1987.

Hegel, G. W. F. *Introduction to Lectures on the Philosophy of World History.* Translated by H. B. Nisbet. New York: Cambridge University Press, 1975.

Heidegger, Martin. *Being and Time.* New York: Harper, 1962.

Hermann, Margaret. "Explaining Foreign Policy Behavior Using Personal Characteristics of Political Leaders." *International Studies Quarterly,* 24 (1980), pp. 7–46.

Hertz, Robert. *Death and The Right Hand.* Glencoe, IL: Free Press, 1960.

Hirschbein, Ron. *Newest Weapons/Oldest Psychology: The Dialetics of American Nuclear Strategy.* New York: Peter Lang, 1989.

Hobbes, Thomas. *Leviathan.* Edited by C. B. Macpherson. New York: Penguin Classics, 1987 (1651).

Holsti, K. J. *The Dividing Discipline: Hegemony and Diversity in International Theory.* Boston: Allen & Unwin, 1985.

Holsti, Ole. "Cognitive Dynamics and Images of the Enemy: Dulles and Russia." In D. Finlay, O. Holsti, and R. Fagen, eds., *Enemies in Politics,* pp. 25–96. Chicago: Rand McNally, 1967.

Howard, Michael. *The Causes of War,* 2nd ed. Cambridge, MA: Harvard University Press, 1983.

Hunt, Michael. *Ideology and U.S. Foreign Policy.* New Haven, CT: Yale University Press, 1987.

Ikle, Fred C. *Every War Must End,* rev. ed. New York: Columbia University Press, 1991.

Janis, Irving, and Leon Mann. *Decision Making: A Psychological Analysis of Conflict, Choice, and Commitment.* New York: Free Press, 1977.

Jeffords, Susan. *The Remasculinization of America: Gender and the Vietnam War.* Indianapolis: Indiana University Press, 1989.

Jeffreys-Jones, Rhodri. *Changing Differences: Women and the Shaping of American Foreign Policy, 1917–1994.* New Brunswick, NJ: Rutgers University Press, 1995.

Jervis, Robert. *Perception and Misperception in International Politics.* Princeton, NJ: Princeton University Press, 1976.

Kantorowicz, Ernst. *The King's Two Bodies.* Princeton, NJ: Princeton University Press, 1957.

Kaplan, Amy, and Donald Pease, eds., *Cultures of United States Imperialism.* Durham, NC: Duke University Press, 1993.

Kastenbaum, Robert, and R. Aisenberg, *The Psychology of Death.* New York: Springer, 1972.

Katzenstein, Peter. *The Culture of National Security.* New York: Columbia University Press, 1996.

Keller, Evelyn Fox. *Secrets of Life, Secrets of Death: Essays on Language, Gender and Science.* New York: Routledge, 1992.

Keohane, Robert, and Judith Goldstein. *Ideas and Foreign Policy: Beliefs, Institutions, and Political Change.* Ithaca, NY: Cornell University Press, 1993.

Khong, Yuen Foong. *Analogies at War: Korea, Munich, Dien Bien Phu, and the Vietnam Decisions of 1965.* Princeton, NJ: Princeton University Press, 1992.

Kierkegaard, Soren. *Fear and Trembling and The Sickness unto Death.* Translated by Walter Lowrie. Princeton, NJ: Princeton University Press, 1954.

King, Gary, Robert Keohane, and Sidney Verba. *Designing Social Inquiry: Scientific Inference in Qualitative Research.* Princeton, NJ: Princeton University Press, 1994.

Kipnis, David. *The Powerholders.* Chicago: University of Chicago Press, 1976.

Kittay, Eva F. "Womb Envy: An Explanatory Concept." In Joyce Trebilcot, ed., *Mothering: Essays in Feminist Theory,* pp. 94–128. Totowa, NJ: Rowman & Allanheld, 1984.

Kubler-Ross, Elizabeth. *On Death and Dying.* London: Macmillan, 1969.

Kuhn, Thomas. *The Structure of Scientific Revolutions,* 2nd ed. Chicago: University of Chicago Press, 1970.

Lakoff, George. "Metaphor and War: The Metaphor System used to Justify War in the Gulf." *Peace Research,* 23 (1991), pp. 25–32.

———. *Women, Fire, and Dangerous Things: What Categories Reveal about the Mind.* Chicago: University of Chicago Press, 1987.

Lakoff, George, and David Johnson. *Metaphors We Live By.* Chicago: University of Chicago Press, 1983.

———. *Philosophy in the Flesh: The Embodied Mind and its Challenge to Western Thought.* New York: Basic Books, 1999.

Lapid, Yusef, and Friedrich Kratochwil, eds., *The Return of Culture and Identity in IR Theory.* Boulder, CO: Lynne Reinner, 1996.

Lasswell, Harold. *Psychopathology and Politics.* Chicago: University of Chicago Press, 1977.

Lebow, Richard Ned. *Between Peace and War: The Nature of International Crisis.* Baltimore, MD: Johns Hopkins University Press, 1981.

Lechte, John. *Fifty Key Contemporary Thinkers: From Structuralism to Postmodernity.* New York: Routledge, 1994.

Lincoln, Bruce. *Death, War, and Sacrifice: Studies in Ideology and Practice.* Chicago: University of Chicago Press, 1991.

Luke, Tim. "Discourses of Disintegration, Texts of Transformation: Re-Reading Realism in the New World Order." *Alternatives,* 18 (1993), pp. 229–258.

Luttwak, Edward. "Toward Post-Heroic Warfare." *Foreign Affairs* 74, no. 3 (May/June 1995), pp. 109–22.

————. "A Post-heroic Military Policy: Post–Cold War U.S. Military Policy." *Foreign Affairs*, 75, no. 4 (July - August 1996), pp. 33–44.

Malinowski, Bronislaw. *Magic, Science, and Religion, and Other Essays*. Garden City, NY: Doubleday, 1954.

March, James, and Johan Olsen. "The New Institutionalism: Organizational Factors in Political Life." *American Political Science Review*, 78, no. 3 (Sept. 1984), pp. 734–47.

————. *Rediscovering Institutions: The Organizational Basis of Politics*. New York: Free Press, 1989.

Martin, Joanne. "Deconstructing Organizational Taboos: The Suppression of Gender Conflict in Organizations." *Organizational Science*, 1, no. 4 (1990), pp. 339–59.

Marx, Karl. "The German Ideology." In Robert C. Tucker, ed., *The Marx-Engels Reader*, 2nd ed. New York: W. W. Norton, 1978.

May, Elaine Tyler. *Homeward Bound: American Families in the Cold War Era*. New York: Basic Books, 1988.

May, Ernest. *"Lessons" of the Past: The Use and Misuse of History in American Foreign Policy*. New York: Oxford University Press, 1973.

McGlen, Nancy, and Meredith Sarkees. *The Status of Women in Foreign Policy*. New York: Foreign Policy Association, 1996.

Metcalf, Peter, and Richard Huntington. *Celebrations of Death: The Anthropology of Mortuary Ritual*, 2nd ed. New York: Cambridge University Press, 1991.

Midlarsky, Manus, ed. *The Handbook of War Studies*. Boston: Unwin Hyman, 1989.

Mills, C. Wright. "Situated Actions and Vocabularies of Motive." In Michael Shapiro, ed., *Language and Politics*. New York: New York University Press, 1984.

Morgenthau, Hans. "Death in the Nuclear Age." In Nathan Scott, ed., *The Modern Vision of Death*. Richmond, VA: John Knox, 1967.

————. *Politics Among Nations*, 5th ed. New York: Knopf, 1985.

————. *Scientific Man Vs. Power Politics*, Midway Reprint. Chicago: University of Chicago Press, 1974.

Mosse, George. *Fallen Soldiers: Reshaping the Memory of the World War*. New York: Oxford University Press, 1990.

Neibuhr, Reinhold. *Moral Man and Immoral Society: A Study in Ethics and Politics*. New York: Charles Scribner's Sons, 1932.

Neustadt, Richard, and Ernest May. *Thinking in Time: The Uses of History for Decision-makers*. New York: Free Press, 1986.

Orwell, George. "Politics and the English Language." In *Shooting an Elephant and Other Essays*, pp. 162–78. New York: Harcourt, Brace, 1950.

Oye, Kenneth, ed. *Cooperation Under Anarchy*. Princeton, NJ: Princeton University Press, 1986.

Paz, Octavio. "The Day of the Dead." In David Fulton, ed., *Death and Identity*, pp. 382–95. New York: Wiley & Sons, 1965.

Peterson, Spike. "Transgressing Boundaries: Theories of Knowledge, Gender, and International Relations." *Millenium*, 21, no. 2 (1992), pp. 183–206.

Pick, Daniel. *The War Machine: The Rationalization of Slaughter in the Modern Age.* New Haven, CT: Yale University Press, 1993.

Plato. *The Republic.* Translated by George M. Grube. Indianapolis, IN: Hackett Pub. Co., 1974.

Putnam, Robert. *Bowling Alone: The Collapse and Revival of American Community.* New York: Simon & Schuster, 2000.

Richardson, Lewis F. *The Statistics of Deadly Quarrels.* Pittsburgh, PA: Boxwood Press, 1960.

Rogin, Michael. *Ronald Reagan, the Movie and other Episodes in Political Demonology.* Berkeley: University of California Press, 1987.

Rosenberg, Emily S. " 'Foreign Affairs' after World War II: Connecting Sexual and International Politics." *Diplomatic History,* 18, no. 1 (Winter 1994), pp. 59–70.

Rosenblatt, Paul, R. Patricia Walsh, and Douglas Jackson, *Grief and Mourning in Cross-cultural Perspective.* Washington, DC: Human Rights Area Files Press, 1976.

Rummel, Rudolph J. *The Dimensions of Nations.* Beverly Hills, CA: Sage Publications, 1972.

Rushing, Janice Hocker, and Thomas S. Frentz. *Projecting the Shadow: The Cyborg Hero in American Film.* Chicago: University of Chicago Press, 1995.

Said, Edward. *Orientalism.* New York: Vintage, 1979.

Sapir, J., and J. Crocker, eds. *The Social Uses of Metaphor: Essays on the Anthropology of Rhetoric.* Philadelphia: University of Pennsylvania Press, 1977.

Saywell, Shelley. *Women in War.* New York: Penguin, 1985.

Scarry, Elaine. *The Body in Pain: The Making and Unmaking of the World.* New York: Oxford University Press, 1985.

Scheff, Thomas J. *Catharsis in Healing, Ritual, and Drama.* Berkeley: University of California Press, 1979.

Schelling, Thomas C. *The Strategy of Conflict.* New York: Oxford University Press, 1963.

———. *Arms and Influence.* New Haven, CT: Yale University Press, 1966.

Schmitt, Carl. *The Concept of the Political.* Translated by George Schwab. New Brunswick, NJ: Rutgers University Press, 1976.

Schutz, Alfred. *Reflections on the Problem of Relevance.* New Haven, CT: Yale University Press, 1970.

Sen, Amartya. "Rational Fools: A Critique of the Behavioral Foundations of Economic Theory," *Philosophy and Public Affairs,* 6 (Summer 1977), pp. 317–44.

Shapiro, Michael J., ed. *Language and Politics.* New York: New York University Press, 1984.

Shapiro, Michael J., and Hayward Alker, eds. *Challenging Boundaries: Global Flows, Territorial Identities.* Minneapolis: University of Minnesota Press, 1996.

Sibley, Mulford Q. "The Limits of Behavioralism," in James C. Charlesworth, ed. *The Limits of Behavioralism in Political Science.* Philadelphia, PA: AAPSS, 1962.

Singer, J. David, and Melvin Small. *Resort to Arms: International and Civil Wars, 1816–1980,* 2nd ed. Beverly Hills, CA: Sage Publications, 1982.

Skocpol, Theda. *Bringing the State Back In.* New York: Cambridge University Press, 1985.

Slotkin, Richard. *Gunfighter Nation: The Myth of the Frontier in Twentieth-Century America.* Tulsa: University of Oklahoma Press, 1998.

Sontag, Susan. *Illness as Metaphor and AIDS and its Metaphors.* New York: Anchor Doubleday, 1990.

Sorokin, Pitirim. *Power and Morality: Who shall Guard the Guardians?* Boston: P. Sargent, 1959.

Stannard, David, ed. *Death in America.* Philadelphia: University of Pennsylvania Press, 1975.

Theweleit, Klaus. *Male Fantasies.* Minneapolis: University of Minnesota Press, 1987.

Thompson, Kenneth W. *Traditions and Values in Politics and Diplomacy: Theory and Practice.* Baton Rouge: Louisiana State University Press, 1992.

Tickner, J. Ann. *Gender in International Relations: Feminist Perspectives on Achieving Global Security.* New York: Columbia University Press, 1992.

Turner, Victor. "Death and the Dead in the Pilgrimage Process." In *Religion and Social Change in Southern Africa,* pp. 107–27. Cape Town: David Philip, 1975.

Turner, Victor, and Edith Turner. *Image and Pilgrimage in Christian Culture.* New York: Columbia University Press, 1978.

Twing, Stephen W. *Myths, Models, and U.S. Foreign Policy: The Cultural Shaping of Three Cold Warriors.* Boulder, CO: Lynne Reinner, 1998.

Underhill-Cady, Joseph. "Doing Battle with Death: U.S. Foreign Policy Elite and the Discourse on War, 1898–1968." Ph.D. Dissertation, University of Michigan, 1995.

———. "Faith and Foreign Policy: Death and Religion in the American Discourse on War." In *Religion, War and Peace,* Conference Proceedings of the Wisconsin Institute. Ripon, WI: Wisconsin Institute, 1997.

———. "Nine Walls to Keep out Nothing," *Dimensions,* 9 (Spring 1995), pp. 90–103.

Underhill-Cady, Joseph, and Andrea Cobery. "The Throat of War: Evolving American Justifications of Death in Battle at the End of the Cold War." Paper presented at the International Studies Association Conference, March 2000, Los Angeles, CA.

Van Evera, Stephan. "The Cult of the Offensive and the Origins of the First World War." *International Security,* 9, no. 1 (1984), pp. 58–107.

Van Gennep, Arnold. *The Rites of Passage.* Chicago: University of Chicago Press, 1960.

Virilio, Paul. *War and Cinema: The Logistics of Perception.* Translated by Patrick Camiller. New York: Verso, 1989.

Walt, Stephen. "Rigor or Rigor Mortis: Rational Choice and Security Studies." *International Security,* 23, no. 4 (Spring 1999), pp. 5–29.

Weldes, Jutta. *Constructing National Interests: The United States and the Cuban Missile Crisis.* Minneapolis: University of Minnesota Press, 1999.

———. "Going Cultural: Star Trek, State Action, and Popular Culture." *Millennium: Journal of International Studies,* 28, no. 1 (Spring 1999), pp. 67–91.

Wendt, Alexander. "Anarchy is What States Make of It: The Social Construction of Power Politics." *International Organization,* 46 (Spring 1992), pp. 391–425.

Winter, David G. "Power, Affliliation, and War: Three Tests of a Motivational Model." *Journal of Personality and Social Psychology*, 65, no. 3 (1993), pp. 532–45.

———. *The Power Motive*. New York: Free Press, 1973.

Wittman, Donald. "How a War Ends: A Rational Model Approach." *Journal of Conflict Resolution*, 23, no. 4 (1979), pp. 743–63.

Zizek, Slavoj. *Looking Awry: An Introduction to Jacques Lacan through Popular Culture*. Cambridge: MIT Press, 1991.

II. Historical and Primary Sources

Acheson, Dean. "Public Opinion and American Foreign Policy," *Department of State Bulletin*, (Aug. 1, 1949).

———. *Present at the Creation: My Years in the State Department*. New York: Norton, 1969.

Adler, Bill, comp. *The Kennedy Reader*. Indianapolis: Bobbs-Merrill Co., 1967.

Aldrich, Nelson W. *Old Money: The Mythology of America's Upper Class*. New York: A. A. Knopf, 1988.

Alger, Russell. *Eulogy on the Late General Philip H. Sheridan*. Detroit: J. F. Eby & Co., 1888.

Ambrose, Stephen. *Citizen Soldiers: The U.S. Army from the Normandy Beaches to the Bulge to the Surrender of Germany, June 7, 1944 to May 7, 1945*. New York: Touchstone Books, 1998.

Amos, James E. *Theodore Roosevelt: Hero to his Valet*. New York: John Day Co., 1927.

Arnold, David, ed. *Imperial Medicine and Indigenous Societies*. New York: St. Martin's, 1988.

Ball, George W. "Top Secret: The Prophecy the President Rejected." *The Atlantic*, 230, no. 1 (July 1972), pp. 36–49.

———. *The Past Has Another Pattern*. New York: Norton, 1982.

Balfour, Arthur J. *Decadence*. Cambridge: Cambridge University Press, 1908.

Bancroft, George, "Abraham Lincoln." In *Memorial Addresses Delivered Before the Two Houses of Congress on the Life and Character of Abraham Lincoln, James A. Garfield, William McKinley*. Washington, DC: GPO, 1903.

Baritz, Loren. *Backfire: A History of how American Culture Led Us into Vietnam and Made Us Fight the Way We Did*. New York: W. Morrow, 1985.

Barnet, Richard. "The National Security Managers and the National Interest." *Politics and Society* (Feb. 1971), pp. 257–68.

Barrett, David. "The Mythology Surrounding Lyndon Johnson, His Advisors, and the 1965 Decision to Escalate the Vietnam War." *Political Science Quarterly*, 103, no. 4 (1988), pp. 637–63.

Berman, Larry. *Lyndon Johnson's War: The Road to Stalemate in Vietnam*. New York: Norton, 1989.

———. *Planning a Tragedy: The Americanization of the War in Vietnam*. New York: W. W. Norton, 1982.

Beschloss, Michael. *Taking Charge: The Johnson White House Tapes, 1963–64*. New York: Simon & Schuster, 1997.

Bourke, Joanna. *An Intimate History of Killing: Face to Face Killing in 20th Century Warfare*. New York: Basic Books, 1999.

Boyer, Paul S. *By the Bomb's Early Light: American Thought and Culture at the Dawn of the Atomic Age*. Chapel Hill: University of North Carolina Press, 1994.

Brecher, Michael, and Michael Wilkenfeld. *Crises in the Twentieth Century*. New York: Pergamon Press, 1988.

Brittain, Vera. *Testament of Youth: An Autobiographical Study of the Years 1900–1925*. New York: Wideview Books, 1980.

Broyles, Jr., William. "Why Men Love War." *Esquire* (November 1984), pp. 55–65.

Bunyan, John. *The Pilgrim's Progress*. Edited by N. H. Keeble. New York: Oxford University Press, 1984.

Burton, David H. "Theodore Roosevelt's Social Darwinism and Views on Imperialism." *Journal of the History of Ideas*, 26 (Jan. 1965), pp. 103–18.

Bush, Barbara. *Barbara Bush: A Memoir*. New York: Scribner's Sons, 1994.

Bush, George. *All the Best, George Bush: My Life in Letters and Other Writings*. New York: Scribner, 1999.

———. "Getting it Right." *Forbes*, 160, no. 6 (Sept. 22, 1997), pp. 114–20.

Caro, Robert. *The Years of Lyndon Johnson, Vol. I: The Path to Power*. New York: Knopf, 1982.

———. *The Years of Lyndon Johnson, Vol. II: The Means of Ascent*. New York: Vintage, 1990.

Clark, Joseph S. *Stalemate in Vietnam*. Report to the Committee of Foreign Relations, United States Senate. Washington, DC: GPO, 1968.

Clifford, Clark, with Richard Holbrooke. *Counsel to the President: A Memoir*. New York: Random House, 1991.

Clymer, Kenton J. *John Hay: The Gentleman as Diplomat*. Ann Arbor: University of Michigan Press, 1975.

Cohen, William S. *A Baker's Nickel*. New York: William Morrow & Co. 1986.

———. *Of Sons and Seasons*. New York: Hamilton Press, 1987.

Cohn, Carol. "The Language of the Gulf War." *Center Review*, 5, no. 2 (Fall 1991), pp. 593–95.

Collins, Richard. *Theodore Roosevelt, Culture, Diplomacy, and Expansion*. Baton Rouge: Louisiana State University Press, 1985.

Colombo, Furio. *God in America: Religion and Politics in the United States*. Translated by Kristin Jarratt. New York: Columbia University Press, 1984.

Congressional Digest Corp. *The Congressional Digest*. Washington, DC: Congressional Digest Corp, 1964–68.

Dawes, Charles G. *A Journal of the McKinley Years*. Chicago: Lakeside Press, 1950.

Dennett, Tyler. *John Hay: From Poetry to Politics*. Port Washington, NY: Kennikat Press, 1963.

Dower, John. *War Without Mercy: Race and Power in the Pacific War*. New York: Pantheon, 1986.

Drinnon, Richard. *Facing West: The Metaphysics of Indian-hating and Empire Building*. Minneapolis: University of Minnesota Press, 1980.

Eisenhower, Dwight D. *At Ease: Stories I Tell to Friends*. Garden City, NY: Doubleday, 1967.

———. *Letters to Mamie*. New York: Doubleday, 1978.

———. *The Eisenhower Diaries*. New York: Norton, 1981.

Farrell, James. *Inventing the American Way of Death*. Philadelphia: Temple University Press, 1980.

Ferguson, Niall. *The Pity of War: Explaining World War I*. New York: Basic Books, 1999.

Finke, Roger, and Rodney Stark. *The Churching of America, 1776–1990: Winners and Losers in our Religious Economy*. New Brunswick, NJ: Rutgers University Press, 1992.

Forrestal, James. *The Forrestal Diaries*. Edited by Walter Millis. New York: Viking Press, 1951.

Fulbright, J. William. *The Arrogance of Power*. New York: Random House, 1967.

Fussell, Paul. *Wartime: Understanding and Behavior in the Second World War*. New York: Oxford University Press, 1989.

Garfield, James. "Strewing Flowers on the Graves of Soldiers, Oration Delivered at Arlington, Virginia, May 30, 1868." In *The Works of James Abram Garfield*. Boston: J. R. Osgood and Co., 1882–83.

Gaustad, Edwin S. "America's Institutions of Faith: A Statistical Postscript." In W. C. McLaoughlin and R. C. Bellah, eds., *Religion in America*. New York: Houghton Mifflin, 1968.

———. *A Religious History of America*. New York: Harper & Row, 1966.

George, Alexander and Juliette George. *Woodrow Wilson and Colonel House: A Personality Study*. New York: Dover, 1964.

Gillett, Frederick H. *George Frisbie Hoar*. New York: Houghton Mifflin, 1934.

Goodwin, Doris Kearns. *Lyndon Johnson and the American Dream*. New York: St. Martin's Press, 1991.

Gould, Lewis L. *The Spanish-American War and President McKinley*. Lawrence: University Press of Kansas, 1982.

Graham, Billy. *Just as I Am: The Autobiography of Billy Graham*. New York: HarperCollins, 1997.

Halberstam, David. *The Best and the Brightest*, 20th anniversary ed. New York: Random House, 1992.

Haraway, Donna. "Teddy Bear Patriarchy." In Amy Kaplan and Donald Pease, eds., *Cultures of United States Imperialism*. Durham, NC: Duke University Press, 1993.

Hay, John. *Addresses of John Hay*. New York: The Century Co., 1906.

———. *A College Friendship: A Series of Letters from John Hay to Hannah Angell*. Boston: Private printing, 1938.

———. "Colonel Baker." *Harper's*, 24, no. 139 (Dec. 1861), pp. 103–10.

———. *The Complete Poetical Works of John Hay*. Boston: Houghton Mifflin Company, 1916.

———. "Ellsworth." *Atlantic Monthly* (July 1861), pp. 119–25.

Hay, John, and John G. Nicolay. *Abraham Lincoln: A History*. New York: The Century Co., 1890.

Hoar, George F. *Autobiography of Seventy Years.* New York: Charles Scribner's Sons, 1903.

Hodgson, Godfrey. *The Colonel: The Life and Wars of Henry Stimson, 1867–1950.* New York: Knopf, 1990.

Hoopes, Townsend. *The Devil and John Foster Dulles.* Boston: Little, Brown, 1973.

———. *The Limits of Intervention.* New York: W. W. Norton, 1987.

Hoopes, Townsend, and Douglas Brinkley. *Driven Patriot: The Life and Times of James Forrestal.* New York: Knopf, 1992.

Humphrey, Hubert H. *The Education of a Public Man: My Life and Politics.* Edited by Norman Sherman. Garden City, NY: Doubleday, 1976.

Huntington, Samuel P. "American Ideals versus American Institutions." In G. John Ikenberry, ed., *American Foreign Policy: Theoretical Essays,* pp. 223–58. Glenview, IL: Scott, Foresman, 1989.

Hutcheson, Richard G. *God in the White House: How Religion has Changed the Modern Presidency.* New York: Macmillan, 1988.

Ignatieff, Michael. *Virtual War: Kosovo and Beyond.* New York: Henry Holt, 2000.

Isaacson, Walter, and Evan Thomas. *The Wise Men: Six Friends and the World They Made.* New York: Touchstone, 1986.

Jessup, Philip. "The Foreign Policy of a Free Democracy." *Department of State Bulletin* (Sept. 5, 1949), pp. 345–49.

Johnson, Lyndon. *The Quotable Lyndon B. Johnson.* Anderson, SC: Droke House, 1968.

Kaldor, Mary. *New and Old Wars.* Stanford, CA: Stanford University Press, 1999.

Kastenbaum, Robert, and Beatrice Kastenbaum, eds. *Encyclopedia of Death.* New York: Avon, 1989.

Keegan, John. *The Face of Battle.* New York: Military Heritage Press, 1986.

Kennan, George. *Around the Cragged Hill: A Personal and Political Philosophy.* New York: W. W. Norton, 1993.

———. *American Diplomacy,* expanded edition. Chicago: The University of Chicago Press, 1984.

———. "The Sources of Soviet Conduct." *Foreign Affairs,* 25 (1947), pp. 566–82.

Kennedy, John F. *Profiles in Courage.* New York: Harper, 1956.

Kraut, Alan M. *Silent Travelers: Germs, Genes, and the "Immigrant Menace."* New York: Basic Books, 1994.

Kushner, Howard, and Anne Sherrill. *John Milton Hay: The Union of Poetry and Politics.* Boston: Twayne Publishers, 1977.

Larson, Deborah. *Origins of Containment: A Psychological Explanation.* Princeton, NJ: Princeton University Press, 1985.

Leech, Margaret. *In the Days of McKinley.* New York: Harper, 1959.

Linderman, Gerald F. *The Mirror of War: American Society and the Spanish-American War.* Ann Arbor: University of Michigan Press, 1974.

Lodge, Henry Cabot. "Theodore Roosevelt." In New York (State) Legislature. *A Memorial to Theodore Roosevelt.* Albany: J. B. Lyon Co., 1919.

———. "Tribute to Senator Hoar." *Massachusetts Historical Society* (Oct. 1904): 385–90.

Long, John D. *After Dinner and Other Speeches.* Cambridge, MA: The Riverside Press, 1895.

———. *America of Yesterday, as Reflected in the Journal of John Davis Long.* Edited by L. S. Mayo. Boston: The Atlantic Monthly Press, 1923.

———. *At the Fireside.* Boston: Albert Harrison Hall, 1914.

———. "The Civil War." *Massachusetts Historical Society Proceedings* (Oct. 1912), pp. 175–79.

———. "General Robert E. Lee." *Massachusetts Historical Society Proceedings* (Apr. 1911), pp. 592–95.

———. *Journal.* Edited by Margaret Long. Rindge, NH: R. R. Smith, 1956.

———. "Reminiscences of my Seventy Years' Education." *Massachusetts Historical Society Proceedings* (June 1909), pp. 348–58.

Manchester, William R. *American Caesar: Douglas MacArthur, 1880–1964.* Boston: Little, Brown, 1978.

Martin, William. *A Prophet with Honor: The Billy Graham Story.* New York: William Morrow, 1991.

Marty, Martin E. *Righteous Empire: The Protestant Experience in America.* New York: Dial Press, 1970.

May, Ernest. *Imperial Democracy: The Emergence of America as a Great Power.* New York: Harcourt, Brace & World, 1961.

McCullough, David. *Mornings on Horseback.* New York: Simon & Schuster, 1981.

McKinley, William. *Speeches and Addresses of William McKinley, 1897–1900.* New York: Doubleday & McClure Co., 1900.

McNamara, Robert S. *In Retrospect: The Tragedy and Lessons of Vietnam.* New York: Times Books, 1995.

———. *The Essence of Security: Reflections in Office.* New York: Harper & Row, 1968.

Miller, Marion M., ed. *Great Debates in American History* (Vol. 3): Foreign Relations, Part II. New York: Current Literature Publishing, 1913.

Miller, Nathan. *Theodore Roosevelt: A Life.* New York: Morrow, 1992.

Morgenthau, Hans. "Globalism: Johnson's Moral Crusade." *The New Republic* (July 3, 1965), pp. 19–22.

Morison, Elting E. *Turmoil and Tradition: A Study of the Life and Times of Henry L. Stimson.* Boston: Houghton Mifflin, 1960.

Morris, Edmund. *Dutch: A Memoir of Ronald Reagan.* New York: Random House 1999.

Mueller, John. "Trends in Popular Support for the Wars in Korea and Vietnam." *American Political Science Review,* 65, no. 2 (1971), pp. 358–72.

Niemi, Robert. "JFK as Jesus: The Politics of Myth in Phil Ochs's 'Crucifixion.'" *Journal of American Culture,* 16, no. 4 (Winter 1993), pp. 35–40.

Nitze, Paul H., et al. *From Hiroshima to Glasnost: At the Center of Decision: A Memoir.* New York: Grove Weidenfeld, 1989.

Nuland, Sherwin. *How We Die: Reflections on Life's Final Chapter.* New York: Knopf, 1994.

O'Toole, Patricia. *The Five of Hearts: An Intimate Portrait of Henry Adams and His Friends, 1880–1918.* New York: C. N. Potter, 1990.

Offner, John L. *An Unwanted War: The Diplomacy of the United States and Spain over Cuba, 1895–1898.* Chapel Hill: University of North Carolina Press, 1992.

Omran, Abdel R. "Epidemiological Transition in the United States: The Health Factor in Population Change." *Population Bulletin,* 32, no. 2 (1977), pp. 3–42.

Raphael, Vincente L. "White Love: Surveillance and Nationalist Resistance in the U.S. Colonization of the Philippines." In Amy Kaplan and Donald Pease, eds., *Cultures of United States Imperialism,* pp. 185–218. Durham, NC: Duke University Press, 1993.

Rogow, Arnold A. *James Forrestal: A Study of Personality, Politics, and Policy.* New York: Macmillan, 1963.

Roosevelt, Franklin D. *Public Papers and Addresses of Franklin D. Roosevelt, 1937.* New York: MacMillan, 1941.

Roosevelt, Kermit, Jr. *A Sentimental Safari.* New York, Knopf, 1963.

———. *Countercoup: The Struggle for the Control of Iran.* New York: McGraw-Hill, 1979.

Roosevelt, Kermit, Sr. *The Happy Hunting Grounds.* New York: Charles Scribner's Sons, 1920.

Roosevelt, Theodore. *African Game Trails: An Account of the African Wanderings of an American Hunter-naturalist.* New York: Charles Scribner's Sons, 1910.

———. *Biological Analogies in History: The 1910 Romanes Lecture.* London: Oxford University Press, 1910.

———. "A Book-lover's Holiday." In *The Works of Theodore Roosevelt,* Vol. IV, memorial ed. New York: Charles Scribner's Sons, 1923–26.

———. "The Cuban Dead." In *The Works of Theodore Roosevelt,* Vol. XII, pp. 625–30, memorial ed. New York: Charles Scribner's Sons, 1923–26.

———. *Diaries of Boyhood and Youth.* New York: Charles Scribner's Sons, 1928.

———. *Fear God and Take Your Own Part.* New York: George H. Doran Co., 1916.

———. *Letters.* Edited by Elting Morison. 8 Vols. Cambridge, MA: Harvard University Press, 1951–54.

———. "The Rough Riders." In *The Works of Theodore Roosevelt,* Vol. XIII, memorial ed. New York: Charles Scribner's Sons, 1924.

———. *Selections from the Correspondence of Theodore Roosevelt and Henry Cabot Lodge, 1884–1918.* New York: Da Capo Press, 1971.

———. *Theodore Roosevelt, an Autobiography.* New York: Charles Scribner's Sons, 1946.

Rusk, Dean. *As I Saw It.* Edited by Daniel S. Papp. New York: W. W. Norton, 1990.

Schmookler, Andrew B. *The Parable of the Tribes: The Problem of Power in Social Evolution.* Boston: Houghton Mifflin, 1984.

Schulzinger, Robert. *The Wise Men of Foreign Affairs: The History of the Council on Foreign Relations.* New York: Columbia University Press, 1984.

Shapley, Deborah. *Promise and Power: The Life and Times of Robert McNamara.* Boston: Little, Brown, 1993.

Sheehan, Neil. *A Bright Shining Lie: John Paul Vann and the American War in Vietnam.* New York: Random House, 1988.

Smith, A. Robert. *The Tiger in the Senate: The Biography of Wayne Morse.* New York: Doubleday, 1962.

Smith, Geoffrey. "National Security and Personal Isolation: Sex, Gender, and Disease in the Cold-War United States." *The International History Review,* 14, no. 2 (May 1992), pp. 307–35.

Stevens, Richard L. *The Trail: A History of the Ho Chi Minh Trail and the Role of Nature in the War in Viet Nam.* New York: Garland, 1993.

Summers, Anthony. *The Arrogance of Power: The Secret World of Richard Nixon.* New York: Viking Press, 2000.

Swaim, Kathleen. *Pilgrim's Progress, Puritan's Progress.* Urbana: University of Illinois Press, 1993.

Terkel, Studs. *The Good War: An Oral History of World War Two,* paperback reprint ed. New York: New Press, 1997.

Tesh, Sylvia. *Hidden Arguments: Political Ideology and Disease Prevention Policy.* New Brunswick, NJ: Rutgers University Press, 1988.

Thayer, William Roscoe. *The Life and Letters of John Hay.* Boston: Houghton Mifflin Company, 1915.

Trewhitt, Henry L. *McNamara.* New York: Harper & Row, 1971.

Truman, Harry. "Public Opinion and American Foreign Policy." *Department of State Bulletin* (Aug. 1, 1949), pp. 145–47.

Umberson, Debra, and Kristen Henderson. "The Social Construction of Death in the Gulf War." *Omega,* 25, no. 1 (1992), pp. 1–15.

United States. Congress. *Congressional Record: Proceedings and Debates of the Congress.* Washington, DC: GPO, 1898–1902; 1962–1968.

———. Congress. *Memorial Addresses in the Congress of the United States and Tributes in Eulogy of John F. Kennedy.* Washington, DC: GPO, 1964.

———. Congress. House. *The Pentagon Papers: Hearings before a subcommittee of the Committee on Government Operations, House of Representatives,* Ninety-second Congress, first [and second] session[s]. Washington, DC: GPO, 1971–72, 9 Volumes.

———. Department of Defense. *Pentagon Papers: The Defense Department History of United States Decisionmaking on Vietnam,* 5 vols., The Senator Gravel ed. Boston: Beacon Press, 1971–72.

———. Department of State. *Foreign Relations of the United States.* Washington, DC: GPO, 1898–1970.

———. President. *Public Papers of the Presidents of the United States: Containing the Public Messages, Speeches, and Statements of the President.* Washington: GPO, 1962–67, and 1989–1993, available at the Bush Digital Library, http://bushlibrary.tamu.edu/papers.

Valenti, Jack. *A Very Human President.* New York: Norton, 1975.

VanDeMark, Brian. *Into the Quagmire: Lyndon Johnson and the Escalation of the Vietnam War.* New York: Oxford University Press, 1991.

Wagenknecht, Edward. *The Seven Worlds of Theodore Roosevelt.* New York: Longmans, Green, 1958.

Welch, Richard E. *Response to Imperialism: The United States and the Philippine-American War, 1899–1902.* Chapel Hill: University of North Carolina Press, 1979.

——. *George Frisbee Hoar and the Half-breed Republicans.* Cambridge, MA: Harvard University Press, 1971.

Wills, Garry. *Under God: Religion and American Politics.* New York: Simon & Schuster, 1990.

Winslow, C. E. A. "The War Against Disease." *Atlantic Monthly,* 91 (Jan. 1903), pp. 43–52.

Wittner, Lawrence. *MacArthur.* Englewood Cliffs, NJ: Prentice Hall, 1971.

INDEX